Albert J. Kuebler, Fred Kraebel

Knights of Pythias Directory

and Buffalo street directory and guide

Albert J. Kuebler, Fred Kraebel

Knights of Pythias Directory
and Buffalo street directory and guide

ISBN/EAN: 9783337299620

Printed in Europe, USA, Canada, Australia, Japan

Cover: Foto ©Andreas Hilbeck / pixelio.de

More available books at **www.hansebooks.com**

KNIGHTS OF PYTHIAS

DIRECTORY

—— AND ——

BUFFALO STREET DIRECTORY AND GUIDE.

PUBLISHED FOR THE BENEFIT OF

George M. Browne Division

Uniformed Rank,   Knights of Pythias,

—— BY ——

ALBERT J. KUEBLER AND FRED. KRAEBEL.

BUFFALO, N. Y.
KRAFT & STERN, PRINTERS, 365 Washington St.

1894.

PUBLISHER'S ANNOUNCEMENT.

In placing the Buffalo Street Guide and Directory and also Knights of Pythias Lodge Directory before the members of the Knights of Pythias, we feel confident that we are supplying a want long felt by many, and though it may be still defective, the labor we have rendered our noble Order and the benefits to be derived therefrom, will be appreciated by all.

For years it has been customary among some lodges in this city to publish lists of the members of their lodges, but never before has any attempt been made to collect the names of all the members of the Order in this city and arrange them alphabetically in lodges, according to numbers, thus enabling anyone to perceive at a glance whether or not any particular person be a member of the Order.

By the publication of this Directory the entire membership of the City of Buffalo and Erie County has been virtually consolidated into one Directory instead of several directories, and also gives us valuable information of the City of Buffalo. It must be apparent to everybody that the publication of this Directory, containing as it does 1,300 names, must be attended with great labor and expense. While the labor would have been cheerfully rendered in so good a cause, it could not be expected that in addition thereto the publishers should also bear the expense to enable us therefore to publish the Directory and Guide and sell it at a very low price, we decided to insert a limited number of business advertisements, and it is due to the pecuniary aid rendered by these advertising members that its publication was made possible. We sincerly hope, therefore, that the generosity of these members will be so fully rewarded by increased patronage of members and their families, that if called upon to do so they will again lend the same aid and assistance in any necessary revision and re-publication of this Directory.

Trusting that the book may accomplish the good for which it is intended, *i e.* the development of a better acquaintance and a more fraternal spirit among all members, we are   Respectfully yours in F.. C. and B.,

ALBERT J. KUEBLER,

Buffalo, May 1, 1894.   FRED. KRAEBEL.

ALBERT J. KUEBLER, P. C.

FRED. KRAEBEL, P. C.

►◄ BUFFALO ►►
STREET AND AVENUE DIRECTORY

EXPLANATION.

It will be noticed that in this Street Directory the names of the streets are set down in alphabetical order, giving the course which they run, according, as near as possible, to the points of the compass, and enumerating all streets which cross the same in the order in which they occur. The streets in the city were renumbered in 1868, and the following method was adopted, to wit: From the starting point of the street, measuring along the line of the street, 20 feet; then making No. 1 to the right-hand side, and No. 2 to the left-hand side, and so on, each 20 feet, whether there be a building or a vacancy or a street crossing. The number on one corner has been given, so that a person wishing to find, say 499 MAIN STREET, on consulting the Street Directory, finds that the right-hand corner of Main and Mohawk is No. 487, consequently the place he seeks is only a few doors above.

ABBREVIATIONS.—N. for North; N. E. for Northeast; N. W. for Northwest; S. for South; S. E. for Southeast; S. W. for Southwest; E. for East; W. for West; Niag. for Niagara; Niag. R. for Niagara River; Junct. for Junction; sq. for square; ave. for avenue; al. for alley; rd. for road; fr. for from; pl. for place; Plk. Rd. for Plank Road; cr'k for creek; bet. for between; acr. for across; nr. for near; tks. for tracks; Boulv'd for Boulevard; B'way for Broadway; Gen. for Genesee; P'kway for Parkway.

A, E. fr. 1013 Fillmore ave. to Mills.

A, N. from William to B'way, third street E. of Bailey ave (in 11th ward) Changed to Garfield in year 1886, and in 1893 changed to Ideal.

Abel, second street E. of Weiss, running N. fr. Griswold to Dingens (N. E. city line).

Abby, S. fr. 569 Abbott rd. to 594 Tifft.
Amelia.
Lackawanna.
Brunck.
Baraga.
Mystic.
Hancock.
Beacon.
Scranton.
Bell ave.
Edmunds.
Lehigh ave.
Lehigh.
Scheu ave.
Burt ave.
Boller ave.
Burrows ave.
Becker.
Roland ave.
Tifft.

Abbott Road, S. E. from 585 Elk to city line.
195 St. Stephen's pl.
Euclid pl.
223 Smith.
250 Owahn pl.
322 Prenatt pl.
344 Lee.
Buffalo creek.
521 Dyer.
569 Abby.
643 Germania.
711 Hopkins.
Kimmel ave.
Buffalo.
799 Triangle.
951 White's Cors. rd (Changed to S. Park ave.)
Melrose.
Rutland.
Milford.
Portland.
Lexington.
Athol.
Salem.
Meriden.
1358 Cazenovia.
Choate ave.
Windemere pl.
1448 Potter's Cors. rd
Woodside ave.
1888 Downing.
1902 City line.

Adams, N. fr. 642 Eagle to 689 Genesee.
37 Clinton.
113 Howard.
179 William.
277 Peckham.
371 Broadway.
Beckwith.
471 Sycamore.
504 Brown.
629 Genesee.

Addison Alley, E. from 215 Bond to 236 Lord.

Alabama, N. fr. Buffalo River to 481 Seneca.
17 South.
83 Tecumseh.
133 Sandusky.
185 Mackinaw.
219 Miami.
261 Elk.
297 Fulton.
335 Perry.
360 Otto.
369 Scott.
405 Main and Hamburgh canal.
429 Mill.
445 Exchange.
485 Carroll.
559 Seneca.

Albany, E. fr. Erie canal to 230 Hampshire.
4 Railroad.

45 Niagara.
106 West ave.
137 Plymouth ave.
143 Hibbard.
161 School.
178 Barton.
185 Thirteenth.
216 Herkimer.
229 Hampshire.

Albemarle, first street E. of Skillen running N. W. fr. Fairmount ave to O'Neil.
North Park ave.
O'Neil.

Albert Avenue, second street E. of Tonawanda running N. W. fr. Rano to See ave.
Hunt ave.
Ontario.
See ave.

Alden, N. fr. Chaucer to Kenmore ave. (N. W. of International Junction) near northerly city line.

Alexander No. 1 (in 25th ward), third street E. of Military rd. running N. from Hertel ave to Race. Changed to Sunset, March 20, 1893.

Alexander No. 2 (in 25th ward), third street W of Main running N. fr. Tyler to Eley (nr. N.city line). Changed to Mildred, March 20, 1893.

Alexander Avenue, second street south of E. Delavan ave., running east from Herbert ave. to Bailey avenue. Changed to Wecker, March 20, 1893.

Alexander Place, N. fr. East Ferry to Puffer (first street west of Jefferson).
Harlow pl.
Elsie pl.

Dexter.
Puffer.

Alleghany, first street W. of White's Corners Plank Road running N. from Tifft to Folger.

Allen, W. from 940 Main to 1 Wadsworth and 79 Clifton pl.
26 N. Pearl.
58 Franklin.
82 Meech.
101 Delaware ave.
135 Irving pl.
159 Park.
191 Elmwood ave.
215 Mariner.
239 College.
253 Wadsworth.
256 Clifton pl.

Alvin, E. from 51 Durrenburger pl.to Johnson (first street north of High).

Alvin Avenue, fourth street N. of E. Hertel ave. running east fr. Main to Bailey ave.
Cordova.
Park Ridge ave.
Lenox ave.
Bailey ave.

Amelia, first street S. of Abbott road running E. from Abbey to Germania.

Amherst, E. from Erie canal, at Black Rock, to 2680 Main.
13 Niagara.
43 Dearborn.
65 East.
117 Thompson.
144 Gorton.
175 Tonawanda.
228 Churchill.
268 Keil.
282 Military rd.
375 Grant.
422 Germain.
448 Peter.
478 Howell.
504 Bush.
533 Yates.

536 Reservation.
580 Bridgeman.
621 Nelson.
698 Elmwood ave., (formerly McPherson).
988 Delaware ave.
1302 Colvin.
Parkside ave.
Woodward ave.
Summit ave.
Crescent ave.
1543 Greenfield.
1610 N. Y. C. R. R. (Belt Line.)
Starin ave.
1700 Fairfield.
Voorhis.
Parker ave.
1788 Main.

Amity, second street S. of Broadway, running east from Quincy street to Deshler.
Swinburne.
Brownell.
Deshler.

Amsterdam (formerly Manhattan), 1st street east of Fillmore ave. (formerly Avenue A) running north from E. Delavan ave.

Anderson Alley, first street north of S. Division running east fr. Emslie to 60 Lord. Changed to Meteor Alley, March 20, 1893.

Anderson Place, E. from 355 Richmond ave. to Elmwood ave.
37 Norwood ave.
81 Ashland ave.
125 Elmwood ave.

Andover, first street E. of Norfolk ave. running north from Warwick ave. to Bayfield.
Duffield.
Bayfield.

Angle, fourth street W. of Main running N. from Tyler to Heath (at Internati'l Junct. near N. city line).

Ann, W. from 200 Terrace to Baker, between Charles and Mechanic.

Annie Place, east from 287 Dewitt to 258 Tryon pl.
61 Herkimer.
127 Grant.
195 Tryon pl.

Ansteth, sixth street N. of Hertel avenue running west from Military road to N. Y. C. R. R. tracks.

Antwerp, (formerly Bommel), E. fr. Bailey ave. to D. L. & W. R. R. Second street south of Genesee.

Appenheimer Ave., first street north of East Delavan ave. running east from Avenue A.

Appleton, S. E fr Erie freight tks. In Union Iron Co.'s tract.

Argus, sixth street east of Tonawanda running north from Esser ave. to O'Neil.
Roesch ave.
O'Neil.

Arizona (formerly Wyoming), 3d street N. of Hertel ave. running W. fr. Military Road to N. Y. C. R. R. tracks.

Arkansas, E. from 887 West avenue to 318 Hampshire.
31 Hibbard.
67 Barton.
105 Herkimer.
135 Sherwood.
187 Grant.
195 Hampshire.

Arlington, S. from 1163 B'way to Concord.

Changed to Houghton, March 20, 1893.

Arlington Avenue, first street E. of Grider running east fr. Kensington ave. to Wyoming ave. Changed to Mendola, March 20, 1893.

Arlington Place, N. fr. 65 Wadsworth to 294 North, and east to 150 College.

Armbruster, south from 1567 Broadway to N. Y. C. Junction (East Buffalo station).

Arnold, E. fr. 71 Grant to Preston (first street north of West Ferry).

Arthur (in 25th ward), east from 2158 Niagara to Tonawanda.
61 East.
Hartmann pl.
Peoria.
Tonawanda.

Arthur Avenue (in 18th ward), N. fr. 700 Walden ave. to Doat (3d street east of Bailey avenue). Changed to Keystone.

Asbury Alley, N. fr. 43 West Huron to rear of 460 Pearl.

Ash, N. fr. 272 Broadway to 357 Genesee.
69 Sycamore.
143 Genesee.

Ashland Avenue, N. fr. 273 Summer to West Forest ave.
145 Bryant,
188 Hodge ave.
231 West Utica.
267 Anderson pl.
321 Lexington ave.
Highland ave.
381 West Ferry.
Breckenridge.
Auburn ave.
Bouck ave.

(Closed bet. Bouck ave and Potomac ave., open from Potomac ave to West Forest ave).
Potomac ave.
Bird ave.
West Forest ave

Ashley, E. from Curtiss to Peck. First street south of Broadway.
Young.
Mohr.
Milburn.
Person.
Krupp.
Peck.

Athol, sixth street S. fr. 951 Abbott road, running N. E. to Cazenovia creek.
Cumberland ave.
Cazenovia creek.

Atlantic, first street W. of Delaware ave. running N. fr. Hodge ave to 155 West Utica.

Atlantic Ave,, 1st street west of Bailey ave. running north fr. E. Delavan ave. to Beverly.
Holborn.
Beverly.

Auburn Avenue, E. fr. Niagara river and 1275 Niagara street to Delaware ave.
19 Mason.
53 Niagara.
71 Gelston.
95 West ave.
133 Dewitt.
205 Herkimer.
267 Grant.
338 Tryon pl.
Preston.
367 Hoyt.
401 Baynes.
Putnam.
Livingston.
501 Richmond ave.
Norwood ave.
Ashland ave.
629 Elmwood ave.

STREET DIRECTORY.

Pacific ave.
Delaware ave.

Auchinvole, first street
north of Brecken-
ridge, running east
from Herkimer to
Grant.

Augusta, third street
east of White's Cor-
ners Plank road run-
ning S. from Down-
ing street to city line.

Aurora, W. fr. 475 Ohio
to Buffalo river.

Aurora Plank Road.
Changed to Seneca
street.

Austin, E. fr. Niagara
river and 1984 Niag-
ara to 168 Military
road.
17 Niagara.
47 Dearborn.
69 East.
99 Hoffman alley.
108 Gurnsey.
121 Thompson.
147 Gorton.
175 Tonawanda.
Pacific.
253 Churchill.
267 Keil.
289 Clay.
323 Glor.
324 Troy alley.
340 Joslyn pl.
355 Military road.

Avenue A, N. fr. North
Parade ave, (near Pa-
rade House) to 2551
Main. Changed to
Fillmore ave. in 1889.
1 N. Parade ave.
27 Puerner ave.
28 Northampton.
69 Fougeron.
79 Girard pl.
105 Urban.
130 Landon.
147 French.
162 East Utica.
Box ave.
210 Woeppel.
215 Glenwood ave.

(formerly Roe-
der).
240 Winslow ave.
276 Woodlawu ave.
301 East Ferry.
Internati'l Park
ave.
Sidney.
462 Puffer.
Buell ave.
Mohican ave.
563 E. Delavan ave.
Appenheimer
ave.
766 Steele.
767 Kensington ave.
907 East Forest ave.
963 Leroy ave.
Brewster.
993 Charlotte ave.
Jewett ave.
1037 Wakefield ave.
Phelps.
Victoria.
Rodney.
Main.

B, east from 967 Fillmore ave. to Mills.

Babcock, N. fr. 266 Prenatt to 1161 William.
75 Elk.
151 Perry.
225 Seneca.
Blank ave.
451 Clinton.
Oscar.
Bergtold.
Fleming.
Lyman.
653 Howard.
872 Hannah.
934 Henricka.
959 William.

Bahama, first street W.
of Hopkins running
N. from Marilla.

Baker, E. fr. Ann (near
200 Terrace) to Erie
canal.

Bailey Ave., (formerly
Williamsville road),
N. from 1505 Seneca
to city line.
Blank ave.
219 Clinton.

422 Howard.
459 Dingens.
717 William.
801 Dempster.
823 Ludington.
Hennepin.
Bogardus.
Lovejoy.
Moreland.
995 Regent.
Stone.
1159 Broadway.
Olmstead.
West Shore.
1449 Walden ave.
Rohe.
1627 Doat.
Moeller.
Antwerp.
Gisel.
1733 Genesee.
1808 East Ferry.
1879 Scajaquada cr'k
Barnett place.
Puffer.
Wecker.
Kirkpatrick.
2101 E. Delavan ave.
Holbern.
Beverly.
2331 Sugar.
2336 Warwick ave.
Duffield.
Bayfield.
Manhart.
2653 Kensington ave.
Cement.
Hewett.
East Hertel ave
Shirley.
La Salle ave.
Minnesota ave.
Lisbon.
Alvin ave.
3081 City line.

Baitz Ave., N. fr. 1340
Clinton to Erie R. R.
tracks.
Manitoba.
Erie R. R. tracks.

Balcom, west from 1630
Main to 557 Linwood
ave.

Balcom, east from Main
to Masten (second

street N. of Junction of Main and Michigan).

Bangor Place, 1st street S. of Kenmore ave. (north city line) east from Delaware ave and north of D. L. & W. R. R. tracks running east from Kasota ave to Sharon ave.
Brocton ave.
Calvin.
Berkshire ave.
Dalton ave.
Kennard ave.
Sharon ave.

Baraga, (formerly Brinker ave.), third street south of Abbott road running east from Abby to Hopkins.
Germania.
Hopkins.

Bardol, east from East Parade ave. to Kehr (first street north of Genesee).
Marshall.
Spiess.
Kehr.

Barker, west from 1210 Main to 829 Delaware ave.
Linwood ave.
Delaware ave.

Barnard, third street E. of Weiss running S. from Griswold street to Buffalo creek.
Clinton.
Beer.
Seward.
Buffalo creek.

Barnett Place, 1st street north of Puffer running east from Herbert ave. to Bailey avenue.

Barr, east from Main to 1444 Jefferson (first street north of Glenwood ave). Changed

Feb., 1888, to Woodlawn ave.

Barry Place, north from 282 Bird ave. to 279 West Forest ave.

Barthel, N. fr. Walden ave. to Urban (sixth street E. of Genesee.)
Genesee.
Fougeron.
Urban.

Barton, N.fr. 178 Albany to 181 Breckenridge.
California.
Arkansas.
West Ferry.
Breckenridge.

Bass, N. fr. 969 Clinton to Howard.

Bass Place, W. from 46 Emslie to N.Y.C.R.R. tracks.

Batavia, north fr. 1710 Broadway (1st street east of Bailey ave.)

Baxter, north fr. Esser ave. to O'Neil (first street east of Tonawanda).
Roesch ave.
O'Neil.

Bayard, 2d street north of Seneca running E. from Troupe to Lester.
Milton.
Harrison.
Lester.

Bayer, N. from 490 East Utica to Glenwood ave. Changed to Portage, March 20, 1893.

Bayfield (formerly Becker, in 25th ward) second street north of Warwick ave. running E. from Norfolk ave. to Bailey ave.
Andover.
Irvington ave.
Tremont ave.
Westchester ave.
Frankfort ave.

Bailey ave.

Baynes, N. from 400 W. Ferry to 370 Bird ave.
45 Breckenridge.
109 Auburn ave.
167 Bouck ave.
239 Delavan ave.
311 Potomac ave.
379 Bird ave.

Beacon (formerly Hancock ave.), fifth street south of Abbott road running east fr. Abby to Hopkins.
Germania.
Hopkins.

Beak, N. from 20 Green to 57 Exchange. (This street closed by N.Y. C. R. R.)

Bean Alley, north fr. 73 W. Mohawk to 64 W. Huron.

Beard Ave., first street N. of Amherst running east from Starin ave. to Parker ave., then north from Parker ave. to Huntington ave.
Voorhis.
Parker ave.
Morris ave.
Wesley.
Depew ave.
Woodbridge ave.
Huntington ave.

Beaver, north from 38 Perry to 37 Scott.

Beck, north from 1012 Broadway to 923 Sycamore.

Becker, (in 5th ward) 1st street north of Tift, running west fr. Abby to B., R. & P. R. R. tracks.

Becker (in 14th ward), N. from 1258 Broadway to 1147 Sycamore

Becker (in 23th ward), second street north of Warwick ave. running east from Norfolk ave. to Bailey ave. Changed to Bayfield, March 20, 1893.

Beckwith, east fr. 461 Sycamore to Adams.
Madison.
Monroe.
Adams.

Beech, N. from 970 Virginia to 381 Carlton.

Beer, 1st street south of Clinton, running east from Weiss to South Ogden.
Weimer.
Cable.
Barnard.
Fenton.
Holly.
Willet.
South Ogden.

Behrends, 7th street N. of Hertel ave. running west from Military road to N. Y. C. R. R. tracks.

Bell Ave., 6th street S. of Abbott road, running east from Abby to Hopkins.
Germania.
Hopkins.

Belmont, second street east of Skillen, running N. W. from Fairmount ave. to O'Neil.
North Park ave.
O'Neil.

Belmont Ave., west fr. Eley to Crosby (first street north of Morton, near north city line). Changed to Brinton, March 20, 1893.

Belmont Ave., 2d street north of East Delavan ave. running E. from Jefferson to Oak Grove ave., then S. to East Delavan avenue Changed to Blaine, March 20, 1893.

Bender Place, S. from 1025 Clinton to W. N. Y. & P. R. R. tracks.

Bennett, north from 146 William to 271 B'way.

Benzinger, N. from 1618 William to B'way (4th street east of Bailey ave.)
Ludington.
Lovejoy.
Vanderbilt.
Reimann.
King.
Broadway.

Bergtold, east fr. Laux to Bushnell ave. (2d street N. of Clinton).
Babcock.
Bushnell ave.

Berkeley Place, first street west of Delaware ave. running north from Bird ave. to The Park.
West Forest ave.
The Park.

Berkshire Avenue, first street east of Colvin running north from Bangor place to Kenmore ave. (north city line).

Berlin, N. fr. 460 High to Best and north fr. Dodge to Northampton (2d street east of Jefferson).

Bernard, second street east of White's Corners Plk Rd., running south from Downing street to City line. Changed to Sibley, March 20, 1893.

Berrick Alley, north fr. 142 Seneca to 171 Swan

Bessie Place, north fr. 414 Bird ave. to 411 West Forest ave.

Best, east fr. 1119 Main to 1132 Genesee.
56 Ellicott.

79 Oak.
117 Elm.
149 Michigan.
225 Masten.
323 Peach.
349 Grape.
379 Jefferson.
415 Handel.
Berlin.
479 Durrenberg'r pl
Roehrer.
Wohlers.
529 Johnson.
St. Michael.
565 Sherman.
599 Fox.
St. Ann.
633 Herman.
634 W. Parade ave.
Guilford.
Rich.
717 Sweeney.
745 Myers.
780 Fillmore ave.
834 Genesee.

Beverly (formerly Kenilworth) fourth street north of E. Delavan ave. running east fr. Olympic ave. to Bailey ave.
Ocean ave.
Atlantic ave.
Bailey ave.

Bidwell Parkway, N. E. from Bidwell place to Soldiers' place.
60 Delavan ave.
168 Potomac ave.
233 Soldiers' place.

Bidwell Place, junction of Richmond ave., Bouck ave. and Bidwell parkway.

Bingham, east fr. Erie canal to 156 Church.

Bird Ave., east fr. Erie canal and 1531 Niagara street to 1538 Delaware ave.
25 Niagara.
79 West ave.
115 Dewitt.
181 Herkimer.
247 Grant.

STREET DIRECTORY.

282 Barry.
313 Tryon pl.
348 Hoyt.
379 Baynes.
389 Lawlin pl.
414 Bessie pl.
441 Carmine pl.
477 Richmond ave.
Norwood ave.
Ashland ave.
Elmwood ave.
Granger pl.
641 Soldiers' pl.
Windsor ave.
Clarendon pl.
Berkeley pl.
835 Delaware ave.
Birdsall, N. E. fr. 62 Mechanic to 128 Church.
Bismarck (in 5th ward) second street south from 569 Abbott rd, running W. fr. Abby to B., R. & P. R. R. tracks. Changed to Brunck March 20, 1893.
Bismarck (in 11th ward) first street south of William running east from South Ogden to city line.
New South Ogden.
City Line.
Bissell Ave., 1st street east of Moselle, running north from Walden ave. to Genesee.
McKibbin.
Genesee.
Bitter, north fr. Woodlawn ave. to E. Delavan avenue. (Second street east of Avenue A).
East Ferry.
Puffer.
East Delavan ave.
Blackwell Canal, S. E. from the mouth of Buffalo River.
Blaine (formerly Belmont ave.) 2d street north of East Delavan ave. running east

from Jefferson to Oak Grove ave., then S. to East Delavan ave.
Meech ave.
Oak Grove ave.
East Delevan ave.
Blank Ave., 1st street south of Clinton running east from Babcock to Bailey ave.
Bushnell ave.
Gilbert ave.
Scoville ave.
Bailey ave.
Bleeker Ave., 5th street east of Tonawanda running N. W. from Rano to Laird ave.
Ross ave.
Laird ave.
Bloomfield Ave., second street south of Tifft running east from S. Park ave. (formerly White's Corners rd.) to Boulevard.
Blossom, north from 54 Broadway to 59 East Huron.
23 Hersee alley.
65 Huron.
Blossom, N. fr. Hampshire to Scajaquada creek. Changed to Grant.
Blum Ave., east from Military rd. to Clayton. (Sixth street N. of Hertel ave).
Bogardus, 4th street N. of William running east from Bailey ave. to Green street.
Boller, 8th street south from 569 Abbott road running west fr. Abby to B., R. & P.R.R. tracks.
Bolton Ave., 2d street east of Colvin running north from Hertel ave. to Taunton place.

Tacoma ave.
Taunton pl.
Bommel, east fr. Bailey ave. to D., L. & W.R. R. (Second street S. of Genesee.) Changed to Antwerp, March 20, 1893.
Bond, north fr. 180 Seymour to 177 Howard.
9 Pink alley.
27 S. Division.
43 Meteor alley.
57 N. Division.
77 Laban alley.
80 Eagle.
101 S. Railroad ave.
103 James.
131 Clinton.
151 Fritz alley.
165 Bristol.
183 San Domingo al.
199 Oneida.
214 Addison alley.
231 Howard.
Boone, north fr. Pembina (between Abby and Hopkins).
Booth Alley, east fr. 297 Washington to 12 Hickory.
Bork. Changed to Detroit.
Boston Alley, north fr. 116 E. Tupper to 675 Virginia. Changed April, 1892, to Demond place.
67 Goodell.
101 Burton.
144 Virginia.
Bouck Ave., east fr. 1319 Niagara to 1776 Main.
19 Gelston.
43 West ave.
83 Dewitt.
147 Herkimer.
184 Congress.
213 Grant.
250 Emily.
279 Tryon pl.
311 Hoyt.
345 Baynes.
371 Putnam.

391 Livingston.
421 Bidwell pl. and
Richmond av.
Norwood ave.
Ashland ave.
569 Elmwood ave.
Pacific ave.
793 Chapin pl. and
Delaware ave.
885 Linwood ave.
Oxford pl.
967 Harvard pl.
1054 Main.

Boulevard, south from
junc. of Abbott road
and South Park ave.
(formerly White's
Corner's rd.) to south
city line.
Mesmer ave.
Hubbell ave.
Columbus pl.
Richfield ave.
Bloomfield ave.
Springfield ave.
Whitefield ave.
Woodside ave.
Downing.
South City line.

Bowen (in 14th ward),
N. fr. 1058 Broadway
to 15 Walden ave.
181 Sycamore.
352 Walden ave.

Bowen (in 25th ward),
7th street east of Col-
vin running north fr.
St. Lawrence ave. to
Kenmore ave. (near
northerly city line).
Changed to Duluth,
March 20, 1893.

Bowery. Changed to
Irving place in 1870.

Box Ave., east fr. Ave-
nue A to Moselle (6th
street north from Pa-
rade grounds).

Boyd, 1st street north
of Breckenridge run-
ning east from Grant
to Preston.

Brace, E. fr. Erie canal
to 1348 Niagara.

Bradford, N. fr. 1156 Elk
to 1301 Seneca.
Perry.
Seneca.

Bradley, east fr. 466 De-
witt to Rees.
25 Danforth.
57 Dart.
83 Hawley.
121 Grant.
150 Rees.

Brantford Pl., 1st street
east of Chapin Park-
way running north
from W. Delavan ave
to Potomac ave.

Brayton, N. fr. 413 Ver-
mont to Massachu-
setts.
Rhode Island.
Massachusetts.

Breckenridge, east from
Erie canal and 1223
Niagara to 525 Elm-
wood ave.
49 Mason.
64 Niagara.
89 Gelston.
113 West ave.
116 Dewitt.
116 Plymouth ave.
181 Barton.
227 Herkimer.
293 Grant.
357 Preston.
389 Hoyt.
423 Baynes.
468 Putnam.
465 Maynard.
495 Iroquois.
498 Livingston.
521 Richmond ave.
Norwood ave.
Ashland ave.
651 Elmwood ave.

Bremen, north from 378
Vermont to 387 Rhode
Island.

Brewster, 1st street N.
of Leroy ave. running
east from Halbert to
Avenue A.

Bridge, E. fr. Erie canal
to 1796 Niagara.

Bridgeman, N. from 580
Amherst to N. Y. C.
(Belt Line) R. R.
Logan.
Grote.
Chandler.
N. Y. C. (Belt Line).

Briggs Ave., 2d street
north of Ontario run-
ning east from Niag-
ara to Tonawanda.
Fuller.
Tonawanda.

Brighton Ave., south fr.
1189 B'way to West
Shore R. R.

Brinker Ave., 3d street
S. of Abbott rd. run-
ning E. from Abby to
Hopkins, Changed to
Baraga, March 20, '93.

Brinkman, 1st street E.
of Bailey ave. run-
ning north from Wal-
den ave. to Doat.
Rohe.
Doat.

Brinton (formerly Bel-
mont ave.), west from
Eley to Crosby (first
street north of Mor-
ton near city line).

Bristol, E. fr. 205 Spring
to 278 Jefferson and
fr. 195 Emslie to 68
Clare. (Not opened
fr. Jefferson to Ems-
lie).
61 Jefferson.
199 Emslie.
243 Bond.
287 Lord.
306 S. Railroad ave.
333 Smith.
373 Montgomery.
415 Clare.

Broadway, N. E. from
421 Washington to E.
line of city.
28 Ellicott.
54 Blossom.
69 Oak.
111 Elm.
155 Michigan.

STREET DIRECTORY.

173 Potter.
State Arsenal.
211 Milnor.
239 Pine.
271 Bennett.
272 Ash.
304 Spruce.
305 Cedar.
335 Walnut.
359 Lutheran.
373 Hickory.
595 Roos.
400 Pratt.
427 Castor al.
453 Spring.
468 Tousey.
489 Mortimer.
499 Jefferson.
563 Madison.
591 Monroe.
616 Adams.
647 Watson.
668 Grey.
679 Emslie.
700 Johnson.
717 Krettner.
735 Sherman.
763 Stanton.
766 Fox.
791 Shumway.
800 Herman.
817 Smith.
840 Guilford.
843 Coit.
876 Reid.
875 Detroit.
899 Townsend.
900 Strauss.
925 Wilson.
947 Fillmore ave.
988 Gibson.
1017 Lombard.
1012 Beck.
1028 Mills.
1035 Clark.
1058 Bowen.
1061 Sears.
1087 Playter.
1090 Loepere.
1113 Sweet ave.
1131 Warner ave.
1136 Sobieski.
1163 Houghton.
1164 Rother ave.
1189 Brighton ave.
1190 Kosciusko

1216 Lathrop.
1225 Curtiss.
1253 Young.
1258 Becker.
1285 Mohr.
1310 Schmarbeck.
1319 Milburn.
Rommel.
1347 Person.
1356 Kuempel ave.
1381 Krupp.
1384 Miller ave.
1409 Titus ave.
1413 Peck.
1427 Quincy. ·
1432 Goodyear ave.
1451 Swinburn.
1458 Koons.
1477 Brownell.
1482 Liddell.
1513 Deshler.
1514 Wick.
1560 Schutrum.
1570 Hirschbeck.
1567 Armbruster.
1604 Shepard.
1619 N. Central ave.
1620 Gatchell.
1633 Bailey ave.
Crocker.
Greene.
1719 Batavia.
Ideal.
1899 King.
Benzinger.
Gold.
Davey.
1966 North Ogden.
1995 Schiller.
Goethe.
2045 City line.

Brocton Ave., 1st street west of Colvin running north fr. Bangor place to Kenmore ave (north city line).

Brooklyn Ave., 3d street east of Jefferson running north from East Utica to Winslow ave Glenwood ave. Winslow ave.

Brown, east fr. 735 Jefferson to 594 Adams.
25 Madison.

57 Monroe.
85 Adams.

Brownell, south fr. 1477 Broadway to Amity.

Bruce, 2d street west of Maine running north from Tyler to Eley (near north city line).

Brunck, (formerly Bismarck, in 5th ward), 2d street south from 569 Abbott rd running west from Abby to B., R. & P. R. R. tracks. Rochester. Pittsburgh. B., R. & P. R. R. tks.

Bryant, west from 1288 Main to 241 Richmond ave.
47 Linwood ave.
105 Delaware ave.
Oakland pl.
265 Elmwood ave.
311 Ashland ave.
355 Norwood ave.
395 Richmond ave.

Buell Ave., 1st street N. of Puffer running E. from Humboldt pky. to Avenue A.
Rex pl.
Avenue A.

Buffalo, 1st street east of Hopkins running south fr. Abbott rd.·

Buffam, north fr. 2215 Seneca to Reservation line.
83 Galloway.
163 Reservation line.

Bull, northeast fr. 1411 West ave. to Dewitt.

Bundy's Alley, north fr. 124 Sycamore.

Burgard Ave., N. fr. 562 Walden ave. to Doat.

Burrows Ave., 2d street north of Tifft running east from Abby to Hopkins.
Germania.

Hopkins.

Burt Ave., 3d street N. of Tifft running east from Abby to Hopkins.
Germania.
Hopkins.

Burton, east from 819 Main to 78 Maple.
19 Washington.
29 Rochevot al.
45 Ellicott.
67 Weaver al.
81 Oak.
106 Boston al.
119 Elm.
137 Werrick al.
142 Ralph al.
155 Michigan.
181 Maple.

Burwell Place, north fr. 48 Perry to 49 Scott.

Busch, 2d street east of Military rd. running north from Race to Kenmore ave. (north city line). Changed to Clayton, March 20, 1893.

Bush, north from 504 Amherst to Grote.

Bushnell Ave., 1st street east of Babcock running north fr. Blank ave. to Bergtold.
Clinton.
Bergtold.

Butler, west from 1064 Delaware avenue to 391 Richmond avenue. Changed in 1888 to Lexington ave.

Byron, north fr. Chaucer to Kenmore ave. (northwest of International Junct.) near northerly city line. Changed to Hecla, March 20, 1893.

Byron Place, 1st street north of E. Delavan ave., running east fr.

Olympic av. to Ocean ave.

C, east from 947 Fillmore ave. to Mills (1st street north of Sycamore).

Cable, south trom Griswold to Buffalo cr'k (2d street E. of Weiss).
Clinton.
Beer.
Buffalo creek.

Caldwell Alley, N. from 114 Wilkeson to 163 Georgia.

California, east from 859 West ave. to Herkimer.
29 Hibbard.
65 Barton.
101 Herkimer.

Calumet Place, 3d street east of Niagara, running north fr. Grace.

Cambridge Avenue, N. fr. E. Ferry to Warwick ave. (4th street E. of Grider).
Puffer.
E. Delavan ave.
Sussex.
Warwick ave.

Camden, 1st street west of Delaware ave. running N. from Olive to Erie R'y tracks.

Camden Ave., 1st street E of Maine running N. from E. Hertel ave to Alvin av. Changed to Cordova, March 20, 1893.

Camp, N. fr. 424 Sycamore to 519 Genesee.

Campbell, 6th street E. of Colvin running N. fr. St. Lawrence ave. to Kenmore ave.(near north city line).

Canal, N.W. fr. 100 Main to 164 Erie. (Between Main and Commer-

cial is called Lake).
1 Hanover.
19 Lloyd.
57 Commercial.
60 Maiden Lane.
84 State.
100 Davenport al.
106 LeCouteulx.
117 Evans.
169 Erie.

Canal Alley. Changed to Court place in 1881.

Carl, 1st street east of Grider running N. fr. East Ferry to 801 East Delavan ave.
Puffer.
E. Delavan ave.

Carlton, east from 909 Main to 740 Genesee.
19 Washington.
49 Ellicott.
75 Oak.
98 Goodlin al.
113 Elm.
130 Neptune.
133 Swiveller al.
149 Michigan.
175 Maple.
201 Mulberry.
227 Locust.
253 Lemon.
277 Orange.
305 Peach.
329 Grape.
355 Rose.
379 Beech.
395 Jefferson.
529 Genesee.

Carlyle Ave., west from Parkside ave. to Stanley place.
Colvin.
Stanley place.

Carmine Place, W. from 448 Bird ave. to 445 West Forest ave.

Carolina, N. E. fr. Erie canal to 168 W. Tupper.
19 Fourth.
39 Efner.
59 Fifth.
83 Front ave.

121 Seventh.
153 Niagara.
180 Fell alley.
189 Prospect ave.
219 Whitney pl.
244 Tenth.
247 Johnson's Park.
268 West ave.
277 Tracy.
292 Garden.
325 Tupper.

Carroll, east from 205 Washington to Indian Reservation line (nr. Seneca street).
28 Ellicott.
87 Wells.
141 Michigan.
243 Chicago.
339 Louisiana.
447 Alabama.
Hamburgh.
545 Jefferson.
553 Red Jacket.
599 Heacock.
661 Van Rensselaer.
725 Hydraulic.
781 Griffin.
815 Reservation line

Carter (in 5th ward) 3d street south of Tifft running east fr. Hopkins to South Park av. (formerly White's Corners rd.)

Carter (in 25th ward) 1st street north of N.Y.C. R. R. (Belt Line) at Cross Cut Junct. running north fr. Pierce Steam Heat'g Works to Hertel ave. (also 1st street east of McpPherson running S.fr. Hertel ave.) Changed to Mandan, March 20, 1893.

Cary, west from 210 Delaware ave.
33 Morgan.

Cass, 6th street east of Military rd. running north fr. Hertel ave. to Race. Changed to

Norris, March 20, 1893.

Cassy, south from 1059 William to lot 58.

Castor Alley, north from 298 William st. to 427 Broadway.

Cattaraugus, 4th street S. of Kensington ave. running E. fr. Bailey ave. to Eggert.
Suffolk.
Orleans.
Ulster.
Eggert.

Cayuga, east fr. 885 Jefferson to 300 Grey.

Cazenovia, N. E. fr. 1358 Abbott road to 2190 Seneca.
Cumberland ave.
Cazenovia creek.
Seneca.

Cecil, 2d street west of Delaware ave. running north fr. Olive to Erie R'y tracks.

Cedar, N. fr. 348 Swan to 305 Broadway.
23 S. Division.
53 N. Division.
85 Eagle.
127 Clinton.
199 William.
313 Broadway.

Cement, east fr. Range ave. to Bailey ave. (2d street south of E. Hertel ave.)
Park Ridge ave.
Lenox ave.
Bailey ave.

Centre, north from 120 Seneca to 101 Swan.
Douglas alley.
Swan.

Centre (in 25th ward) 1st street north of Warwick ave. running E. from Andover street to Bailey av. Changed to Duffield, March 20, 1893.

Central Ave., north fr. 1404 William to N. Y. C. R. R. tracks.

Central Wharf, west fr. foot of Main to foot of Commercial.

Chadduck Ave., east fr. Tonawanda to Harold ave. (6th street N. of Ontario).
Condon ave.
Harold ave.

Chain Alley, north from 254 Amherst.

Champlin, northeast fr. 493 Spring to 212 Mortimer.
27 Tousey.
39 Mortimer.

Chandler, east fr. Military road to Bridgeman (2d street north of Amherst).

Chapin Parkway, northwest fr. Chapin place to Soldiers' place.
St. James pl.
47 W. Delavan ave.
140 Potomac ave.
189 Soldiers' place.

Chapin Place, at junct. of Delaware avenue, Bouck ave. and Chapin parkway.

Charles, east from Erie canal to 188 Terrace.

Charlotte Ave., east fr. 993 Avenue A to Hill.
Holden.
Hill.

Chatam, northeast fr. Arlington to Brighton (1st street south of Broadway .

Chatham, east fr. Elmwood ave. to Atlantic (1st st. N. of Hodge ave.)

Chaucer, 1st street S. of Kenmore ave (north city line) running W from Crosby to A1

den (N. W. from International Junct).
Hawthorne.
Hecla.
Dryden.
Alden.

Chautauqua, 1st street S. of Kensington ave. running east fr. Bailey ave. to Eggert.
Suffolk.
Orleans.
Ulster.
Eggert.

Cheektowaga (formerly Spencer ave.), second street east of Scajaquada creek running south from Genesee (near east city line).

Chelsea Place (formerly Miller place) N. from Puffer to E. Delavan ave. (4th street E. of Fillmore ave.) Formerly Avenue A.

Chemung, 3d street S. of Kensington ave. running east fr. Bailey ave to Eggert.
Suffolk.·
Orleans.
Ulster.
Eggert.

Chenango, northwest fr. 459 West Utica to 399 West Ferry.
Rhode Island.
Massachusetts.
West Ferry.

Cherry, N. E. from 727 Michigan to 955 Virginia.
31 Spruce.
34 Maple.
68 Mulberry.
88 Goodell.
89 Hickory.
104 Locust.
140 Lemon.
151 Spring.
174 Orange.
199 Mortimer.
208 Peach.

248 Grape.
298 Virginia.

Chester, north from 178 Glenwood ave. to Puffer.
47 Woodlawn ave.
97 East Ferry.
Dexter.
Puffer.

Chestnut, N. from 224 Swan to 227 N. Division.
Booth alley.
25 S. Division.
55 N. Division.

Chicago, N. fr. Buffalo river to 267 Swan.
25 Ohio.
73 Mackinaw.
107 Miami.
149 Elk.
185 Fulton.
205 Hamill alley.
221 Perry.
248 Scott.
251 Warren.
287 Granger.
291 Main and Hamburgh canal.
341 Exchange.
369 Carroll.
395 Seneca.
419 Myrtle.
443 Swan.

Child, east from Hamburgh turnpike to Buffalo creek.

Chippewa, E. from 587 Main to 102 Genesee.
19 Washington.
53 Ellicott.
68 Genesee.

Chippewa, W. from 590 Main to junct. Georgia and Whitney pl.
25 Pearl.
42 Asbury alley.
55 Franklin.
97 Delaware ave.
142 Morgan.
177 Whitney pl.
186 Georgia.

Choate, 1st street S. of Cazenovia, running

W. from Abbott rd.

Church, W. fr. 312 Main to Erie canal.
21 Pearl.
43 Franklin.
83 Delaware ave.
97 Terrace.
128 Birdsall.
156 Bingham.
157 Jackson.
171 W. Genesee
183 Fourth.
Erie canal.

Churchill, N. fr. 228 Amherst to 253 Austin.

Cincinnati, S. from 257 Ohio to Buffalo river.

Circle, Junction North, Wadsworth, Fourteenth and Pennsylvania sts., and Porter and Richm'd aves.

City Ship Canal, from Buffalo river, near lighthouse, to south channel.

Clare (formerly Raze), N. from 916 Eagle to 347 Howard.
3 James.
45 Clinton.
Fritz alley.
68 Bristol.
San Domingo al
105 Oneida.
Steuben al.
Olga place.
S. Railroad ave.
165 Howard.

Clarence, 3d street W. of Delaware ave. running north fr. Olive to Erie R'y tracks.

Clarendon Place, second street W. of Delaware ave. running N. fr. Bird ave. to The Park.
West Forest ave.
The Park.

Clarion Place, north fr. Philadelphia ave. to Skillen.
Evelyn.

STREET DIRECTORY.

South Newfield.
Skillen.

Clark, N. fr. 88 Curtiss to 1035 Broadway.
Peckham.
Lovejoy.
214 Grimes.
Broadway.

Clark and Skinner Canal from Buffalo river to Hamburgh canal, E. of Mississippi street.

Clay, N. fr. 36 Military rd. to 289 Austin.

Clayton (form'ly Busch) 2d street east of Military rd. running N. fr. Race to Kenmore ave. (north city line).
Layer ave.
Kofler ave.
Ruhl ave.
Sherriff ave.
Blum ave.
Ritt ave.
Kenmore ave.

Clement Place, 1st street N. of E. Delavan ave. running east fr. Gillette ave. to N. Y. C. R. R. (belt line) tks.

Clemo, N. fr. 1094 Clinton to Fleming.

Cleveland, W. fr. Delaware avenue to Elmwood ave. (1st street N. of West Ferry).
Pacific ave.
Elmwood ave.

Clevelad Ave., N. fr. 452 West Ferry to 495 Breck'ri'ge. Changed to Iroquois, March 20, 1893.

Clifford, east from 375 Smith to Selkirk.

Clifton north from 264 East Utica to 221 East Ferry. Changed to Verplanck.

Clifton Place, N. E. from 109 Cottage to 256 Al-

len. Changed to Day's Park, March 20, 1893.

Clinton, east fr. 411 Main to east line of city.
19 Washington.
51 Ellicott.
87 Oak.
123 Elm.
159 Michigan.
241 Union.
258 Picard alley.
273 Pine.
302 W. Bennett.
Clinton Market.
322 E. Bennett.
330 Cedar.
373 Walnut.
390 Sylvan alley.
407 Hickory.
439 Pratt.
471 Spring.
545 Jefferson.
573 Madison.
603 Monroe.
629 Adams.
657 Watson.
685 Emslie.
S. Railroad ave.
725 Bond.
777 Lord.
813 Smith.
855 Montgomery.
897 Clare.
939 Fillmore ave.
962 Metcalfe.
969 Bass.
1000 Jones.
1025 Bender.
Lewis.
1094 Clemo.
Laux.
1214 Babcock.
1250 Bushnell ave.
1270 Gilbert ave.
1290 Scoville ave.
1340 Baitz ave.
Faxon.
1525 Bailey ave.
Olsen.
Snow ave.
Roberts ave.
Spaulding ave.
1832 Weiss.
1851 Weimar.

1873 Cable.
1880 Pulaski.
1893 Barnard.
Fenton.
Holly.
Weaver ave.
Willet.
Seifert.
2009 S. Ogden.
2040 Wheelock.
Cochrane.
2071 City line.

Clinton Ave., E. fr. Erie canal and 1471 Niagara to 1474 Delaware ave. Changed to Potomac ave., March 20, 1893.
21 Niagara.
75 West ave.
111 Dewitt.
187 Herkimer.
231 Congress.
251 Grant.
287 Emily.
319 Tryon place.
351 Hoyt.
385 Baynes.
485 Richmond ave.
Howard ave.
Ashland ave.
Elmwood ave.
611 Bidwell park'y.
Brantford pl.
731 Chapin parkw'y
Windsor ave.
751 Delaware ave.

Coatsworth Alley, east from 17 Hayward to 272 Hamburgh.

Cochrane, N. fr. Clinton to Griswold street (at eastern city line).

Coe, east from 1215 Main to Ellicott.

Coit, N. fr. 292 Howard to 843 Broadway.
55 William.
159 Peckham.
223 Lovejoy.
298 Broadway.

Colchester (formerly Westchester), 1st st. S. of Kensington ave.

STREET DIRECTORY.

running east fr. Chautauqua to Eggert.
Suffolk.
Orleans.
Eggert.

Coleman Alley, S. from Vine, between Michigan and Elm.

Colfax Ave., E. fr. Grider to Wyoming ave. (1st street S. of Kensington ave.)
Deerfield ave.
Wyoming ave.

Collaton, east from 2287 Niagara to Fuller.

College, N. from 25 Cottage to 260 North.
52 Maryland.
87 Allen.
150 Arlington pl.
189 North.

College Place, N. from Johnson's pl. to Park place.

Colorado Ave., N. from Genesee to E. Ferry (5th street E. of Moselle).

Colson Ave., N. from Humboldt street to Dingens (4th street west of city line). Changed Oct. 1891, to Weaver ave.

Colton, W. from Erie canal to Lake Erie (from towpath opposite Pennsylvania.)

Columbia, N. fr. Buffalo river to 129 Scott.
7 Ohio.
27 Elk.
93 Perry.
Scott.

Columbus Ave., 3d st. north of E. Hertel av. running east fr. Main to Bailey avenue. Changed to Lisbon, March 20, 1893.

Columbus Place, 1st st. S. of Triangle running east from South Park ave. (formerly White's Corners rd.) to Boulevard.

Colvin, N. fr. 1302 Amherst to N. city line (Kenmore ave.)
Tillinghast.
Crescent ave.
121 N.Y.C.R.R. (belt line station).
Linden ave.
Dryden ave.
Carlyle ave.
273 Hertel ave.
Tacoma ave.
Taunton pl.
Bangor pl.
Kenmore avenue (north city line).

Comet (formerly Crescent), 4th street west of Delaware ave. running north fr. Olive to Erie R'y tracks.

Commercial, N. E. from Buffalo river to 8 Terrace.
13 Prime.
22 Water.
60 Canal.
76 Erie canal.
106 Pearl.
121 Terrace.

Compromise Alley, N. W. fr. 312 Maryland to 177 West avenue. Changed to Malta pl., January, 1890.

Concord, W. fr. Curtiss to Arlington (second street N. of Lovejoy).

Condon Ave., N. from Crowley ave. to Esser ave. (1st street east of Tonawanda).
Ross ave.
Laird ave.
Chadduck ave.
Esser ave.

Congress, N. from 184 Bouck av. to 231 Clinton ave.

W. Delavan ave.
Potomac ave.

Connecticut, N. E. from 656 Front ave. to 222 Richmond ave.
125 Seventh.
150 Niagara.
197 Prospect ave.
239 Fargo ave.
275 West ave.
311 Plymouth ave.
347 Thirteenth.
383 Fourteenth.
419 Fifteenth.
454 Sixteenth.
485 Seventeenth.
516 Ripley pl.
519 Eighteenth.
524 Richmond ave.

Cooper, E. fr. 2334 Main to N.Y.C.R.R. Belt line. Changed to Oakwood place.

Cordova (form'ly Camden ave.), 1st street east of Main running north fr. East Hertel ave. to Alvin ave.
La Salle ave.
Minnesota ave.
Lisbon.
Alvin ave.

Cornelia, N. E. from 274 Seymour to Eagle.
3 Smith.
61 N. Division.
115 Eagle.

Cornell, 1st street west of Main running N. fr. Tyler to Eley (near north city line).
Hendricks.
Heath.
Eley.

Cornell, 1st street east of Tonawanda running N. W. fr. Martin to Ontario. Changed to Gallatin, March 20, 1893.

Cornwall Ave., N. from East Ferry to Warwick ave. (5th street east of Grider.

STREET DIRECTORY.

Puffer.
E. Delavan ave.
Sussex.
Warwick ave.

Cottage, N. W. from 370
Virginia to 297 Hudson.
  25 College.
  75 Maryland.
  109 Clifton pl.
    Day's park.
  125 Norris pl.
  151 Hudson.

Coulson, 8th street N.
of Hertel ave., running west fr. Military rd. to N.Y.C.R.R. tks.

Court, W. fr. 428 Main to Erie canal.
  23 Pearl.
  53 Franklin.
  78 Delaware ave.
  125 Niagara square.
  141 Morgan.
  167 Staats.
  185 Terrace.
  209 Seventh.
  215 Front ave.
  220 Court pl.
  242 Wilkeson.
  257 Fifth.
  325 Fourth.
  339 Georgia.
  363 Erie canal.

Courtland, 1st street E.
of Bailey av. running north from E. Delavan ave. to Sugar st.

Court Place, S. from 220
Court to 124 Jackson.

Crescent, 4th street W.
of Delaware ave. running north fr. Olive to Erie Railway tracks. Changed to Comet, March 20, 1893.

Crescent Ave., 1st street
W. fr. Main, running N. W. fr. Humboldt pk'way to Colvin st.
  Robie.
  Florence.
  Oakwood pl.
  Jewett ave.

Elam pl.
Russell.
Amherst.
Summit ave.
Woodward ave.
Parkside ave.
Colvin.

Crocker, N. fr. Lovejoy
to Broadway (first st. east of Bailey ave.)
  Moreland.
  Regent.
  Stone.
  Broadway.

Crosby, N. fr. Brinton
to Kenmore ave. (N. city line) near International junction.

Crowley Ave., east from
Niagara to Welland (5th street north of Ontario).
  Palace ave.
  Tonawanda.
  Condon ave.
  Welland ave.

Crystal Ave., 1st street
south of Tifft, running W. fr. South Park av. (form'ly White's Corners road).

Cumberland Ave., N.W.
fr. Cazenovia to Melrose (1st street east of Abbott road).
  Meridan.
  Salem.
  Athol.
  Tamarack.
  Portland.
  Milford.
  Rutland.
  Melrose.

Curtiss, N. fr. 772 William to 1225 Broadw'y
  Lombard.
  Gibson.
  88 Clark.
  Sears.
  Playter.
  302 Lovejoy.
  Newton.
  Concord.
  _ Grimes.

Geneva.
Dover.
Ashley.
Broadway.

Custer (formerly Sheridan), 1st street N. of
Hertel ave. running west from Main to D., L. & W. R. R. tracks.

Cypress, N. E. from 571
Michigan to 318 Pine.

Daisy, 4th street east of
Jefferson, running N. from Florida to East Delavan ave.

Dakota, 1st street S. of
Hertel ave. running east fr. Delaware ave to Fairchild place.

Dalton, 1st street east of
White's Cors. plank rd., running south fr. Downing to southerly city line. Changed to Hines, March 20, 1893.

Dalton Ave., 2d street
east of Colvin, running north fr. Bangor place to Kenmore ave (north city line.)

Dana Ave., 4th street
east of Tonawanda running N. W. from Rano to Crowley ave. Changed to Welland, March 20, 1883.

Danforth, N. fr. 158 W.
Forest av. to 25 Bradley.

Dann, north from foot
of Amherst to foot of Hamilton.

Danube, north fr. Genesee to E. Ferry street
(2d street east of Moselle).

Dart, N. fr. 188 W. Forest ave. to Scajaquada creek.
  97 Bradley.
  Letchworth.
  163 Scajaquada cr'k

Daugherty's Alley, N. from 248 Seneca to 59 Myrtle. Changed to Seneca pl. in 1884.

Davenport Alley, S. E. fr. 100 Canal to 26 Fly.

Davey, north from 1648 William to Broadw'y (6th street east of Bailey ave.)
Ludington.
Lovejoy.
Vanderbilt.
Reimann.
Broadway.

Davis, N. W. from 702 Jefferson to 551 Genesee.

Davis Ave., 2d street west fr. Main running N. W. fr. Humboldt parkway to Crescent avenue. Changed to Woodward avenue, March 20, 1893.

Day's Park, north from 107 Cottage to 256 Allen and 2 Wadsworth.

Dayton, west from 48 Main to 35 Prime.

Dearborn, N. from 44 Tonaw'nda to 49 Hertel ave.
49 Wayne.
134 Parish.
195 Amherst.
263 Hamilton.
335 Austin.
401 Farmer.
445 Hertel ave.

Deer, 2d street east of N. Y. C. R. R. tracks running north from Hertel ave. to Gladstone.

Deerfield Ave. (formerly Huntingdon ave.) 2d street east of Grider running north fr. East Delavan ave. to Kensington ave.
Litchfield ave.
Sussex.

Gratiot ave.
Maple Ridge ave.
Pembroke ave.
Warwick ave.
Colfax ave.
Mendola.
Kensington ave.

Delavan Ave. East, fr. 1851 Main to city line.
81 Jefferson.
Pleasant pl.
Meech ave.
Hager.
Pansy.
Oak Grove ave.
Daisy.
Blaine.
Humboldt pk'y.
Gillette ave.
473 Fillmore ave.
Winchester ave.
Bitter.
Harrison ave.
Chelsea pl.
Dutton ave.
Sheridan ave.
Amsterdam.
Pfaudler.
750 Grider.
801 Carl.
Durham ave.
Deerfield ave.
Schuele ave.
Wyoming ave.
Cambridge ave.
Cornwall ave.
Northumberland ave.
Norfolk.
Herbert ave.
Olympic ave.
Ocean ave.
Atlantic ave.
1163 Bailey ave.
Gruner.
Rumsey.
Courtland.
Desquesne ave.
Hazelwood ave.
Floss ave.
Wilkes ave.
Harriett.
Edison.
Hickman.
Wright ave.
1555 City line.

Delavan Ave. West, E. from Black Rock harbor to 1397 Niagara to 1850 Main.
25 Niagara.
79 West ave.
115 Dewitt.
181 Herkimer.
215 Congress.
247 Grant.
281 Emily.
315 Tryon pl.
347 Hoyt.
379 Baynes.
479 Richmond ave.
501 Norwood ave.
533 Bidwell p'kway.
579 Elmwood ave.
Brantford pl.
785 Chapin p'kway.
855 Delaware ave.
923 Linwood ave.
993 Harvard pl.
1117 Main.

Delaware Place, W. fr. 376 Delaware ave. to 327 Virginia. Changed to Trinity, March 20, 1893.

Delaware Ave., N. from 223 Terrace to north line of city.
13 Church.
51 Eagle.
89 Niagara square.
119 West Mohawk.
173 West Huron.
202 Cary.
227 West Chippewa.
274 Johnson's park.
286 Johnson's park.
314 Tracy.
349 Tupper.
376 Trinity.
419 Edward.
457 Virginia.
553 Allen.
661 North.
748 Summer.
829 Barker.
907 Bryant.
954 Hodge ave.
999 West Utica.
1064 Lexington ave.
Highland ave.
1151 West Ferry.

Cleveland st.
Auburn ave.
1337 Chapin pl. and
Bouck ave.
1401 W. Delavan ave.
Forest Lawn
Cemetery.
1474 Potomac ave.
1538 Bird ave.
1616 W. Forest ave.
2069 Amherst.
N. Y. C. belt line
R. R.
Duncan.
Tioga.
Dakota.
2333 Hertel ave.
Delaware Ave.
Cemetery.
Olive.
Erie R'y and D.
L. & W. R. tks.
Hinman ave.
Sessions.
Ramsdell ave.
Villa ave.
Kenmore ave.
2736 City line.

Demond Place, N. from
160 E. Tupper to 675
Virginia.
67 Goodell.
101 Burton.
144 Virginia.

Dempster, E from 801
Bailey ave. to Greene
street (1st street N. of
William).

Denver, 4th street N. of
Hertel ave. running
west from Military
rd. to N.Y.C.R.R. tks.

Depew Ave., 2d street
N. of Amherst run-
ning west from Main
to Linden ave.
Wesley.
Parker ave.
Voorhis.
Starin ave.
Linden ave.

Depot, south from 1067
William to lot No. 58.

De Rutte, north fr. 414

Virginia to rear of 57
Fremont place.

Deshler, S. from 1513
Broadway to Amity.
Grand.
Amity.

Desquesne Ave., third
street east of Bailey
ave. running south fr.
East Delavan ave.

Detroit, N. fr. 318 How-
ard to 875 Broadway.
55 William.
159 Peckham.
223 Lovejoy.
323 Broadway.

Dewitt, north from 116
Breckenridge to Sca-
jaquada creek.
50 Auburn ave.
111 Bouck ave.
147 Helen.
179 W. Delavan ave.
217 Perkins pl.
251 Potomac ave.
287 Annie place.
319 Bird ave.
357 Pooley pl.
387 West Forest av.
469 Bradley.
481 Bull.
513 Scajaquada c'rk

Dexter, east from 1625
Main and 1597 Michi-
gan to International
Exposition Grounds.
Masten.
Chester.
Waverly.
Purdy.
Alexandria pl.
Jefferson.
International Expo-
sition Grounds.

Dickens Alley (formerly
Orlando alley), east
from 259 Washington
to 18 Ellicott.

Dillon (formerly Ricker
ave.) 1st street north
of Seneca running E.
from Fillmore ave.

Dingens, E. fr 459 Bai-
ley ave. to city line.

187 Weiss.
Weaver ave.
Abel.
363 S. Ogden.
New S. Ogden.
425 City line.

Doat, E. fr. Genesee to
east city line (fourth
street E. of Moselle).
Zimmermann.
Philip.
Rawlins.
Willard.
Burgard ave.
Bailey ave.
Brinkmann.
Sumner pl.
Keystone.
Poplar ave.
Petri.
Jahle.
City line.

Dock, S. from 32 Water
to Buffalo river.

Dodge, east from 1177
Main to St. Michael.
51 Ellicott.
133 Michgan.
207 Masten.
363 Jefferson.
Gerhardt.
Berlin.
Timon.
Roehrer.
Wohlers.
St. Michael.

Dold, Tifft to Whitfield.
Changed to Ithaca,
March 20, 1883.

Dole, north from 1237
Elk to 1359 Seneca.
52 Perry.
103 Seneca.

Doll, 2d street west of
Bailey ave. running
N. from Walden ave.
Changed to May,
March 20, 1893.

Doll Ave., S. fr. Walden
ave. to West Shore
street (3d street W. of
Bailey ave.) Changed
to May, March 20, '93.

Douglas Alley, E fr. 23 Ellicott to Centre.

Dover, W. fr. Curtiss to Brighton (1st street S. of Broadway).

Downing, east from 1045 South Park ave. (formerly White's Cors. rd.) to 1888 Abbott rd.
Hines.
Sibley.
Augusta.
Boulevard.
Abbott road.

Dryden, N. fr. Chaucer to Kenmore ave. (N. W. of International junct.) near northerly city line.

Dryden Ave., 2d street south of Hertel ave. running west fr. Colvin street to Stanley place.

Duchess, east from Suffolk to Eggert (second street south of Kensington ave.)
Orleans.
Ulster.
Eggert.

Duckwitz, N. fr. 450 E. Utica to Glenwood avenue.

Duerstein, 1st street S. of Indian Church rd. running east fr. Seneca to city line.

Duffield (formerly Centre, in 25th ward), 1st street north of Warwick ave. running E. from Andover to Bailey ave.
Irvington ave.
Tremont ave.
Westchester ave.
Frankfort ave.
Bailey ave.

Duluth (formerly Bowen, in 25th ward), 7th street east of Colvin running north fr. St.

Lawrence av. to Kenmore av. (near northerly city line).

Duncan, 3d street S. of Hertel ave. running east from Delaware ave. to Fairchild pl.

Dupont, N. fr. 342 East Utica to 303 E. Ferry.
31 Glenwood ave.
Winslow ave.
Woodlawn ave.
125 East Ferry.

Durham Ave., 1st street east of Grider running north from East Delavan ave. to Sussex.
Litchfield ave.
Sussex.

Durrenberger Pl. (formerly Urban alley) N. from 492 High to 479 Best.
51 Alvin.
71 East North.
140 Best.

Dutton Ave., 4th street east of Avenue A running north from East Ferry to East Delavan ave.
Puffer.
E. Delavan ave.

Dyer, 1st street west of Abby running south from 521 Abbott rd. to D., L. & W. R. R. tks.

Eagle, east fr. 377 Main to 176 Fillmore ave.
18 Washington.
53 Ellicott.
89 Oak.
125 Elm.
149 Mead alley
161 Michigan.
250 Union.
281 Pine.
355 Cedar.
376 Walnut.
415 Hickory.
448 Pratt.
490 Spring.
565 Jefferson.

586 Madison.
614 Monroe.
624 Grosvenor.
642 Adams.
670 Watson.
696 Emslie.
743 Bond.
789 Lord.
832 Smith.
874 Montgomery.
Elizabeth.
916 Clare.
Cornelia.
956 Fillmore ave.

Eagle, West, W. fr. 368 Main to 269 Terrace.
31 Pearl.
52 Franklin.
93 Delaware ave.
139 Morgan.
139 W. Genesee.
140 Terrace.

East, from 65 Wayne to 61 Arthur.
66 Parish.
119 Amherst.
87 Hamilton.
57 Austin.
323 Farmer.
374 Hertel ave.
388 Grace.
Garfield.
421 Arthur.

East Bennett, N. fr. 322 Clinton to 159 William.

East Delavan Ave. See Delavan ave., East.

East Ferry. See Ferry, East.

East Forest Ave. See Forest ave., East.

East Genesee. Changed to Genesee.

East Hertel Ave., E. fr. 2995 Main to Bailey av.
Cordova.
Range ave.
Park Ridge ave.
Lenox ave.
Bailey ave.

East Huron. See Huron, East.

East Market, N. fr. 138 Elk to Hamburgh canal.
29 Fulton.
65 Perry.
109 Scott.
133 Hamburgh can'l

East Mohawk. See Mohawk, East.

East North. See North, East.

East Parade Ave., N. fr. 1186 Genesee to Puerner ave.
Bardol.
N. Parade ave.
Puerner ave.

East Seneca. Changed to Seneca.

East Summer, 1st street N. of Best running east from Ellicott to Masten. Changed to Edna place, March 20, 1893.

East Swan. Changed to Swan.

East Tupper. See Tupper, East.

East Utica. See Utica, East.

Eastwood Place (formerly Humboldt Pl.) 2d street N. of Jegerson running east from Main to Humboldt parkway.

Eaton, E. fr. 1283 Michigan to 1246 Jefferson.
Masten.
Jefferson.

Eckhardt Avenue, first street S. of Mineral Spring rd., running N. E. from Seneca st. to Mineral Spring rd. Changed to Hayden, March 20, 1893.

Echhert, N. from Esser ave. to O'Neil (fourth street east of Tonawanda).

Roesch ave.
O'Neil.

Edison, 5th street east of Bailey avenue running N. from E. Delavan ave. to Sugar.

Edmunds, 6th street S. of 569 Abbott rd. running west from Abby to Hopkins.

Edmunds Avenue, 7th street S. of Abbott rd. running east fr. Abby to Hopkins. Changed to Edmunds, March 20, 1893.

Edna Place (formerly East Summer), first street N. of Best running east from Ellicott to Masten.
Michigan.
Masten.

Edson, 2d street south of Indian Church rd. running east fr. Seneca to city line.

Edward, west from 776 Main to 357 Virginia.
51 Franklin.
91 Delaware ave.
135 N. Morgan.
187 Virginia.

Edwin Place (formerly Goodell alley), N. 154 East Tupper to 159 Goodell.

Efner, N. W. from 100 Georgia to 46 Hudson.
97 Carolina.
167 Virginia.
237 Maryland.
Hudson.

Eggert, N. from 387 Sugar at east city line to northeast city line.
Cattaraugus.
Chemung.
Rockland.
Chautauqua.
Duchess.
Oswego.
Ulster.

Colchester.
507 Kensington.
775 N. E. city line.

Eighteenth, fr. 516 Connecticut to 428 Vermont. Changed to Ripley place in 1889.

Eighteenth, N. W. from 429 Vermont to 388 W. Ferry.
West Utica.
Rhode Island.
Massachusetts.
Hampshire.
West Ferry.

Elam Place, west from Greenfield to Crescent ave. (1st street north of Jewett ave.)

Eleventh. Changed to West ave. in year 1881.

Eley, N. W. fr. 3276 Main to north city line.
Gallatin.
Bruce.
Mildred.
Brinton.
Nicholson ave.
Emerson street.
North city line.

Elgas, 7th street east of Tonawanda, running north from Esser ave. to O'Neil.
Zinns ave.
Roesch ave.
O'Neil.

Elizabeth, N. E. fr. 252 Seymour to Eagle.
32 Smith.
59 N. Division.
Eagle.

Elk, E. from 73 Ohio to junct. with 1627 Seneca.
8 Illinois.
29 Mississippi.
71 Columbia.
102 Michigan.
120 W. Market.
138 E. Market.
153 Moore.
172 Marvin.

205 Chicago.
299 Louisiana.
340 Hayward.
405 Alabama.
467 Hamburgh.
497 Sidway.
514 Red Jacket.
527 Katharine.
559 Fitzgerald.
585 Abbott road.
627 Van Rensselaer.
765 Euclid place.
809 Smith.
871 Selkirk.
933 Lee.
950 Peabody.
996 Walter.
1021 Maurice.
1043 Orlando.
1090 Babcock.
1106 Gorham.
1134 Winona.
1156 Bradford.
1237 Dole.
1397 Melvin place.
    Keppel.
1490 Seneca.

Ellicott, N. from 60 Exchange to Riley st. (Opened fr. Exchange to Seneca in 1886).
    Carroll.
    Seneca.
18 Dickens alley.
23 Douglas.
41 Swan.
73 S. Division.
104 N. Division.
133 Eagle.
183 Clinton.
213 Broadway.
246 East Mohawk.
255 Hersee alley.
299 East Huron.
341 Genesee.
353 East Chippewa.
471 East Tupper.
537 Goodell.
577 Burton.
617 Virginia.
661 Carlton.
747 High.
783 Goodrich.
817 E. North.
    St. Paul.
897 Best.

    Edna place.
963 Dodge.
    Coe.
995 Southampton.
1029 Northampton.
    Riley.

Ellicott Turnpike, N. E. fr. 767 Avenue A to city line. Changed to Kensington av. in '87.

Elm, N. from 124 Swan to 117 Best.
23 S. Division.
51 N. Division.
81 Eagle.
123 Clinton.
157 Vine.
195 Broadway.
269 Sycamore.
343 Genesee.
411 East Tupper.
485 Goodell.
524 Burton.
571 Virginia.
637 Carlton.
699 High.
732 Goodrich.
771 East North.
845 Best.

Elmwood Ave., N. from 392 Virginia to 581 W. Forest ave.
87 Allen.
189 North.
299 Summer.
440 Bryant.
    Hodge ave.
    Chatham.
    West Utica.
    Anderson pl.
    Lexington ave.
    Highland ave.
    West Ferry.
    Breckenridge.
    Cleveland.
    Auburn ave.
    Lancaster ave.
    Bouck ave.
    St. James pl.
    W. Delavan ave.
    Bidwell park'y.
    Potomac ave.
    Bird ave.
    W. Forest ave.

Elsie Place, 2d street N.

of East Ferry, running east from Purdy to Alexandria pl.

Emerson (formerly Linden ave. No. 2, in 25th ward), east fr. Eley to Crosby, 1st street south of Kenmore av. (north city line).

Emerson Pl., 1st street N. of Glenwood ave. running east fr. Michigan to Masten.

Emily, N. fr. 250 Bouck ave. to 287 Clinton av.
61 W. Delavan ave.
235 Potomac ave.

Empire (formerly Harrison ave., 14th ward) east from Miller ave. to Goodyear ave.

Emslie, N. fr. 738 Seneca to 679 Broadway.
    Schuyler.
31 Seymour.
46 Bass pl.
57 S. Division.
    Meteor alley.
87 N. Division.
93 S. Railroad ave.
119 Eagle.
135 James.
163 Clinton.
    Fritz alley.
195 Bristol.
    San Domingo al.
227 Oneida.
249 Howard.
313 William.
411 Peckham.
477 Lovejoy.
527 Broadway.

Emson. See Imson.

Englewood Ave. See Eley.

Ensign, E. fr. Katharine to Buffalo river.

Erie, S. W. fr. 308 Main to 134 Water.
33 Pearl.
66 Franklin.
53 Swan.
82 Terrace.

120 W. Seneca.
128 Lock.
147 Erie Canal.
164 Canal.
170 Peacock.
179 Ship canal.
195 River.
Jane.
270 Water.

Erie Canal, N.W. fr. 110 Main st. to city line.

Esser Ave., E. fr. Niagara to Skillen (eighth street N. of Ontario).
Palace ave.
Tonawanda.
Baxter.
Kertz.
Stephen pl.
Ruth ave.
Eckhert.
Ullman.
Argus.
Elgas.
Philadelphia ave.
Evelyn.
S. Newfield.
Skillen.

Essex, N. fr. 530 Rhode Island to 511 Massachusetts.

Euclid, E. fr. Bailey ave to Greene (3d street north of William st.) Changed to Hennepin, March 20, 1893.

Euclid Ave., N. fr. Leroy ave. to Rodney (3d street east of Fillmore ave.) (formerly Avenue A). Changed to Richlawn avenue, March 20, 1893.

Euclid Place, S. fr. 765 Elk to Abbott road.
Prenatt.
Abbott road.

Eugene, 1st street west of Delaware ave. running N. fr. D., L. & W. R. R. tks to Kenmore ave. (near northerly city line).

Hinman ave.
Ramsdell ave.
Kenmore ave.

Eureka Place (formerly German) N. from 338 Sycamore to 431 Genesee.

Evans, N. E. from 69 Water to 82 Terrace.
6 Norton.
23 Fly.
46 Peacock.
53 Canal.
86 Terrace.

Evans Ship Canal, N.E. fr. Buffalo river to Erie street.

Evelyn, S. W. fr. Esser ave. to Clarion place (fifth street east of Tonawanda).
Ontario.
Clarion place.

Excelsior (in Union Iron Co.'s tract, So. Buffalo), from Packer to Buffalo river.

Exchange, E. from 177 Main to 987 Seneca.
23 Washington.
57 Beak.
60 Ellicott.
121 N. Y. C. R. R. depot.
122 Wells.
179 Michigan.
Erie R'y depot.
281 Chicago.
383 Louisiana.
489 Alabama.
557 Hamburgh.
598 Jefferson.
609 Red Jacket.
660 Peacock.
727 Van Rensselaer.
794 Hydraulic.
837 Griffin.
921 Smith.
981 Selkirk.
1007 Seneca.

Exeter Ave., 1st street east of Delaware ave. running north from

Hertel ave. to Taunton place.
Tacoma ave.
Taunton place.

Express, W. fr. 222 Pearl to 121 Franklin.

Fairchild Place (formerly Stanley place), 1st street east of Delaware ave. running N. from Duncan to Hertel ave.
Tioga.
Dakota.
Hertel ave.

Fairfield, N. W. fr. about 2470 Main to abo't 1700 Amherst.
Orchard place.
Russell.
Vernon.
Amherst.

Fairmount Avenue, 1st street north of Ontario running N. E. fr. Skillen to city line.
Albemarle.
Belmont.
Seabrook.
City line.

Fargo Ave., N.W. from 234 Hudson to 1075 Niagara.
61 Pennsylvania.
129 Jersey.
197 Porter ave.
263 Connecticut.
331 Vermont.
399 Rhode Island.
467 Massachusetts.
535 Hampshire.
579 School.
636 Niagara.

Farmer, E. fr. Erie canal to 442 Tonawanda.
17 Niagara.
47 Dearborn.
71 East.
110 Gurnsey.
121 Thompson.
149 Gorton.
177 Tonawanda.

Faxon, N. fr. 1552 Clinton.

STREET DIRECTORY.

Fay (formerly Leo ave.)
S. from Walden ave.
to West Shore st. (1st
street west of Bailey
avenue).

Federal Ave. (formerly
Livingston ave.) N. fr.
Kensington ave. to
Rodney (2d street E.
of Grider).
  Shawnee ave.
  Rodney.

Fell Alley, N. fr. 180 Carolina to 181 Virginia.

Fenton, 4th street east
of Weiss running S.
from Clinton street to
Buffalo creek.
  Beer.
  Seward.
  Buffalo creek.

Ferguson, E. fr. Herkimer to Grant (1st st.
north of West Ferry).

Ferry, East, E. fr. 1531
Main to 1808 Bailey
avenue.
  24 Otis place.
  47 Michigan.
    Maple.
    Mulberry.
 123 Masten.
 149 Chester.
 173 Waverly.
 197 Purdy.
 221 Verplanck.
 247 Welker.
    Alexander pl.
 273 Jefferson.
 303 Dupont.
    N. Dupont.
    Roehrer.
    Wohlers.
 531 Humboldt pk'y.
 671 Avenue A.
 767 Quaranti'e Hospital.
    Winchester ave.
    Bitter.
    Harrison ave.
    Dutton ave.
    Sheridan ave.
    N. Y. C. (Belt
     Line) R. R.

    Grider.
    Carl.
    Schuele ave.
1207 Moselle.
    Wyoming ave.
    Rhine.
    Cambridge ave.
    Danube ave.
    Cornwall ave.
    Nevada ave.
    Northumberla'd
     avenue.
    Montana ave.
    Norfolk ave.
    Colorado ave.
    Leslie.
    Kilhoffer.
    Zenner.
    Wende.
    Logan.
    Walther's.
1353 Bailey ave.

Ferry, West, E. fr. Erie
canal to 1530 Main.
  57 Niagara.
  84 Gelston.
 113 West ave.
 151 Hibbard.
 187 Barton.
 223 Herkimer.
 303 Grant.
 338 Eighteenth.
 344 Preston.
 353 Nineteenth.
 355 Hampshire.
 356 Hoyt.
 399 Chenango.
 400 Baynes.
 428 Maynard
 452 Iroquois.
 469 Massachusetts.
 499 Richmond ave.
 584 Norwood ave.
 609 Ashland ave.
 635 Elmwood ave.
 841 Delaware ave.
 901 Linwood ave.
    Oxford pl.
 953 Main.

Fifteenth, from 404 Jersey to 141 York street.
Changed to Ketchum
place.

Fifteenth, N. W. from

142 York to 273 Hampshire.
131 Connecticut.
199 Vermont.
215 Rhode Island.
265 West Utica.
281 Massachusetts.
409 Hampshire.

Fifth, N. W. from 257
Court to 79 Pennsylvania.
 59 Georgia.
135 Carolina.
210 Virginia.
277 Maryland.
348 Hudson.
382 Root.
419 Pennsylvania.

Fillmore Ave., N. fr. 898
Seneca to 2551 Main.
(From North Parade
ave. to 2551 Main was
known as Ave A, and
was changed in 1889
to Fillmore ave.)
  2 Schuyler.
    Dillon.
 94 N. Division.
176 Eagle.
194 James.
225 Clinton.
282 Oneida.
    Steuben alley.
285 Norton.
328 Olga place.
364 S. Railroad ave.
367 Howard.
427 William.
532 Peckham.
597 Lovejoy.
719 Broadway.
893 Sycamore.
947 C street.
967 B street.
1013 A street.
1025 Peterson.
1061 Genesee.
1107 Best.
    Parade grounds
    N. Parade ave.
    Puerner ave.
    Northampton.
    Fougeron.
    Girard pl.
    Urban.

Landon.
French.
East Utica.
Box ave.
Woepple.
Glenwood ave.
Winslow ave.
Woodlawn ave.
East Ferry.
International
Park ave.
Sidney.
Puffer.
Buell ave.
Mohican ave.
E. Delavan ave.
Appenheim'r av
Steele.
Kensington ave.
E. Forest ave.
Leroy ave.
Brewster.
Charlotte ave.
Jewett ave.
Wakefield ave.
Phelps.
Victoria.
Rodney.
Main.

Fischer (in 25th ward)
E. fr. Grant to Rees
(3d street north from
West Forest ave.)

Fisher (in 5th ward), 2d
street E. of Dole run-
ning N. from Elk to
Seneca. Changed to
Keppel, March 20, '93.

Fitch Alley, N. from 198
Seneca to 15 Myrtle.

Fitzgerald (in 2d ward),
N. from 262 Sandus-
key to 559 Elk.
    63 Mackinaw.
    159 Elk.

Fitzgerald (in 25th ward)
5th street east of Col-
vin running north fr.
St. Lawrence ave. to
Kenmore ave. (near
north city line).

Fleming (formerly Nor-
ton, in 11th ward), 1st
street north of Clin-
ton running east fr.
Metcalfe to Babcock.
    Jones.
    Lewis.
    Clemo.
    Laux.
    Babcock.

Fletcher, east from 1076
Hamburgh turnpike
to Lake Shore R'y.
    208 Sophia.
    285 Lake Shore R'y.

Flint, N. fr. Leroy ave.
to Rodney (2d street
east of Fillmore ave.)
Changed to Hill.
    Charlotte ave.
    Wakefield ave.
    Victoria.
    Rodney.

Florence, W. from Main
to Parkside ave. (2d
street north of Hum-
boldt parkway).
    Crescent ave.
    Woodward ave.
    Parkside ave.

Florida, east from 1769
Main to Humboldt
parkway.
    Jefferson.
    Pleasant pl.
    Hager.
    Pansy.
    Daisy.
    Regina pl.
    Humboldt parkw'y

Floss Ave., 2d street E.
of Bailey avenue run-
ning north from Gen-
esee to East Delavan
avenue.

Flower (form'ly Lautz),
1st street W. of Main
running west fr. Ty-
ler to D.,L. & W.R.R.
tks (at International
Junction near north
city line).

Fly, N.W. from 8 Maid-
en lane to 22 Evans.
    13 State.
    26 Davenport al.
    37 Le Couteulx.
    49 Evans.

Folger, 2d street west of
White's Cors. plank
rd. running north fr.
Tifft to Triangle.

Folsom. Changed to
Myrtle in year 1884.

Fordham Place, second
street east of Ave. A
running north fr. E.
Forest ave. to Leroy
ave.

Forest Ave., East, E. fr.
2270 Main to Kensing-
ton ave.
    146 Halbert.
    180 Sanford.
    214 Fillmore ave.
    Holden.
    Fordham pl.
    Worcester pl.
    439 Kensington ave.

Forest Ave., West, E.
from Erie canal and
1580 Niagara to 1616
Delaware ave.
    31 Niagara.
    85 West ave.
    121 Dewitt.
    158 Danforth.
    188 Dart.
    220 Hawley.
    251 Grant.
    279 Barry pl.
    286 Rees.
    313 Tryon pl.
    341 Hoyt.
    379 Lawlin pl.
    400 Baynes.
    411 Bessie pl.
    445 Carmine pl.
    475 Richmond ave.
    Norwood ave.
    Ashland ave.
    578 N. Elmwood av.
    581 Elmwood ave.
    Granger pl.
    663 Lincoln parkw'y
    Windsor ave.
    Clarendon pl.
    Berkeley pl.
    831 Delaware ave.

Fort, W. fr. 970 Niagara
to Erie canal. (This

STREET DIRECTORY.

street is partly occupied by the Niagara St. R. R. car barns).

Fort Porter, on triangle bounded by Vermont, Front ave. and Erie canal.

Fougeron, E. fr. 69 Ave. A to 1486 Genesee.
Josephine.
Kehr.
N. Y. R. (Belt Line) R. R.
Barthel.
Genesee.

Foundry, 1st street east of N. Y. C. R. R. tks. running north fr. Hertel ave. to Gladstone.

Fourteenth, N. W. from 384 Pennsylvania to 237 Hampshire.
31 Porter ave.
61 Jersey.
129 York.
197 Connecticut.
265 Vermont.
333 Rhode Island.
403 Massachusetts.
473 Hampshire.

Fourth, N. W. from 275 West Genesee to 52 Porter ave.
81 Wilkeson.
133 Court.
153 Georgia.
227 Carolina.
297 Virginia.
365 Maryland.
Opened halfway fr. Maryland to Hudson, then is closed to Pennsylvania, then continued from Pennsylvania to Porter ave.

Fox, N. from 767 Broadway to 559 Best.
139 Sycamore.
285 Genesee.
311 High.
379 E. North.
447 Best.

Frank Ave., S. fr. Mineral Spring road (1st street N. of Seneca).

Frankfort Avenue, 5th street east of Norfolk ave. running north from Warwick ave. to Bayfield.
Duffield.
Bayfield.

Franklin, north from 63 Terrace to North.
19 W. Seneca.
39 Erie.
47 W. Swan.
77 Church.
City and County Hall.
105 W. Eagle.
113 Niagara.
121 Express.
135 Court.
159 W. Genesee.
164 W. Mohawk.
201 W. Huron.
239 W. Chippewa.
333 W. Tupper.
385 Edward.
419 Virginia.
491 Allen.
571 North.

Fremont Place, N. from 392 Virginia to 210 North st. Changed March, 1888, to Elmwood ave.

French, E. fr. 147 Avenue A to 244 Moselle.
Kehr.
N. Y. C. R. R. (Belt Line).
Moselle.

Frey Place, E. from 1679 Main to Masten.

Fritz Alley, 1st street N. of Clinton running E. from Emslie to Clare.

Front, east from foot of Main to Clark and Skinner ship canal.

Front Ave. (formerly Sixth street), N. W.

from 215 Court to 979 Niagara.
17 Wilkeson.
88 Georgia.
158 Carolina.
228 Virginia.
304 Maryland.
374 Hudson.
445 Pennsylvania.
516 Jersey.
586 Porter ave.
656 Connecticut.
734 Vermont.
795 Rhode Island.
865 Massachusetts.
915 Seventh.
940 Hampshire.
969 Niagara.

Fuller, N. fr. 74 Ontario to Briggs ave.
Collaton.
Briggs ave.

Fulton, E. fr. 87 Michigan to 278 Smith.
11 W. Market.
19 E. Market.
61 Marvin.
93 Chicago.
183 Louisiana.
221 Hayward.
285 Alabama.
349 Hamburgh.
395 Red Jacket.
509 Van Rensselaer.
689 Smith.

Gallatin (formerly Cornell), 1st street east of Tonawanda running N. W. fr. Martin to Ontario.
Hunt ave.
Ontario.

Galloway, S. E. from 83 Buffum to Indian Church ground.

Ganson, N. W. from 17 Hamburgh turnpike to Peck Slip, opp. ft. Main.

Garden, N. fr. 292 Carolina to 293 Virginia.

Garfield (in 11th word). N. fr. 1588 William to

Broadway (3d street east of Bailey ave.) Changed to Ideal, March 20, 1893.

Garfield (in 25th ward), E. fr. 2131 Niagara to 580 Tonawanda.
  East.
  Hartmann place.
  Peoria.
  Tonawanda.

Gatchell, N. from 1620 Broadway to West Shore R'y tks. (1st st. west from Bailey av.)
  Olmstead.
  West Shore R. R. tracks.

Gay, N. E. fr. 487 Michigan to 34 Potter.
  15 Mark.
  31 Potter.

Geary, N. E. fr. Seneca to Frank ave. (3d st. S. of Mineral Spring road).

Gelston, N. fr. 48 West Ferry to 17 Bouck av.
  53 Breckenridge.
  113 Auburn ave.
  165 Bouck ave.

Genesee, N. E. from 539 Main to city line.
  19 Washington.
  39 E. Huron.
  72 Ellicott.
  102 E. Chippewa.
  125 Oak.
  175 Elm.
  235 Michigan.
  257 Ash.
  291 Spruce.
  317 Walnut.
  347 Hickory.
  379 Pratt.
  413 Spring.
  431 Eureka place.
  462 Mortimer.
  495 Kane.
  519 Camp.
  551 Davis.
  595 Jefferson.
  689 Adams.
  725 Grey.

740 Carlton.
767 Johnson.
805 Sherman.
852 Fox.
881 Herman.
882 High.
919 Guilford.
948 Rich.
951 Reed.
974 Sweeney.
975 Strauss.
1010 Myers.
1021 Wilson.
1047 Fillmore ave.
  Mills.
1132 Best.
1139 Walden ave.
1186 E. Parade ave.
  Marshall.
  Spiess.
  Latour.
  Kehr.
  Kiefer.
  Rohr.
  Roetzer.
  N. Y. C. R. R. (Belt Line).
  Wasmuth ave.
  Barthel.
  Ivy.
1486 Fougeron.
1507 Moselle.
  Bissell ave.
  Rhine.
  Danube.
  Goodyear ave.
  Koons ave.
  Nevada.
  Doat.
  Montana ave.
  Colorado ave.
  Leslie.
  Zimmerman.
  Kilhoffer.
  Philip.
  Rawlins.
  Willard.
1831 Bailey ave.
  Theodore.
  Gruner.
  Zelmer.
2077 Scajaquada cr'k
  Floss ave.
  Randle.
  Cheektowaga.
2190 City line.

Genesee, West, S. W. fr. 522 Main to Lake Erie.
  29 Pearl.
  57 W. Mohawk.
  79 Franklin.
  Delaware ave.
  Niagara Square
  183 Morgan.
  W. Eagle.
  Terrace.
  247 Jackson.
  Gas Works.
  275 Fourth.
  285 Church.
  Erie Canal.
  342 Rock.
  343 River.
  363 Lake Erie.

Geneva, 2d street south of Broadway running west from Curtiss to Arlington.

George, E. fr. 205 Mortimer to Jefferson.

Georgia, east from Lake Erie to junct. of W. Chippewa and Whitney place.
  Erie canal.
  69 Court.
  86 Fourth.
  100 Efner.
  121 Fifth.
  145 Front ave.
  181 Seventh.
  203 Utley alley.
  213 Niagara.
  249 Prospect ave.
  244 Whitney pl.
  277 W. Chippewa.

Gerhardt, 1st street east of Jefferson running north from Dodge to Northampton.

Germain, N. from 422 Amherst to Grote.

German, N. fr. 338 Sycamore to 431 Genesee. Changed Oct, 7, 1890, to Eureka pl.

Germania, S. from 643 Abbott road to Tifft.
  Amelia.
  Lackawanna.

Pembina.
Baraga.
Mystic.
Beacon.
Bell ave.
Edmunds.
Lehigh ave.
Scheu ave.
Burt Ave.
Burrows ave.
Roland ave.
Tifft.

Gibson, N. fr. Curtiss to 988 Broadway (2d st. east of Fillmore ave.)
Peckham.
Lovejoy.
Broadway.

Gibson, 1st street north of Glenwood av. running east from Michigan to Masten street. Changed to Tompkins in year 1881.

Gilbert Ave., 2d street east of Babcock running north fr. Blank ave. to Erie R'y tks.
Clinton.
Manitoba.
Erie R'y tracks.

Gillette Ave., 1st street E. of Humboldt parkpay running north fr. East Delavan ave. to Oak Grove ave.
Clement ave.
Oak Grove ave.

Girard Place, east from Humboldt parkway, (2d street north of Parade grounds),to Fillmore ave.

Gisel, E. fr. Bailey ave. to D., L. & W R. R. (1st street south of Genesee).

Gittere, 2d street east of N.Y.C. (Belt Line) R. R. running south fr. Walden ave.

Gladstone, 1st street N. of Hertel ave. running west from Mili-

tary road to N. Y. C. R. R. tracks.
Short.
Deer.
Foundry.

Glenwood Ave., E. fr. 1425 Main to 830 Humboldt parkway and from Avenue A to Moselle.
Otis place.
75 Michigan.
151 Masten.
178 Chester.
204 Waverly.
227 Purdy.
251 Verplanck.
275 Welker.
301 Jefferson.
327 Dupont.
353 Hauf.
Brooklyn ave.
Storz ave.
Roehrer.
Wohlers.
Duckwitz.
Portage.
Humboldt pk'y.
Avenue A
Kehr.
N. Y. C. R. R. (Belt Line).
Moselle.

Glor, N. fr. 68 Military rd. to 323 Austin, and continued N. about 800 feet.

Goembel Ave., 1st street west of Bailey ave. running north from Walden ave.

Goethe, N. fr. 1780 William to Broadway.
Ludington.
Lovejoy.
Reimann.
Broadway.

Gold, N. from 1648 William to Broadway, 5th street east from Bailey ave.
Ludington.
Lovejoy.
Vanderbilt.

Reimann.
Broadway.

Goodlin Alley, N. from 665 Virginia to 98 Carlton.

Goodell, east from 785 Main to 88 Cherry.
19 Washington.
53 Ellicott.
76 Weaver alley.
89 Oak.
125 Boston alley.
135 Elm.
154 Werrick alley.
159 Goodell alley.
171 Michigan.
197 Maple.
223 Mulberry.
246 Cherry.

Goodell Alley, N. fr. 154 East Tupper to 159 Goodell. Changed to Edwin pl., May, 1891.

Goodliffe, 1st street S. of Tifft running E. fr. Hopkins to So. Park ave. (form'ly White's Corners road).

Goodrich, E. from 1005 Main to 794 Michigan.
51 Ellicott.
127 Elm.
165 Michigan.

Goodyear Avenue, N. from 1432 Broadway to Genesee.
West Shore street.
Sycamore.
Walden ave.
McKibben.
Genesee.

Gorham, north fr. 1106 Elk to Perry.

Gorton, N. fr. 144 Amherst to 145 Hertel av.
59 Hamilton.
133 Austin.
199 Farmer.
303 Hertel ave.

Grace (in 25th ward) E. from 2107 Niagara to Cornelius creek.
59 East.

Hartmann pl.
Peoria.
Calumet pl.
Tonawanda.
Cornelius creek.

Grace Ave. (in 5th ward) west from Hopkins to Germania, ne'r Abbott rd. Changed to Pembina, Mar. 20, '93.

Grand, 1st street S. of Broadw'y running E. from Quincy to Deshler.
Swinburne.
Brownell.
Deshler.

Granger, east from 287 Chicago to Ohio slip.

Granger Place, 1st street east of Elmwood ave. running N. from Bird ave. to W. Forest av.

Grant, N. fr. junction of Hampshire and Arkansas to Scajaquada creek, and 375 Amherst to 151 Military road.
4 Arkansas.
47 W. Ferry.
69 Ferguson.
79 Arnold.
100 Breckenridge.
Boyd.
Auchinvole.
161 Auburn ave.
223 Bouck ave.
293 W. Delavan ave.
367 Potomac ave.
401 Annie pl.
425 Bird ave.
468 Pooley pl.
501 W. Forest ave.
583 Bradley.
667 Letchworth.
Fisher.
Jessemine.
845 Scajaquada cr'k
Amherst.
Military road.

Grape, north from 248 Cherry to 349 Best.
27 Virginia.

95 Carlton.
159 High.
229 E. North.
393 Best.

Gratiot Ave. (formerly Summit View ave.), 4th street north of E. Delavan av. running east fr. Grider street to Wyoming ave.
Deerfield ave.
Wyoming ave.

Greely, 5th street E. of Military rd. running north fr. Hertel ave. to Race.

Green, E. fr. 147 Washington to 212 Michig'n.
20 Beak.
112 Michigan.

Greene, 1st street E. of Bailey ave. running north from 1550 William to Broadway.
Dempster.
Ludington.
Hennepin.
Bogardus.
Lovejoy.
Moreland.
Regent.
Vanderbilt.
Reimann.
King.
Stone.
Broadway.

Greenfield, N. W. from 2436 Main to 1543 Amherst.
Elam place.
Russell.
Amherst.

Grey, north from 668 Broadway to High.
129 Sycamore.
251 Genesee.
259 Carlton.
300 Cayuga.
381 High.

Grider, 6th street east of Ave. A running N. from East Ferry to 437 Leroy ave.
Puffer.

780 E. Delavan ave.
Litchfield ave.
Sussex.
Gratiot ave.
Maple Ridge av.
Pembroke ave.
Warwick ave.
Colfax ave.
Kensington ave.
Leroy ave.

Griffin, 2d street east of Van Rensselaer running N. fr. 160 Roseville to Schuyler.
19 Railroad.
45 Exchange.
63 Carroll.
89 Seneca.
Schuyler.

Grimes, east from 214 Clark to Krupp.
Sears.
Playter.
Sweet ave.
(Closed bet. Sweet ave. and Curtiss.)
Curtiss.
Young.
Mohr.
Milburn.
Persons.
Krupp.

Griswold(form'ly Humboldt), east fr. Weiss to east city line (first street N. of Clinton).
Weimar.
Cable.
Barnard.
Pulaski.
Weaver ave.
Abel.
Seifert.
South Ogden.
Wheelock.
Cochrane.
City line.

Grosvenor, N. from 30 Seymour to 624 Eagle.
19 S. Division.
Laban alley.
49 N. Division.
85 Eagle.

Grote, 1st street north of Amherst running

CATON'S
NATIONAL BUSINESS
COLLEGE

Offers to Young Men and Women unequalled facilities for obtaining a thorough training in Business, English and Shorthand. Largest attendance of any college in Western New York. . . . . First = class instructors. First = class appointments in every particular. Day and Evening Sessions the entire year. Students may enter at any time. . . . . . For further information call on or address . . . .

CATON'S NATIONAL BUSINESS COLLEGE,

460 Main Street, Buffalo, N. Y.

east from Military rd.
to Bridgeman.
  Germain.
  Peter.
  Howell.
  Bush.
  Reservation.
  Bridgeman.

Grove, 4th street east of Military rd. running north from Hertel av. to Kenmore avenue (north city line).
  Lawn ave.
  Race
  Hinman ave.
  Ramsdell ave.
  Kenmore ave.

Gruner, 1st street east of Bailey ave. running north from Genesee to E. Delavan av.
  Kerns ave.
  Navel ave.
  Lang ave.
  E. Delavan ave.

Gurnsey, N. W. fr. 110 Austin to 109 Hertel avenue.
  59 Farmer.
  113 Hertel ave.

Guilford, N. from 840 Broadway to Best.
  Sycamore.
  Genesee.
  Best.

Gull, E. from Erie canal to 1144 Niagara.

Gunnell, 8th street east of Colvin running N. fr. St. Lawrence ave. to Kenmore ave. (near north city line).

Hagen, 2d street E. of Bailey ave. running south from E. Delavan ave. Changed to Rumsey, Mar. 20, '93.

Hager, 1st street east of Jefferson running N. from Puffer to East Delavan ave.
  Florida.
  E. Delavan ave.

Hagerman, north fr. 682 Swan to 113 Seymour.
  11 Schuyler.
  21 Seymour.

Halbert, N. from 146 E. Forest ave. to Main.
  Leroy ave.
  Brewster.
  Jewett ave.
  Phelps.
  Rodney.
  Main.

Hamburgh, north fr. 160 South to 551 Seneca.
  2 South.
  55 Erie Railroad.
  67 Tecumseh.
  117 Sandusky.
  169 Mackinaw.
  203 Miami.
  245 Elk.
  272 Coatsworth al.
  281 Fulton.
  317 Perry.
  345 Scott.
  385 Hamburgh can'l
  421 Railroad.
  435 Exchange.
  453 Carroll.
  489 Seneca.

Hamburgh Canal, E. fr. 117 Main to 385 Hamburgh.

Hamburgh Turnpike, S. from Buffalo river and 549 Ohio to city line.
  17 Ganson.
  Child.
  202 Buffalo Crk. R.R.
  784 Tifft.
  1076 Fletcher.
  1145 City line.

Hamilton, east from Niagara river to 300 Tonawanda.
  15 Niagara.
  45 Dearborn.
  67 East.
  99 Hoffmann alley.
  116 Thompson.
  144 Gorton.
  171 Tonawanda.

Hamilton, E. from 227

Emslie to 282 Fillmore ave. Changed to Oneida.

Hamilton, E. from 227 Spring to 310 Jefferson. Changed in 1884 to Superior.

Hamill Alley, E. fr. 205 Chicago to rear 135 Fulton.

Hampshire, N. E. fr. 941 Front ave. to junct. W. Ferry and Hoyt.
  13 Niagara.
  49 Prospect ave.
  91 Fargo ave.
  129 West ave.
  165 Plymouth ave.
  201 Thirteenth.
  230 Albany.
  237 Fourteenth.
  250 Sherwood.
  273 Fifteenth.
  311 Lawrence pl.
  318 Arkansas.
  318 Grant.
  Winter.
  385 Eighteenth.
  Nineteenth.
  413 West Ferry.
  430 Hoyt.

Hancock, west fr. Abby to B., R. & P.R.R. tks. (4th street south of 569 Abbott road).
  Newerf.
  Rochester.
  Pittsburgh.
  B., R. & P. R.R. tks.

Hancock Avenue, 5th st. S. of Abbott rd. running east from Abby to Hopkins. Changed to Beacon, Mar. 20, '93.

Handel, north from 409 High to 415 Best.

Hannah, S. fr. 1123 William to 872 Babcock.

Hanover, N. E. from 55 Prime to 106 Main.

Harlow Place, 1st street N. of East Ferry running east from Purdy to Alexandria place.

Harmonia, N. from 1046 Sycamore to Walden ave.

Harold Ave., 6th street east of Tonawanda running N. W. from Rano to Chadduck avenue.

Harriett (form'ly Weber) 4th street east of Bailey ave. running N. from East Delavan ave. to Sugar.

Harrison, 4th street east of Babcock running north fr. Perry, across Seneca at 1325, to W. N. Y. & P. R. R. tks.

Harrison Ave. (in 14th ward), east from Miller ave. to Goodyear ave. Changed to Empire, March 20, 1893.

Harrison Ave. (in 18th ward), 3d street east of Ave. A running N. from East Ferry st. to East Delavan ave.
Puffer.
E. Delavan ave.

Harrison Pl., 3d street east of Delaware ave. running north from Sessions ave. to Villa ave. Changed to Medford pl., March 20, '93.

Hartmann Pl., 1st street east of East street running north from Grace to Arthur.
Garfield street.
Arthur street.

Harvard Place (in 24th ward), N. fr. 1614 Main to 993 West Delavan ave. (formerly Michigan street).
Balcom.
Bouck ave.
W. Delavan ave.

Harvard Place (in 25th ward) 1st street west of Wyoming ave. running north fr. Mendola to Kensington ave. Changed to Palos pl., March 20, 1893.

Harvest (form'rly Hopman), 10th street east of Colvin running N. from St. Lawrence ave. to Kenmore ave. (near northerly city line).

Harwood Place, E. from Jefferson to International Expo. Grounds (between Dexter and Puffer).

Hatch Slip, opp. foot of Mississippi.

Hauf, N. fr. 355 E. Utica to 353 Glenwood ave.

Hawley, N. fr. 220 W. Forest ave. to Letchworth.
Bradley.
Letchworth.

Hawthorne, N. fr. Chaucer to Kenmore ave. (northwest of International Junct.), near northerly city line.

Hawthorne Place, N. fr. Massachusetts ave. to 311 Hampshire street. Changed to Lawrence pl., March 20, 1893.

Hayden (formerly Eckhardt ave.), 1st street S. of Mineral Spring road running N. from Seneca street to Mineral Spring road.

Hayward, N. from 340 Elk to Otto.
17 Coatsworth al.
29 Fulton.
67 Perry.
93 Otto.

Hazlewood Ave., second street east of Bailey ave. running north fr. East Delavan ave. to Sugar.

Heacock, N. from 618 Scott to 645 Seneca.
213 Roseville.
251 Railroad.
267 Exchange.
285 Carroll.
321 Seneca.

Heath (formerly Morton), W. fr. 3226 Main to N. Y., L. E. & W. R. R tracks.
Cornell.
Bruce.
Mildred.
Angle.
N. Y., L. E. & W. R. R. tracks.

Hecla (formerly Byron) N. from Chaucer to Kenmore ave. (N. W. of International junction, near northerly city line).

Hedley Place, 1st street north of E. Delavan ave. running east fr. Jefferson st. to Oak Grove ave.
Meech ave.
Oak Grove ave.

Helen, E. fr. 147 Dewitt to 298 Herkimer.

Hendricks, 2d street N. of Hertel ave. running west from Main to D., L. & W. R. R. tks. (at International Junction, near north city line). Changed to Merrimac, March 20, 1893.

Hennepin (form'ly Euclid), 3d street north of William running east from Bailey ave. to Greene.

Henricka, S. from 1151 William to 959 Babcock.

Henry, east from Erie canal to 160 Terrace.

Herbert Ave., 1st street west of Bailey ave.

running north fr. Puffer to E. Delavan ave.
Barnett place.
Wecker.
Kirkpatrick.
E. Delavan ave.

Herkimer, N. fr. 216 Albany to 181 Bird ave.
24 California.
51 Arkansas.
85 West Ferry.
Ferguson.
141 Breckenridge.
Auchinvole.
201 Auburn ave.
263 Bouck ave.
298 Helen.
331 W. Delavan av.
365 Perkins place.
403 Potomac ave.
437 Annie place.
471 Bird ave.

Herman, north from 800 Broadway to 663 Best.
143 Sycamore.
291 Genesee.
High.
382 E. North.
413 Best.

Hersee Alley (formerly Koons alley) east fr. 255 Ellicott to 168 Oak.
13 Blossom.
59 Oak.

Hertel Ave., east from Niagara river and 2079 Niagara street to 3002 Main.
13 Niagara.
49 Dearborn.
67 East.
109 Gurnsey.
145 Gorton.
175 Tonawanda.
203 Pacific.
N. Y. C. tracks.
Foundry.
Deer.
Short.
445 Military road.
La Force place.
604 Page.
Sunset.
Grove.
Greeley.

Norris.
811 McPherson (N. Elmwood av.)
Mandan.
Ledger.
Sarvis.
Steward.
Rosalia.
1069 Delaware ave.
Fairchild pl.
Exeter ave.
1323 Colvin.
Saranac ave.
Bolton ave.
Norwalk ave.
Sterling ave.
Parkside ave.
Wallace ave.
Starin ave.
Voorhis ave.
Parker ave.
Wesley.
2091 Main.

Hertel Ave., East. See East Hertel ave.

Hewett, 1st street S. of East Hertel eve. running west fr. Range ave. to Bailey ave.

Hibbard, north from 143 Albany to 116 Breckenridge. Changed to Plymouth ave., April 1892.
21 California.
49 Arkansas.
75 W. Ferry.
125 Breckenridge.

Hickman, 6th street E. of Bailey ave. running north from East Delavan ave. to Sugar (at east city line).

Hickory, north from 414 Swan to 89 Cherry.
12 Booth alley.
23 S. Division.
53 N. Division.
84 Eagle.
127 Clinton.
220 William.
253 Broadway.
445 Sycamore.
527 Genesee.

557 Cherry.

High, E. from 967 Main to junction of Genesee and Herman.
17 Washington.
51 Ellicott.
89 Oak.
125 Elm.
139 Neptune.
161 Michigan.
188 Maple.
213 Mulberry.
239 Locust.
265 Lemon.
291 Orange.
317 Peach.
341 Grape.
367 Rose.
393 Jefferson.
409 Handel.
460 Berlin.
492 Durrenberger pl
545 Johnson.
577 Sherman.
609 Fox.
631 Genesee.
642 Herman.

Highland Place, 3d st. east of Fillmore ave. (formerly Avenue A) running north from E. Forest ave. to Leroy ave. Changed to Worcester pl., March 20, 1893.

Highland Avenue, first street north of Lexington ave. (formerly Butler street), running west from Delaware ave. to Richmond ave.
Elmwood ave.
Ashland ave.
Norwood ave.
Richmond ave.

Hill, 2d street east of Avenue A running N. from Leroy ave. to Rodney.
Charlotte ave.
Wakefield ave.
Lexington ave.
Victoria.
Rodney.

Hillery Place, E. fr. 3275 Main to Bailey ave.

Hinckley. Changed to West Peckham.

Hines (formerly Dalton), 1st street east of So. Park ave. (formerly White's Corners road) running south fr. Downing to southerly city line.

Hinman Ave., 2d street south of Kenmore av. (near northerly city line), running west fr. Delaware avenue to Grove.

Hirschbeck, N. fr. 1570 Broadway to West Shore R. R.
Olmstead.
W. S. R. R. tracks.

Hodge, N. W. from 342 Vermont to 351 Rhode Island: Changed to Lowell pl., Mar. 20, '93.

Hodge Ave., west from 954 Delaware ave. to 188 Ashland ave.
Atlantic.
159 Elmwood ave.
205 Ashland ave.

Hoffmann, 1st street E. of Bailey ave. running south from Walden ave. to W.S.R.R. tks. Changed to Keystone, March 20, 1893.

Hoffmann Alley, S. from 93 Hamilton and N. from 96 Hamilton to 99 Austin.

Holborn (form'ly Windsor), 2d street north of Delavan ave. running east fr. Olympic ave. to Bailey ave.
Ocean ave.
Atlantic ave.
Bailey ave.

Holden, N. from E. Forest ave. to Rodney

(first street east of Avenue A.)
Leroy ave.
Charlotte ave.
Wakefield ave.
Victoria.
Rodney.

Holland Place (formerly North Elm street), N. from 96 Northampton to Riley.

Hollister, east from 399 Spring to 122 Mortimer.

Holly, 5th street east of Weiss, running south from Clinton street to Buffalo creek.
Beer.
Seward.
Buffalo creek.

Holt, east from Indian Reservation line to ½ lot 57, across Jones and Lewis (1st street south of Howard).

Hopkins, N. fr. 208 Marilla to 711 Abbott rd.
Carter.
Larabee.
Goodliffe.
343 Tifft.
Roland ave.
Burrows ave.
Burt ave.
Scheu ave.
Trowbridge.
Wilbur.
Lehigh ave.
Osage.
Edmunds.
Bell ave.
Houston.
Spaulding.
Beacon.
Sirrett.
Mystic.
Baraga.
Pembina.
743 Abbott road.

Hopman, 10th street E. of Colvin running N. from St. Lawrence ave. to Kenmore ave.

(near northerly city line). Changed to Harvest, Mar. 20, '93.

Houghton (form'rly Arlington). S. from 1163 Broad'ay to Concord.

Houston, 3d street S. of 711 Abbott road running east fr. Hopkins.

Howard, E. fr. 297 Jefferson to 422 Bailey ave.
21 Madison.
47 Monroe.
75 Adams.
105 Watson.
133 Emslie.
162 Krettner.
177 Bond.
188 Sherman.
214 Stanton.
221 Lord.
238 Shumway.
265 Smith.
292 Coit.
305 Montgomery.
318 Detroit.
347 Clare.
389 S. Railroad ave.
389 Fillmore ave.
Bass.
Stetson.
Thomas.
514 Metcalfe.
568 Newell.
Lewis.
740 Babcock.
1049 Bailey ave.

Howard Ave., north fr. 313 Summer to West Forest ave. Changed to Norwood avenue, March 20, 1893.
145 Bryant.
231 W. Utica.
265 Anderson pl.
361 Lexington ave.
Highland ave.
381 W. Ferry.
Breckenridge.
Auburn ave.
Bouck ave.
W. Delavan ave.
Potomac ave.

Bird ave.
W. Forest ave.

Howell, north from 478 Amherst to Grote.

Howlett (formerly Ullman, in 14th ward) N. from 1148 Sycamore to Walden ave.

Hoyer Place, 2d street E. of Delaware ave. running N. from Sessions ave. to Villa av.

Hoyt, N. from 356 W. Ferry to 347 W. Forest ave.
41 Breckenridge.
103 Auburn ave.
163 Bouck ave.
233 W. Delavan ave.
307 Potomac ave.
373 Bird ave.
439 W. Forest ave.

Hubbell Ave., 2d street south of Abbott road running east from S. Park ave. (formerly White's Corners rd.) to Boulevard.

Hudson, E. fr. Niagara river to 28 Wadsworth.
Erie canal.
46 Effner.
67 Fifth.
93 Front ave.
112 Osborne alley.
127 Seventh.
161 Niagara.
195 Prospect ave.
221 Whitney pl.
234 Fargo ave.
247 Tenth.
269 West ave.
297 Cottage.
306 Plymouth ave.
354 Orton pl.
393 Wadsworth.

Hughes (form'ly Parkway ave.), 3d street north of E. Delavan ave. running east fr. Jefferson st. to Oak Grove ave.
Meech ave.

Oak Grove ave.

Humber Ave., 3d street east of Grider running north from East Delavan av to Sussex.
Litchfield ave.
Sussex.

Humboldt, E. fr. Weiss to east city line (first street north of Clinton st.) Changed to Griswold Mar. 20, '93.

Humboldt Parkway, S. W. from The Park to The Parade grounds.
Parkside ave.
Woodward ave.
Crescent ave.
169 Main.
179 Steele.
Eastwood pl.
Loring ave.
Oak Grove ave.
471 E. Delavan ave.
Mohican ave.
542 Florida.
Buell ave.
573 Puffer.
Sidney.
Internat'al Park avenue.
737 E. Ferry.
765 Woodlawn ave.
790 Winslow ave.
830 Glenwood ave.
841 Woepple.
872 East Utica.
905 Landon.
Riley.
Girard pl.
Kingsley.
1107 Northampton.
Parade grounds

Humboldt Place, second street north of Jefferson running east from Main to Humboldt pkway. Changed to Eastwood pl., March 20, 1893.

Hunt Ave., 4th street N. of Cornelius creek running east fr. Tonawanda street to Norman ave.

Gallatin.
Mayer ave.
Albert ave.
Norman ave.

Huntingdon Ave., 2d st. east of Grider running north from East Delavan ave. to Kensington av. Changed to Deerfield avenue, March 20, 1893.

Huntington Avenue, 4th street north of Amherst running west fr. Main to Starin ave.
Beard ave.
Wesley.
Parker Ave.
Voorhis.
Starin ave.

Hurlbert, E. from L. S. R. R. tks. to 1094 South Park ave. (formerly White's Cors. rd.) 1st street north of south city line.

Huron, East, east from 543 Main to 238 Oak.
8 Genesee.
15 Washington.
39 Ellicott.
59 Blossom.
75 Oak.

Huron, West, W. fr. 544 Main to 193 Niagara.
23 Pearl.
43 Asbury alley.
53 Franklin.
64 Bean alley.
95 Delaware ave.
139 Morgan.
165 Prospect ave.
217 Niagara.

Hydraulic, N. from 746 Scott to 783 Seneca.
27 Roseville.
52 Railroad.
75 Exchange.
93 Carroll.
134 Seneca.

Idaho, 5th street north of Hertel ave. running west from Military road to N. Y. C. R. R. tracks.

Ideal (form'ly Garfield, in 11th ward), north from 1588 William to Broadway (3d street east of Bailey ave.)
Ludington.
Lovejoy.
Vanderbilt.
Reimann.
King.
Broadway.

Illinois, N. from Buffalo river to 67 Scott.
9 Ohio.
54 Mary.
85 Perry.
135 Scott.

Imson, 1st street east of Babcock running N. from Perry to W. N. Y. & P. R. R. tracks.

Indiana, N. fr. Buffalo river to 41 Perry.
11 Ohio.
41 Mary.
73 Perry.

Indian Church Road, E. from 2270 Seneca to city line.

Indian Reservation Line —on old maps—now located at or near Fillmore ave.

Inkerman. See Woodside ave.

International Junction, N. W. fr. Main street near Buffalo Plains Postoffice (near north city line).

International Park Ave., 1st street north of E. Ferry running east fr. Humboldt parkway to Avenue A.

Iroquois (form'ly Cleveland ave.), N. fr. 452 West Ferry to 495 Breckenridge.

Irving Place, N. fr. 135 Allen to 152 North.

Irvington Ave., 2d street east of Norfolk ave.

running N. of Warwick ave. to Bayfield.
Duffield.
Bayfield.

Ithaca (formerly Dold), east from Tifft to Whitfield.

Ivy (formerly Oakland) N. fr. Walden ave. to Genesee (3d street E. of N. Y. C. Belt Line R. R.)

Jackson, north from 143 Church to Court pl.
25 W. Genesee.
124 Court pl.

Jahle, second street E. of Baily ave. running north from Doat to Scajaquada creek.

James, E. fr. 135 Emslie to 194 Fillmore ave.
40 Bond.
84 Lord.
128 Smith.
170 Montgomery.
212 Clare.
251 Fillmore ave.

James, N. fr. 36 Military road to 289 Austin. Changed to Clay.

Jane, W. fr. Erie street to Coit slip (1st street south of river).

Jefferson, N. fr. 598 Exchange to 1975 Main.
25 Carroll.
61 Seneca.
86 Myrtle.
107 Swan.
137 S. Division.
167 N. Division.
199 Eagle.
226 Vary.
241 Clinton.
278 Bristol.
297 Howard.
310 Superior.
367 William.
465 Peckham.
474 W. Peckham.
537 Broadway.
586 Rey.
George.

616 Mathews.
661 Sycamore.
702 Davis.
735 Brown.
771 Genesee.
786 Virginia.
797 Jefferson alley.
851 Carlton.
885 Cayuga.
917 High.
983 E. North.
1051 Best.
1119 Dodge.
1154 Southampton.
1191 Northampton.
1221 Kingsley.
1246 Eaton.
1267 Riley.
1280 Laurel.
1287 Landon.
1317 E. Utica.
1362 Glenwood ave.
1414 Woodlawn ave.
1456 E. Ferry.
Dexter.
Harwood pl.
Lyth place.
1615 Puffer.
Florida.
1715 E. Delavan ave.
Hedley pl.
Blaine.
Hughes.
1831 Main.

Jefferson Alley, east fr. 797 Jefferson.

Jerry, 3d street north of Clinton running east from Clare to 328 Fillmore ave. Changed to Olga pl., Mar. 20, '93.

Jessemine, E. fr. Grant to Rees (4th street N. of W. Forest ave.)

Jersey, N. E. from Lake Erie to 56 Richmond avenue.
Erie canal.
29 Fourth.
61 Lake View ave.
90 Front ave.
127 Seventh.
161 Niagara.
195 Prospect ave.
235 Fargo ave.

271 West ave.
307 Plymouth ave.
341 Porter ave.
350 Thirteenth.
377 Fourteenth.
404 Ketchum pl.
432 Richmond ave.

Jewett Ave., W. fr. 2420 Main to The Park and east from 2419 Main to Avenue A.
West Crossings:
Crescent ave.
Summit ave.
Woodward ave.
Parkside ave.
The Park.
East Crossings:
Halbert.
Avenue A.

John, S. from 14 West Seneca.

Johnson, north from 700 Broadway to 529 Best.
131 Sycamore.
265 Genesee.
272 Carlton.
324 High.
Alvin.
390 E. North.
457 Best.

Johnson Ave., 1st street east of Bailey avenue running north from Kerns ave. to Lang ave. Changed to Texas, March 20, 1893.

Johnson Place, W. from 274 Delaware ave. to 247 Carolina. Chang'd to Johnson's Park, March 20, 1893.

Jones, N. fr. 1000 Clinton to Lyman.
Fleming.
Klaus.
Lyman.

Joseph, 1st street south of East Forest ave. running west from Kensington ave.

Josephine, 1st street E. of East Parade ave.

running north from Puerner av. to Urban.
Fougeron.
Urban.

Joslyn Place, N. fr. 340 Austin.

Joy, W. fr. 118 Water to Erie basin.

Juliet, 1st street north of Cornelius. creek running southeast fr. Tonawanda.

Juniata Ave., 1st street south of South Park ave. running N.E. fr. Seneca st. to Buffalo river.

Kamper Ave., N. E. fr. Seneca to Frank ave. (5th street south of Mineral Spring road).

Kane, N. fr. 400 Sycamore to 495 Genesee.

Kasota Ave., 1st street east of Delaware ave. running north from Bangor place to Kenmore ave. (north city line.)

Katharine, N. fr. Buffalo creek ne'r Union Iron Works to 527 Elk.
Ensign.
253 Sandusky.
305 Mackinaw.
381 Elk.

Keep Alley, N. fr. 336 Virginia street to 43 Twelfth.

Kehr, N. fr. Genesee to Woodlawn ave. (4th street east of Parade grounds).
Bardol.
Puerner ave.
Fougeron.
Urban.
French.
Box ave.
Glenwood ave.
Winslow ave.
Woodlawn ave.

Keil, N. from 263 Amherst to 267 Austin.

Kenilworth, 4th street north of East Delavan ave. running east from Olympic ave. to Bailey ave. Changed to Beverly, March 20, 1893.

Kenmore Ave., (northerly city line), east fr. O'Neil to Main.
North Park ave.
Fairmount ave.
Ontario.
Military road.
Clayton.
Grove.
N. Elmwood ave.
Eugene.
Delaware ave.
Myron ave.
Winthrop place.
Kasota ave.
Brocton ave.
Colvin.
Berkshire ave.
Dalton ave.
Kennard ave.
Sharon ave.
Fitzgerald.
Campbell.
Duluth.
Gunnell.
Redmond.
Harvest.
Newport.
Alden.
Dryden street.
Hecla.
Hawthorne.
Crosby.
Eley.
Kennelworth.
Richards ave.
Sawyer ave.
Main.

Kennard Ave., 3d street east of Colvin running north fr. Bangor pl. to Kenmore ave. (north city line).

Kennelworth, 1st street north of Eley running north fr. Main to north city line.

Kensington Ave. (formerly Ellicott turnpike), N. E. from 767 Ave. A to city line.
303 Grider.
Mendola.
370 Leroy ave.
Deerfield ave.
Federal ave.
Harvard pl.
Liberty ave.
Wyoming ave.
Kensington Station (Erie R'y.)
Park Ridge ave.
Northumberla'd ave.
Norfolk ave.
Lenox ave.
784 Bailey ave.
Suffolk.
Orleans.
1099 Eggert.
1225 City line.

Kent, E. fr. Sweet ave. to Houghton (first street S. of Broadway).
Warner ave.
Houghton.

Kentucky, N. fr. 42 St. Clair to 141 Mackinaw.
45 South.
99 Tecumseh.
163 Sandusky.
215 Mackinaw.

Keppel (form'ly Fisher, in 5th ward), 2d street east of Dole running N. fr. Elk to Seneca.

Kerns Ave., first street north of Genesee running west from Gruner to Texas.

Kertz, north from Esser ave. to Eckhert (2d st. east of Tonawanda.)
Roesch ave.
Eckhert ave.

Ketchum Alley, N. from

130 Carlton to 139 High. Changed to Neptune street, Mar. 20, 1893.

Ketchum Place, N. W. from 404 Jersey to 141 York.

Keystone (formerly Arthur, in 18th ward, and Hoffman), north from 700 Walden ave. to W. S. R. R. tks.

Kiefer, N. from Walden ave. to Genesee (2d street east of Parade House).

Kilhoffer, 1st street W. of Bailey ave. running north fr. Genesee to Puffer.
East Ferry.
Puffer.

Kimmel Ave., 1st street east of Hopkins, running north from Abbott road to Buffalo creek.

King, east from Greene to 1890 Broadway.
Longnecker.
Ideal.
Benzinger.
Broadway.

Kingsley, E. fr 1221 Jefferson to Humboldt parkway.
Roehrer.
Wohlers.
Humboldt parkw'y

Kirkpatrick (formerly Spencer ave.), first street south of East Delavan ave. running east fr. Herbert ave. to Bailey ave.

Klaus, E. from Metcalfe to Jones (2d street N. of Clinton).

Knoerl Ave., 1st street south of Mineral Sp'g road running S. W. fr.

Seneca street to Cazenovia creek.

Kofler Ave., 3d street N. of Hertel av. running east from Military road to Clayton.

Koons Alley, E. from 255 Ellicott to 198 Oak. Changed to Hersee alley, March 20, 1893.

Koons Ave., north from 1458 Broadway to Genesee.
West Shore street.
Sycamore.
Walden ave.
McKibbin.
Genesee.

Kosciuszko, north from 1190 Broadway to Walden ave.
Stanislaus.
Sycamore.
Walden ave.

Kozlowaki, S. fr. Piatti to Scajaquada creek (between Yates and Nelson).

Krettner, N. from 162 Howard to 717 Broadway.
57 William.
159 Peckham.
225 Lovejoy.
281 Broadway.

Krupp, S. fr. 1381 Broadway to N. Y. C. R. R.
Ashley.
Grimes.
N. Y. C. R. R.

Kuempel Ave., N. from 1356 Broadway to Walden ave.

Laban Alley, east from Grosvenor to Smith (bet. No. Division and So. Division).

Lackawanna, W. from Germania to B., R. & P. R. R. tks. (second street south from 603 Abbott road).
Abbey.

Parnell.
B., R. & P. R. R. tks.

Lacy, S. fr. 49 St. Clair to Buffalo river.

Lafayette, E. from 447 Main to 436 Washington.

La Force Place, first st. east of Military road running north from Hertel ave.

Laird Ave., E. fr. Tonawanda to Bleeker av. (5th street N. of Ontario).
Condon ave.
Bleeker ave.

Lake, E. from Erie basin to 84 River street.

Lake, W. from 100 Main to Commercial.

Lakeview Ave., N. W. from 78 Pennsylvania to 147 Porter ave.
71 Jersey.
131 Porter ave.

Lancaster Ave., 1st st. north of Auburn ave. running east fr. Elmwood ave. to Pacific avenue.

Landon, E. fr. 1287 Jefferson to 130 Ave. A.
Roehrer.
Wohlers.
269 Humboldt pk'y.
Avenue A.

Lang Ave., 3d street N. of Genesee running west from Gruner to Texas.

Lansing, 1st street N. of Austin runninng W. fr. Military rd. to Joslyn place.

Larabee, 2d street south of Tifft running east from Hopkins to So. Park ave. (formerly White's Cors. road).

Lark, 1st street east of Humboldt parkway

running north fr. Sidney st. to Scajaquada creek.

La Salle Ave., 1st street north of East Hertel ave. running east fr. Main to Bailey ave.
Cordova.
Park Ridge ave.
Lenox ave.
Bailey ave.

Last. (In Union Iron Co.'s tract).

Lathrop, N. from 1216 Broadway to 167 Walden ave.
Stanislaus.
Sycamore.
Walden ave.

Latour, N. fr. Walden ave. to Genesee (first street east of Parade House).

Laurel, E. tr. 1351 Michigan to 1280 Jefferson.
69 Masten.
Purdy.
221 Jefferson.

Lautz, 1st street west of Main running west fr. Tyler to D., L. & W R. R. tks. (at International junction, near north city line.) Changed to Flower, March 20, 1893.

Laux, N. from Clinton to Fleming (1st street west of Babcock).
Oscar.
Bergtold.
Fleming.

Lawn Ave., 1st street north of Hertel ave. running east fr. Page to Norris.
Sunset.
Grove.
Greeley.
Norris.

Lawlin Place, N. fr. 380 Bird ave. to 379 West Forest ave.

Lawrence Place (formerly Hawthorne pl.), north fr. Massachusetts to 311 Hampshire.

Layer Ave., east from Military rd. to Clayton (1st street north of Race and second north of Hertel ave.)
Simon.
Clayton.

Le Couteulx, from 61 Water to 106 Canal.
17 Fly.
57 Canal.

Ledger, 1st street E. of Pierce Steam Heating Works running N. fr. N. Y. C. R. R. (belt line) at Cross-Cut junction to Hertel av. also 2d street east of North Elmwood ave. running south from Hertel ave.

Lee, N. from 344 Abbott road to 933 Elk.
71 Prenatt.
149 Elk.

Lehigh, No. 1 (in 5th ward) west fr. Abby to B., R. & P. R. R. tks. (7th street south fr. 569 Abbott road).
Rochester.
Pittsburg.
B., R. & P. R. R. tks.

Lehigh, No. 2 (in 5th ward) 2d street west of Hopkins running north fr. Marilla.

Lehigh Ave., 8th street south of Abbott road running east fr. Abby to Hopkins.
Germania.
Hopkins.

Lemon, N. fr. 140 Cherry to 267 East North.
81 Virginia.
149 Carlton.
219 High.
291 East North.

Lenox Ave., 1st street west of Bailey ave. rnnning north from Kensington avenue to Alvin avenue.

Leo, S. fr. Genesee to Doat (2d street west of Bailey avenue). Changed to Rawlins, March 20, 1893.

Leo Ave., S. fr. Walden ave. to West Shore street. (1st street W. of Bailey ave.)

Leroy Ave., E. fr. 2341 Main to 370 Kensington ave.
    N. Y. C. (Belt Line) R. R.
    101 Halbert.
    135 Sanford.
    169 Avenue A.
    Holden.
    Fordam place.
    Hill.
    Worcester pl.
    Richlawn ave.
    Marigold.
    437 Grider.
    Manhattan ave.
    Montclair ave.
    487 Kensington ave.

Leslie, 2d street west of Bailey ave. running north fr. Genesee to Puffer.
    East Ferry.
    Puffer.

Lester, N. fr. 1342 Seneca to W. N. Y. & P. R. R. tks.

Letchworth, 2d street north of West Forest ave. running east fr. Dart to 156 Rees.
    Hawley.
    Grant.
    Rees.

Lewis, N. fr. 268 Amherst to 267 Austin. Changed to Keil.

Lewis, 2d street east of Metcalfe running E.

fr. Clinton to William.
    Fleming.
    Lyman.
    Holt.
    Howard st.
    William.

Lewis Place, 4th street east of Delaware ave. running north fr. Sessions av. to Kenmore av. Changed to Winthrop pl., Mar. 20, '93.

Lexington (in 5th ward), 5th street south from 951 Abbott road running N. E. to Cazenovia creek. Changed to Tamarack, March 20, 1893.

Lexington Ave. (in 24th ward), formerly Butler street, west from 1064 Delaware ave. to 391 Richmond ave.
    186 Elmwood ave.
    230 Ashland ave.
    274 Norwood ave.
    320 Richmond ave.

Lexington Ave. (in 25th ward), 1st street N. of Leroy ave. running east from Hill (formerly Flint) to Liberty avenue. Changed to Shawnee ave. March 20, 1893.

Liberty Avenue (in 18th ward), 1st street S. of East Delavan avenue running E. fr. Queens pl. to Ave. A. Chang'd to Mohican ave. Mar. 20, 1893.

Liberty Avenue (in 25th ward), 3d street east of Grider running N. fr. Kensington ave. to Rodney.
    Shawnee ave.
    Rodney.

Liddell, N. from 1482 Broadway to W. S. R. R. tracks.

Lincoln, W. fr. Abby to B., R. & P. R. R. tks. (3d street south fr. 569 Abbott rd.) Changed to Mystic, Mar. 20, '93.

Lincoln Ave., 4th street south of Abbott road running east fr. Abby to Hopkins. Changed to Mystic, Mar. 20, '93.

Lincoln Parkway, N. fr. Soldier's place to The Park Lake.
    47 W. Forest ave.
    169 The Park.

Linden Ave. No. 1 (in 25th ward) 1st street N. of Amherst running west fr. Starin ave. to Colvin street.
    Morris ave.
    Wallace ave.
    Depew ave.
    Parkside ave.
    Colvin street.

Linden Ave. No. 2 (in 25th ward) east from Eley to Crosby, first street south of Kenmore ave. (north city line). Changed to Emerson street, Mar. 20, 1893.

Linwood Ave., N. fr. 41 North to 923 W. Delavan ave.
    87 Summer.
    161 Barker.
    237 Bryant.
    314 W. Utica.
    475 W. Ferry.
    557 Balcom.
    664 Bouck ave.
    731 W. Delavan ave.

Lisbon (form'ly Columbus ave), 3d street N. of East Hertel avenue running east fr. Main to Bailey ave.

Litchfield Ave., first st. north of East Delavan ave. running east fr. Grider street to Wyoming ave.

Durham ave.
Deerfield ave.
Humber ave.
Wyoming ave.
Livingston, 1st street W. of Richmond av. running north fr. Breckenridge to Bouck ave.
Auburn ave.
Bouck ave.
Livingston Ave., N. fr. Kensington ave. to Rodney (2d street E. of Grider). Changed to Federal ave., Mar. 20, 1893.
Lloyd, N. E. fr. Buffalo river to 132 Main.
10 Prime.
49 Canal.
94 Main.
Lock, N. W. fr. 92 Terrace to 128 Erie.
Lockwood, N. from 832 Eagle to 817 Broadway. Changed to Smith.
Locust, N. fr. 104 Cherry to 241 E. North.
101 Virginia.
169 Carlton.
235 High.
305 E. North.
Loepere, N. from 1090 Broadway to Walden ave.
Stanislaus.
Sycamore.
Walden ave.
Logan (in 18th ward), 2d street west of Bailey ave. running south fr. E. Ferry. Changed to Zenner, Mar. 20, '93.
Logan No. 1 (in 25th ward), 1st street N. of Amherst running E. fr. Reservation street to Bridgeman.
Logan No. 2 (in 25th ward), 2d street N. of Hertel ave. running west from Military

road to N. Y. C. R. R. tracks. Changed to Sayre, March 20, 1893.
Lombard, 1st street east of Fillmore ave. running north fr. Curtiss to 1017 Broadway.
Peckham.
Lovejoy.
Broadway.
Longnecker, 2d street E. of Bailey avenue running north from 1570 William to King.
Ludington.
Lovejoy.
Vanderbilt.
Reimann.
King.
Long Wharf, W. from foot of Commercial to Evans ship canal.
Lord, N. from 230 Seymour to 221 Howard.
24 Pink alley.
37 S. Division.
60 Meteor alley.
70 N. Division.
85 Laban alley.
99 Eagle.
117 James.
143 Clinton.
148 S. Railroad ave.
161 Fritz alley.
178 Bristol.
195 San Domingo al.
209 Oneida.
227 Pink.
236 Addison al.
251 Howard.
Loring Ave., 1st street N. of Jefferson running east from Main to Humboldt p'kway.
Meech ave.
Humboldt p'kway.
Louessen, N. from 240 Puerner ave. to 239 Fougeron.
Louisiana, N. fr. Buffalo river to 375 Seneca.
47 St. Clair.
64 Ohio.
121 South.

193 Tecumseh.
237 Sandusky.
297 Mackinaw.
327 Miami.
369 Elk.
405 Fulton.
441 Perry.
Hamburg canal
560 Exchange.
586 Carroll.
611 Seneca.
Love Alley, N. from 92 Ohio to rear of 40 Illinois.
Lovejoy, E. fr. 47 Emslie to 302 Curtiss, then closed by N. Y. C. R. R. to Trestle alley, then continued to city line.
21 Krettner.
49 Sherman.
75 Stanton.
101 Shumway.
127 Smith.
153 Coit.
177 Detroit.
203 Townsend.
229 Wilson.
249 Fillmore ave.
Lombard.
Gibson.
333 Clark.
357 Sears.
379 Playter.
404 Sweet ave.
505 Curtiss.
851 Trestle alley.
897 Central ave.
919 Bailey ave.
Crocker.
1039 Greene.
1067 Longnecker.
1101 Ideal.
1131 Benzinger.
1161 Gold.
1205 Davy.
1235 N. Ogden.
1271 Schiller.
1305 Goethe.
1318 City line.
Lowell Place (formerly Hodge street), N. W. from 342 Vermont to 351 Rhode Island.
Ludington, E. from 823

STREET DIRECTORY.

Bailey avenue to city
line.
  Greene.
  Longnecker.
  Ideal.
  Benzinger.
  Gold.
  Davey.
  North Ogden.
  Schiller.
  Goethe.
  City line.
Lutheran, N. from 234
  William to 359 Broad-
  way.
Lyman, E. fr. Metcalfe
  to Babcock (1st street
  south of Howard).
  Jones.
  Lewis.
  Babcock.
Lyth Place, E. fr. Purdy
  to Jefferson (1st street
  south of Puffer).
Mackinaw, E. from 250
  Ohio to Indian Reser-
  vation line.
  27 Chicago.
    Wabash (Aban-
    doned in 1888).
  115 Louisiana.
  141 Kentucky.
  167 Tennessee.
  193 Vincennes.
  225 Alabama.
  247 Vandalia.
  283 Hamburgh.
  309 Sidway.
  343 Katharine.
  373 Fitzgerald.
  415 Indian Reserva-
    tion line.
Madison, N. from 586
  Eagle to 25 Brown.
  35 Clinton.
  97 Howard.
  167 William.
  265 Peckham.
  345 Broadway.
  459 Beckwith.
  469 Sycamore.
  551 Brown.
Maiden Lane, E. fr. 11
  Water to 60 Canal.

8 Fly.
37 Canal.
Main, N. from Buffalo
  river to north line of
  city.
  2 Central Wharf.
  3 Ohio.
  24 Prime.
  47 Perry.
  48 Dayton.
  97 Scott.
  100 Canal.
  106 Hanover.
  117 Main and Ham-
    burgh canal.
  119 Quay.
  132 Lloyd.
  156 Terrace.
  177 Exchange.
  225 Seneca.
  275 Swan.
  308 Erie.
  309 S. Division.
  312 Church.
  333 N. Division.
  344 Niagara.
  377 Eagle.
  411 Clinton.
  428 Court.
    Lafayette Squ're
  447 Lafayette.
  487 E. Mohawk.
  488 W Mohawk.
  539 Genesee.
  543 E. Huron.
  544 W. Huron.
  589 E. Chippewa.
  590 W. Chippewa.
  707 E. Tupper.
  716 W. Tupper.
  776 Edward.
  785 Goodell.
  819 Burton.
  837 Virginia.
  909 Carlton.
  938 Allen.
  967 High.
  1005 Goodrich.
  1039 E. North.
  1040 North.
  1081 St. Paul.
  1119 Best.
  1130 Summer.
  1177 Dodge.
  1210 Barker.
  1215 Coe.

1249 Northampton.
1288 Bryant.
1321 Riley.
1381 E. Utica.
1382 W. Utica.
1425 Glenwood ave.
1477 Woodlawn ave.
1530 W. Ferry.
1531 E. Ferry.
1614 Harvard pl.
1619 Michigan.
1625 Dexter.
1630 Balcom.
1679 Frey pl.
1727 Puffer.
1751 Masten.
1769 Florida.
1776 Bouck ave.
1850 E. Delavan ave.
1851 W. Delavan ave.
1893 Scajaquada cr'k
1975 Jefferson.
  Loring ave.
  Eastwood pl.
2095 Steele.
2100 Humboldt pk'y.
  Robie.
  Florence.
2270 E. Forest ave.
2320 } Oakwood pl.
2334 }
2341 Leroy ave.
2420 Jewett ave.
2429 N. Y. C. R. R.
  Junction.
2436 Greenfield.
  Halbert.
2470 Fairfield.
  Orchard pl.
2500 Russell.
2351 Fillmore ave.
2600 Vernon.
2680 Amherst.
  Morris ave.
  Depew ave.
  Woodbridge av.
  Huntington ave.
2995 E. Hertel ave.
3002 Hertel ave.
  Custer.
  La Salle ave.
  Minnesota ave.
  Erie R. R. junct.
  Lisbon.
  Alvin ave.
  Tyler.

Hendricks.
3026 Public School No. 22.
3219 Sutton Lane.
3226 Heath.
3275 Hillery pl.
3276 Eley.
3399 Erie Co. Poorhouse.
Kennelworth.
Richards ave.
Sawyer ave.
Kenmore ave.
3470 City line.

Main and Hamburgh Canal, E. fr. 117 Main to 385 Hamburgh.

Malta Place, N. W. fr. 312 Maryland to 177 West avenue.

Manhart, 3d street N. of Warwick ave. running east fr. Norfolk ave. to Bailey ave.

Mandan (formerly Carter, in 25th ward), 1st st. N. of N. Y. C. R. R. Belt Line at Cross Cut junct. running N. fr. Pierce Steam Heating W'ks to Hertel ave. (Also 1st st. E. of McPherson running S. of Hertel av).

Manhattan, 1st street east of Fillmore ave. running N. fr. East Delavan av. Changed to Amsterdam, Mar. 20, 1893.

Manhattan Ave., N. fr. Leroy ave. to Rodney (fifth street east of Avenue A).
Shawnee ave.
Rodney.

Manitoba (formerly Oneida, in 10th ward), 1st street north of 1270 Clinton running east fr. Gilbert to Baitz ave.
Scoville ave.
Baitz ave.

Maple, N. fr. 34 Cherry to 189 East North. (Closed fr. E. North to Tompkins st., then opened to E. Ferry).
37 Goodell.
78 Burton.
137 Virginia.
202 Carltou.
271 High.
338 E. North.

Maple Ridge Ave., third street north of East Delavan av. running east from Grider to Wyoming ave.
Deerfield ave.
Wyoming ave.

Marigold (formerly Pleasant ave.), 4th st. east of Fillmore ave. (formerly Avenue A) running north fr. Leroy ave. to Rodney.

Mariner, N. fr. 370 Virginia to 234 North.
89 Allen.
191 North.

Marilla, E. fr. L. S. R. R. tks. to 960 South Park ave. (form'ly White's Corners road).
Lehigh.
Bahama.
208 Hopkins.
437 So. Park ave.

Marion, 1st street north of Amherst, running west fr. N. Elmwood ave. (formerly McPherson st.) to inner lot.

Mark, N. from 22 William to 15 Gay.

Markham Place, 1st st. east of Delaware ave. running north from Sessions ave. to Villa avenue.

Marquette Place (formerly Milton pl.), 3d street north of East Delavan av. running

east fr. Olympic ave. to Ocean ave.

Marshall, N. fr. Genesee to Puerner avenue (2d street east of Parade House).
Bardol.
Puerner ave.

Martin Ave., 3d street north of Grace running east from Tonawanda to Mayer ave.
Gallatin.
Mayer ave.

Marvin, N. fr. 172 Elk to 231 Perry.
29 Fulton.
65 Perry.

Mary, E. fr. 41 Indiana to 54 Illinois.

Mary, S. fr. 1095 William st. Changed to Spencer.

Maryland, E. from Erie canal to 52 College.
21 Fourth.
44 Effner.
69 Fifth.
95 Front ave.
127 Seventh.
163 Niagara.
197 Prospect ave.
226 Whitney pl.
251 Tenth.
275 West ave.
311 Twelfth.
312 Malta pl.
328 Cottage.
392 College.

Mason, N. fr. 16 Breckenridge to 19 Auburn avenue.

Massachusetts Ave., N. E. fr. 865 Front ave. to 469 West Ferry.
25 Seventh.
57 Niagara.
93 Prospect ave.
129 Fargo ave.
165 West ave.
201 Plymouth ave.
237 Thirteenth.
273 Fourteenth.
Fifteenth.

293 W. Utica.
Sixteenth.
Lawrence pl.
Shields ave.
Brayton.
Winter.
Eighteenth.
Nineteenth.
473 Chenango
511 Essex.
555 W. Ferry.

Masten, N. fr. 236 East North to 1751 Main.
57 Best.
Edna pl.
121 Dodge
Southampton.
189 Northampton.
Eaton.
259 Riley.
286 Laurel.
319 E. Utica.
365 Glenwood ave.
Emerson pl.
Tompkins.
421 Woodlawn ave.
469 East Ferry.
Dexter.
Balcom.
Frey pl.
619 Puffer.
638 Main.

Mathews, E. fr. 227 Mortimer to 616 Jefferson.

Maurice, N. fr. 200 Prenatt to 1141 Seneca.
Elk.
Perry.
Seneca.

May (formerly Doll st. and Doll ave.), 2d and 3d streets west of Bailey ave. running N. fr. W. S. R. R. tracks across Walden ave. to an inner lot.

Mayer Ave., 1st street E. of Tonawanda running N. W. from Rano to Royal ave.
Martin ave.
Hunt ave.
Ontario.
Royal ave.

Maynard (form'ly Webster), N. W. from 428 West Ferry to 465 Breckenridge.

McKibbin, 1st street N. of Walden ave. running east from Moselle to Koons ave.
Bissell ave.
Goodyear ave.
Koons ave.

McPherson, N. from 698 Amherst to 811 Hertel ave. (see North Elmwood ave.)

Mead Alley, N. fr. 146 N. Division to 149 Eagle.

Mechanic, E. from Erie canal to 216 Terrace.
62 Birdsall.
Terrace.

Medford Place (formerly Harrison pl.), 3d street E. of Delaware ave. running north fr. Sessions ave. to Villa avenue.

Medina, fr. Church to Erie canal, bet. Terrace and W. Genesee.

Meech Ave., 1st street east of Jefferson running north from East Delavan ave. to Loring ave.
Hedley pl.
Blaine.
Parkway ave.
Loring ave.

Meech, N. fr. 472 Virginia to 82 Allen.

Meldrum (formerly Whitney), 2d street N. of Amherst running west fr. N. Elmwood ave. (formerly McPherson).

Melvin Place (formerly Sloan pl.), south from 1397 Elk to Buffalo river.

Melrose, 1st street S. fr.

951 Abbott rd. running N. E. to Cazenovia creek.
Cumberland ave.
Cazenovia creek.

Mendola (formerly Arlington ave.), 1st st. east of Grider running east fr. Kensington ave. to Wyoming avenue.
Deerfield ave.
Palos place.
Wyoming ave.

Meriden, 8th street S. fr. 951 Abbott road running N. E. to Cazenovia creek.
Cumberland ave.
Cazenovia creek.

Merrimac (form'ly Hendricks), 2d street N. of Hertel ave. running west fr. Main to D. L. & W. R. R. tks. (at Internatio'l junct. near north city line).
Gallatin.
Bruce.
Mildred.
Angle.
D. L. & W. R. R. tks.

Mesmer Ave., 1st street south of Abbott road running east from S. Park ave. (formerly White's Cors. road) to Boulevard.

Metcalfe, N. fr. 962 Clinton to 895 William.
Bass.
Stetson.
Fleming.
Klaus.
Thomas.
Lyman.
Howard.
William.

Meteor Alley (formerly Anderson alley), first alley north of S. Division running east fr. Emslie to 60 Lord.

STREET DIRECTORY.

Miami, E. fr. 196 Ohio
to 203 Hamburgh.
  1 Moore.
  45 Chicago.
  Ohio slip.
  135 Louisiana.
  241 Alabama.
  305 Hamburgh.

Michigan, N. fr. Buffalo
river to 1619 Main.
  12 Ohio.
  52 Elk.
  87 Fulton.
  128 Perry.
  171 Scott.
  196 Main and Ham-
    burgh canal.
  212 Greene.
  N. Y. C. depot.
  Erie R'y depot.
  238 Exchange.
  262 Carroll.
  282 Seneca.
  303 Myrtle.
  326 Swan.
  350 S. Division.
  376 N. Division.
  402 Eagle.
  440 Clinton.
  465 William.
  474 Vine.
  487 Gay.
  530 Broadway.
  571 Cypress.
  605 Sycamore.
  682 Genesee.
  718 E. Tupper.
  727 Cherry.
  794 Goodell.
  832 Burton.
  882 Virginia.
  942 Carlton.
  1008 High.
  1044 Goodrich.
  1072 E. North.
  1130 Best.
  Edna place.
  1189 Dodge.
  Southampton.
  1229 Northampton.
  1283 Eaton.
  Riley.
  1351 Laurel.
  1386 E. Utica.
  1425 Glenwood ave.
  Emerson pl.

Tompkins.
  1479 Woodlawn ave.
  1531 E. Ferry.
  1580 Main.

Milburn, S. from 1319
Broadway to N. Y. C.
R. R. tracks.
  Ashley.
  Grimes.
  N. Y. C. R. R. tracks.

Mildred (form'ly Alex-
ander street, in 25th
ward), third street W.
of Main running N.
fr. Tyler to Eley (near
north city line).
  Hendricks.
  Heath.
  Eley.

Milford, 3d street S. fr.
951 Abbott road run-
ning N. E. to Cazeno-
via creek.
  Cumberland ave.
  Cazenovia creek.

Military Road, N. fr. 282
Amherst to city line.
  2 Keil.
  36 Clay.
  68 Glor.
  151 Grant.
  168 Austin.
  Lansing.
  Grote.
  Chandler.
  N. Y. C. (Belt
    Line) R. R.
  342 Hertel ave.
  Gladstone.
  Sayre.
  Arizona.
  Denver.
  Idaho.
  Ansteth.
  Behrends.
  Race.
  Coulson.
  Layer ave.
  Kofler ave.
  Ruhl ave.
  Skillen.
  Sherriff ave.
  Blum ave.
  Ritt ave.
  777 Kenmore ave.

City line.

Mill, E. from 421 Ham-
burgh to 19 Griffin.
Changed to Railroad,
March 20, 1893.

Mill, E. from Erie canal
to 1796 Niagara st.
Changed to Bridge.

Miller, S. fr. 1427 Broad-
way to Amity street.
Changed to Quincy,
March 20, 1893.

Miller Ave., N. fr. 1384
Broadway to 1228
Sycamore.
  West Shore street.
  Sycamore.

Miller Place, N. fr. Puf-
fer to East Delavan
ave. (4th street east of
Fillmore ave., form-
erly Avenue A).
Changed to Chelsea
pl., March 20, 1893.

Mills, N. fr. 1028 Broad-
way to Genesee.
  Sycamore.
  C street.
  B street.
  A street.
  Peterson.
  Genesee.

Milnor, N. fr. 82 William
to 211 Broadway.

Milton, N. fr. 1296 Sen-
eca to W. N. Y. & P.
R. R. tks.

Milton Place, 3d street
north of E. Delavan
ave. running east fr.
Olympic ave. to Pa-
cific ave. Changed to
Marquette pl., March
20, 1893.

Mineral Spring Road, E.
from 1940 Seneca to
city line.
  Hayden.
  Frank ave.
  308 S. Ogden.
  365 City line.

Minnesota Ave. (form-
erly Summit Park

STREET DIRECTORY.

ave.), 2d street north of East Hertel ave. running east fr. Main to Bailey ave.
Cordova.
Park Ridge ave.
Lenox ave.
Bailey ave.

Minton, 2d street north of Perry running east fr. Smith to Selkirk.

Mississippi, N. fr. Buffalo river to 93 Scott.
7 Ohio.
15 Elk.
81 Perry.
125 Scott.

Moeller, E. from Bailey ave. to D., L. & W. R. R. (3d street south of Genesee).

Mohawk, East, E. fr. 487 Main to 246 Ellicott.
19 Washington.
55 Ellicott.

Mohawk, West, west fr. 488 Main to 145 Wilkeson.
24 Pearl.
36 W. Genesee.
55 Franklin.
97 Delaware ave.
143 Morgan.
161 Niagara.
184 Staats.
201 Utley alley.
202 Wilkeson.

Mohican Ave. (formerly Liberty ave., in 18th ward), 1st street south of East Delavan ave. running east fr. Regina pl. to Fillmore ave. (formerly Avenue A).
Humboldt parkw'y
Fillmore ave.

Mohr, S. fr. 1285 Broadway to Grimes.
Ashley.
Grimes.

Monitor (Uniontown), E. from Packer to Buffalo river.

Monroe, north from 614 Eagle to 57 Brown.
37 Clinton.
105 Howard.
173 William.
271 Peckham.
359 Broadway.
467 Beckwith.
485 Sycamore.
575 Brown.

Montana Ave., N. from Genesee to E. Ferry (4th street east of Moselle).

Montclair Ave., 1st st. E. of Grider (junction Kensington ave. and Leroy ave.) running N. from Leroy ave. to Rodney street.
Shawnee ave.
Rodney.

Montgomery, N. fr. 874 Eagle to 305 Howard.
9 James.
33 Clinton.
Fritz alley.
73 Bristol.
San Domingo al.
105 Oneida.
S. Railroad ave.
144 Pink.
167 Howard.

Moore, N. fr. 214 Ohio to 153 Elk.
13 Miami.
55 Elk.

Moreland, E. fr. Bailey ave. to Greene, first street north of Lovejoy.

Morgan, N. fr. 139 West Eagle to 142 W. Chippewa and fr. 135 Edward to 411 Virginia.
7 W. Genesee.
33 Court.
63 Niagara.
79 W. Mohawk.
133 W. Huron.
162 Cary.
189 W. Chippewa.

Morris Ave., 1st street N. of Amherst run-

ning west from Main to Linden ave.
Beard ave.
Parker ave.
Voorhis.
Starin ave.
Linden ave.

Mortimer, N. from 342 William street to 199 Cherry.
91 W. Peckham.
93 Peckham.
122 Hollister.
151 Broadway.
183 Rey.
205 George.
212 Champlin.
227 Mathews.
257 Sycamore.
349 Genesee.
379 Cherry.

Morton, west from 3226 Main to N. Y., L. E. & W.R.R. tks. Changed to Heath, Mar. 20, '93.

Moselle, N. fr. 318 Walden ave. to 1207 East Ferry.
McKibbin.
177 Genesee.
216 Urban.
244 French.
Box ave.
Glenwood ave.
Winslow ave.
Woodlawn ave.
359 E. Ferry.

Mugler, 4th street south of Mineral Spring rd. running S.W. fr. Seneca street to Cazenovia creek.

Mulberry, N. fr. 68 Cherry to 215 East North. (Closed fr. E. North to Tompkins, and then opened to East Ferry).
13 Goodell.
115 Virginia.
183 Carlton.
249 High.
319 E. North.

Myers, N. fr. 1010 Genesee to 745 Best.

Myron Ave., 1st street east of Delaware ave. running north from Villa av. to Kenmore ave. (at north city line).

Myrtle (formerly Folsom), east fr. 303 Michigan to 86 Jefferson.
  15 Fitch alley.
  59 Seneca pl.
  97 Chicago.
  203 S. Cedar.
  313 Spring.
  401 Jefferson.

Mystic (formerly Lincoln street and Lincoln ave.), 3d and 4th streets south of 569 Abbott road running east from Hopkins to B., R. & P. R. R. tks.
  Germania.
  Abby.
  Newerf.
  Rochester.
  Pittsburgh.
  B., R. & P. R. R. tks.

Navel Ave., 2d street N. of Genesee running west from Gruner to Johnson avenue.

Nelson, S. fr. 621 Amherst to Scajaquada creek.
  Piatti.
  Scajaquada creek.

Neptune (formerly Ketchum alley) N. fr. 130 Carlton to 139 High street.

Nevada Ave., N. from Genesee to E. Ferry (3d street east of Moselle).

New (in Union Iron Co. tract), South Buffalo.

Newell, N. fr. 568 Howard to 965 William.

Newell Ave., E. fr. Niagara to Mayer ave.

(third street north of Ontario). Changed to Royal ave., March 20, 1893.

Newerf, 1st street west of Abby running S. fr. Mystic to Hancock.

Newport, 11th street E. of Colvin running N. fr. St. Lawrence ave. to Kenmore av. (near north city line).

Newfield, N.W.fr. Zinns ave. to O'Neil (1st st. west of Skillen).
  Roesch ave.
  O'Neil.

New South Ogden, N. fr. Dingens to 1763 William (1st street W. of city line).

Newton, 1st street N. of Lovejoy running W. from Curtiss to Warner ave.

Niagara, N. W. from 344 Main to city line.
  34 Pearl.
  33 W. Eagle.
  51 Franklin.
  75 Niagara Square.
  111 Morgan.
  123 W. Mohawk.
  134 Staats.
  193 W. Huron.
  208 Georgia.
  273 Carolina.
  338 Virginia.
  397 Maryland.
  462 Hudson.
  524 Pennsylvania.
  585 Jersey.
  647 Porter ave.
  Prospect parks.
  709 Connecticut.
  Prospect reservoir.
  771 Vermont.
  833 Rhode Island.
  895 Massachusetts.
  957 Hampshire.
  970 Fort.
  979 Front ave.
  995 School.

  1017 Prospect ave.
  1075 Fargo ave.
  1088 Albany.
  1144 Gull.
  1160 W. Ferry.
  1225 Breckenridge.
  1275 Auburn ave.
  1319 Bouck ave.
  1348 Brace.
  1363 Penfield.
  1397 W.Delavan ave.
  1422 Sloan.
  1471 Potomac ave.
  1531 Bird ave.
  1589 W. Forest ave.
  1619 Scajaquada cr'k
  1649 Tonawanda.
  1707 Wayne.
  1775 Parish.
  1796 Bridge.
  1857 Amherst.
  1917 Hamilton.
  1987 Austin.
  2047 Farmer.
  2079 Hertel ave.
  2107 Grace.
  2131 Garfield.
  2159 Arthur.
  Cornelius creek.
  2261 Ontario.
  2287 Collaton.
  Briggs ave.
  Royal ave.
  See ave.
  Crowley ave.
  Esser ave.
  Germania Park.
  Roesch ave.
  2687 O'Neil.
  2825 City line.

Niagara Square, at junction of Court, W.Genesee, Delaware ave. and Niagara.

Nichols Alley, N. fr. 160 Seneca. Changed to Nichols pl., Jan. 1891.

Nichols Place, N. fr. 160 Seneca street.

Nicholson Ave., east fr. Eley to Crosby, 2d st. south of Kenmore av. (north city line).

Ninth. Changed to

Prospect ave. in 1876.

Nineteenth, north from Rhode Island to 353 West Ferry.
Massachusetts.
Hampshire.
W. Ferry.

Norfolk Ave., 7th street east of Grider running north fr. E. Ferry street to Kensington ave.
Puffer.
E. Delavan ave.
Erie R'y and D., L. and W.R.R.crossing.
Warwick ave.
Bayfield.
Kensington ave.

Norman Ave., 3d street east of Tonawanda running N. W. from Rano to See ave.
Hunt ave.
Ontario.
See ave.

Norris (formerly Cass), 6th street east of Military road running N. fr. Hertel av. to Race.

Norris Place, N.E. from 125 Cottage street to 2 Wadsworth. Changed to Day's Park, March 20, 1893.

North, W. fr. 1040 Main to the Circle.
27 N. Pearl.
44 Linwood ave.
60 Franklin.
97 Delaware ave.
152 Irving pl.
178 Park.
209 Elmwood ave.
234 Mariner.
260 College.
394 Arlington pl.
317 The Circle.

North, East, E. fr. 1039 Main to 382 Herman.
51 Ellicott.
91 Oak.
127 Elm.

163 Michigan.
189 Maple.
215 Mulberry.
236 Masten.
241 Locust.
267 Lemon.
291 Orange.
319 Peach.
343 Grape.
365 Rose.
383 Jefferson.
419 Handel alley.
451 Berlin.
Durrenberg'r pl
533 Johnson.
567 Sherman.
599 Fox.
663 Herman.

Northampton, E. fr. 1249 Main to 28 Ave. A.
49 Ellicott.
96 Holland pl.
115 Michigan.
191 Masten.
343 Jefferson.
Gerhardt.
Berlin.
Timon.
Roehrer.
Wohlers.
St. Michael.
St. Ann.
W. Parade ave.
Humboldt pk'y
Avenue A.

North Adams, N. fr. 143 Albany to 116 Breckenridge. Changed to Hibbard in year 1881.

North Central Ave., S. from 1619 Broadway to N. Y. C. & H. R. R. tracks.

North Division, E. fr. 333 Main to 94 Fillmore ave.
19 Washington.
51 Ellicott.
87 Oak.
123 Elm.
146 Mead alley.
159 Michigan.
227 Chestnut.
277 Pine.
343 Cedar.

409 Hickory.
475 Spring.
561 Jefferson.
575 Grosvenor.
705 Emslie.
749 Bond.
795 Lord.
839 Smith.
869 Elizabeth.
895 Cornelia.
919 Fillmore ave.

North Dupont, first st. east of Jefferson running north from East Ferry. (Parallel with Internat'l Exhibition grounds).

North Elm, N. from 96 Northampt'n to Riley Changed to Holland place in 1891.

North Elmwood Ave., north from 578 W. Forest ave. to north city line.
Scajaquada creek.
Amherst.
Marion.
Meldrum.
N. Y. C. (Belt Line) Cross-Cut Junct.
Hertel ave.
Hinman ave.
Ramsdell ave.
Kenmore ave.
North city line.

North Jefferson. Changed to Herkimer.

North Ogden, N. from 1714 William to 911 Walden ave.
Ludington.
Lovejoy.
Vanderbilt.
Reimann.
Broadway.
Walden ave.

North Parade Ave., east from 1 Avenue A to East Parade pl. (first street north of Parade grounds).

North Park Ave., 1st st. north of Ontario run-

ning east from Skillen to Kenmore ave.
Albemarle.
Belmont.
Seabrook.
Kenmore ave.

North Pearl, N. fr. 522 Virginia to 27 North.
89 Allen.
195 North.

North Smith. Changed to Batavia.

North Swan. Changed to Seymour.

North Washington. Changed to West ave.

North William. Changed to Fremont pl. and in year 1887 changed to Elmwood ave.

Norton (in 11th ward), 1st street north of Clinton running east fr. Metcalfe to Babcock. Changed to Fleming, Mar. 20, '93.

Norton (in 19th ward), N. from 77 Water to Peacock.

Northumberland Ave., N. fr. East Ferry to Kensington ave. (6th street east of Grider).
Puffer.
E. Delavan ave
Sussex.
Warwick ave.
Kensington ave.

Norwalk Ave., 3d street east of Colvin running north fr. Hertel avenue to Taunton place.
Tacoma ave.
Taunton pl.

Norwood Ave., (formerly Howard ave.), N. from 313 Summer to West Forest ave.
145 Bryant.
231 W. Utica.
265 Anderson pl.
361 Lexington ave.

Highland ave.
381 W. Ferry.
Breckenridge.
Auburn ave.
Bouck ave.
W. Delavan ave.
Potomac ave.
Bird ave.
W. Forest ave.

Oak, N. fr. 88 Swan to 79 Best. (Closed bet. High and E. North.)
21 S. Division.
49 N. Division.
81 Eagle.
123 Clinton.
157 Vine.
175 Broadway.
198 Hersee alley.
238 E. Huron.
239 Sycamore.
322 Genesee.
413 E. Tupper.
487 Goodell.
525 Burton.
568 Virginia.
639 Carlton.
705 High.
772 E. North.
806 St. Paul.
839 Best.

Oak Grove Ave., second street east of Jefferson running north fr. East Delavan ave. to N. Y. C. R. R. (Belt Line) tracks.
Hedley pl.
Blaine.
Hughes.
Humboldt parkw'y
Gillette ave.
N. Y. C. R. R. Belt Line.

Oakland, N. fr. Walden ave. to Genesee (3d street east of N. Y. C. [Belt Line] R. R.) Changed to Ivy, Mar. 20, 1893.

Oakland Ave., N. fr. 165 Summer to Bryant (1st street west of Delaware ave.)

Oakwood Place, 3d st. north of Humboldt parkway running W fr. 2320 Main to Parkside ave. and fr. 2334 Main to N. Y. C. (Belt Line) R. R.
Crescent ave.
Summit ave.
Woodward ave.
Parkside ave.

Oberlin (formerly St. Louis ave.), south fr. Walden ave. across Sycamore (4th street east of N. Y. C. [Belt Line] R. R.)

Ocean Ave. (formerly Pacific ave., in 12th ward), 2d street west of Bailey avenue running north from East Delavan ave. to Beverly.
Byron pl.
Holborn.
Marquette pl.
Beverly.

Ohio, S. E. from 3 Main to Buffalo river and 1 Hamburgh turnpike.
21 Washington.
45 Indiana.
68 Elk.
73 Illinois.
92 Love alley.
95 Mississippi.
Clark and Skinner canal.
131 Columbia.
161 Michigan.
N. Y. C. freight depot.
196 Miami.
214 Moore.
238 Mackinaw.
300 Chicago.
Ohio Basin.
442 South.
Freight dept. N. Y., L. E. & W. R. R.
475 Aurora.
498 Louisiana.
524 St. Clair.

548 Buffalo river.

549 Hamburgh turn pike.

Ohio Basin, bounded S. by Ohio street, east by Louisiana street, north by Mackinaw street and west by Wabash street.

Ohio Basin Slip, fr. Ohio basin to Main and Hamburgh canal.

Olga Place (formerly Jerry) 3d street north of Clinton running east fr. Clare to 328 Fillmore ave.

Olive, (in 5th ward), 3d street S. of White's Corners plank road running east fr. Seneca street to Buffalo creek. Changed to Pomona pl., March 20, 1893.

Olive, (in 25th ward), 1st street north of Delaware Ave. Cemetery, running W. fr. Delaware ave. to Erie R'y tracks.
Camden.
Cecil.
Clarence.
Steward.
Comet.
Sarvis.
Erie R'y tracks.

Olmstead, E. fr. Schutrum to Bailey ave. (1st street N. of Broadway).
Hirschbeck.
Shepard.
Gatchell.
Bailey ave.

Olsen, 1st street east of Bailey ave. running N. fr. Clinton street.

Olympic Ave., 3d street west of Bailey ave. running north fr. E. Delavan ave. to Warwick ave.

Byron pl.
Holborn.
Milton pl.
Kenilworth.
Warwick.

Oneida, (in 10th ward), east fr. 227 Emslie to 282 Fillmore ave.
41 Bond.
85 Lord.
123 Smith.
153 S. Railroad ave.
179 Montgomery.
213 Clare.
452 Fillmore ave.

Oneida, (in 10th ward), 1st street north of 1279 Clinton running east fr. Gilbert to Baitz avenue. Changed to Manitoba, Mar. 20, '93.

O'Neil, E. from 2687 Niagara to city line.
Palace ave.
117 Tonawanda.
Baxter.
Kertz.
Eckhert.
Ullman.
Argus.
Elgas.
Ziegeler.
Newfield.
265 Skillen.
Albemarle.
Belmont.
Seabrook.
495 City line.

Ontario, E. from 2261 Niagara to city line.
74 Fuller.
165 Tonawanda.
Saratoga.
Mayer ave.
Albert ave.
Norman ave.
Dana ave.
Bleeker ave.
Harold ave.
Ruth ave.
Philadelphia av.
Evelyn.
S. Newfield.
574 Skillen.
689 City line.

Orange, N. fr. 174 Cherry to 291 East North.
62 Virginia.
133 Carlton.
203 High.
273 E. North.

Orchard Place, 2d street S. of Amherst running west fr. Main to N. Y. C. R. R. (Belt Line) tracks.

Orlando, N. fr. 232 Prenatt to 1169 Seneca.
Elk.
Perry.
Seneca.

Orlando Alley, E. fr. 259 Washington to 18 Ellicott. Changed to Dickens alley, March 20, 1893.

Orleans, 2d street east of Bailey ave. running north fr. Sugar to Kensington ave.

Orton Place, N. fr 354 Hudson to 355 Pennsylvania.

Osage, 4th street south of 711 Abbott road, running east fr. Hopkins.

Oscar, E. from Laux to Babcock (1st street N. of Clinton).

Oswego, E. fr. Winchester street to Eggert.

Otis Place, 1st street E. of Main running N. fr. Glenwood ave. to East Ferry street.
Woodlawn ave.
East Ferry.

Ottawa, E. fr. Louisiana and Ohio basin to 55 Hamburgh. (Discontinued by Common Council, July 14, 1879).

Otto, E. fr. 73 Hayward to 360 Alabama.

Owahn Place, N. E. fr.

STREET DIRECTORY.

250 Abbott road to Prenatt.

Oxford Place, 1st street west of Main running north fr. West Ferry street to Bouck ave.
  Balcom.
  Bouck ave.

Pacific, N. fr. Austin to 203 Hertel ave. (1st st. east of Tonawanda).

Pacific Avenue (in 12th ward), 2d street west of Bailey ave., running north fr. E. Delavan ave. to Beverly. Changed to Ocean av. March 20, 1893.

Pacific Avenue (in 25th ward), 1st street west of Delaware ave. running north fr. Cleveland street to Bouck avenue.
  Auburn ave.
  Lancaster ave.
  Bouck ave.

Page, N. fr. 605 Hertel ave. to Race.
  Lawn ave.
  Whitlock.
  Race.

Palace Ave., N. fr. Esser ave. to O'Neil (1st st. east of Niagara near Germania Park).

Palmer. Changed to Whitney pl. in 1875.

Palos Place (formerly Harvard pl., in 25th ward), 1st street west of Wyoming av. running north fr. Mendola to Kensington ave.

Pansy, 2d street east of Jefferson running N. fr. Florida to East Delavan ave.

Parish, E. fr. 1775 Niagara to 222 Tonawanda.
  10 Niagara.
  42 Dearborn.
  72 East.

120 Thompson.
170 Tonawanda.

Park, N. fr. 422 Virginia to 178 North.
  87 Allen.
  189 North.

Park Place, W. from 286 Delaware avenue to Johnson pl. Changed to Johnson Park's, March 20, 1893.

Parker Ave., 1st street west of Main, running north fr. Amherst to Hertel ave.
  Beard ave.
  Morris ave.
  Depew ave.
  Woodbridge ave.
  Huntington ave.
  Hertel ave.

Park Ridge Ave., 2d st. west of Bailey avenue running north from Kensington ave. to Alvin avenue.
  Cement.
  Hewett.
  Shirley ave.
  La Salle ave.
  Minnesota ave.
  Lisbon.
  Alvin ave.

Parkside Ave., 1st street east of the Park grounds and 3d street west of Main running northwest fr. Humboldt parkway to Hertel avenue.
  Robie.
  Florence.
  Oakwood pl.
  Jewett ave.
  Russell.
  Amherst.
  Tillinghast.
  Crescent ave.
  Linden ave.
  Woodbridge ave.
  Carlisle ave.
  Hertel ave.

Parkway Ave., 3d street north of East Delavan ave. running east fr.

Jefferson st. to Oak Grove ave. Changed to Hughes, March 20, 1893.

Parnell, 1st street west of Abby running W. fr. Lackawanna st. to B., R. & P.R.R. tks.
  Rochester.
  Pittsburg.
  B., R. & P. R. R. tks.

Pauline, N. from Steele (bet. Humboldt parkway and Ave. A).

Peabody, N. fr. 950 Elk to 1069 Seneca.
  Perry.
  Seneca.

Peach, N. fr. 208 Cherry to 323 Best.
  45 Virginia.
  118 Carlton.
  185 High.
  257 E. North.
  32 Best.

Peacock, N. W. from 46 Evans to 179 Erie.
  Norton.
  Erie.

Pearl, N. fr. Erie canal and 99 Commercial to 24 West Tupper.
  3 Commercial.
  29 Terrace.
  72 W. Seneca.
  111 W. Swan.
  122 Erie.
  146 Church.
  178 Niagara.
  189 W. Eagle.
  222 Express.
  245 Court.
  293 W. Mohawk.
  308 W. Genesee.
  350 W. Huron.
  398 W. Chippewa.
  518 W. Tupper.

Pearl Place, S. from 521 Virginia (opp. North Pearl) to rear of St. Louis Church.

Peck, S. fr. 1413 Broadway to N. Y. C. R. R. tracks.

Peckham, E. fr. 465 Jefferson to 200 feet west of Curtiss.
  21 Madison.
  51 Monroe.
  79 Adams.
  107 Watson.
  137 Emslie.
  166 Krettner.
  193 Sherman.
  219 Stanton.
  247 Shumway.
  273 Smith.
  301 Coit.
  327 Detroit.
  353 Townsend.
  379 Wilson.
  399 Fillmore ave.
  Lombard.
  Gibson.
  485 Clark.
  509 Sears.
  531 Playter.
  655 Curtiss.
Peckham, E. fr. 823 Bailey ave. Changed to Ludington.
Peck Slip, opp. foot of Main.
Pembina (form'ly Grace ave. in 5th ward), W. fr. Hopkins to Germania, near Abbott road.
  Boone.
  Germania.
Pembroke Ave., E. from Grider to Wyoming ave. (5th street N. E. of Delavan ave.)
  Deerfield ave.
  Wyoming ave.
Penfield, E. fr. 1363 Niagara to 1142 West ave.
Pennsylvania, E. from Erie canal to The Circle.
  Fourth.
  78 Lakeview ave.
  79 Fifth.
  105 Front ave.
  115 Osborne alley.
  139 Seventh.
  173 Niagara.

207 Prospect ave.
249 Fargo ave.
277 West ave.
327 Plymouth ave.
355 Orton pl.
350 Thirteenth.
384 Fourteenth.
385 Wadsworth.
  The Circle.
Peoria (form'ly Thompson), N. W. fr. Grace to Arthur (1st street west of Tonawanda).
  Garfield.
  Arthur.
Perkins Place, E. fr. 217 Dewitt to 368 Herkimer.
Perry, E. from 47 Main to 52 Dole.
  19 Washington.
  38 Beaver.
  41 Indiana.
  48 Burwell pl.
  67 Illinois.
  95 Mississippi.
  Clark and Skinner canal.
  137 Columbia.
  165 Michigan.
  185 W. Market.
  Elk st. Market.
  196 E. Market.
  231 Marvin.
  269 Chicago.
  Ohio Basin slip.
  363 Louisiana.
  405 Hayward.
  469 Alabama.
  533 Hamburgh.
  569 Red Jacket.
  687 Van Rensselaer.
  867 Smith.
  931 Selkirk.
  Peabody.
  Walter.
  Maurice.
  Orlando.
  1139 Babcock.
  Gorham.
  Imson.
  Winona.
  Bradford.
  Harrison.
  1305 Dole.

Person, south from 1347 Broadway to N. Y. C. R. R. tks.
  Ashley.
  Grimes.
  N. Y. C. R. R. tks.
Peter, N. fr. 448 Amherst to Grote.
Peterson, E. fr. 1025 Fillmore ave. to Mills.
Petri, 1st street east of Bailey ave. running N. from Doat to Scajaquada creek.
Pfaudler, 2d street east of Ave. A running N. fr. E. Delaware ave.
Phelps, E. fr. Halbert to Ave. A (3d street N. of Leroy ave.)
Philadelphia Ave., S. E. fr. Esser ave. to Clarion pl. (4th street east of Tonawanda).
  Ontario.
  Clarion pl.
Philip, S. from Genesee to Doat, 3d street W. of Bailey ave.
Piatti, 1st street south of Amherst running east fr. Yates to Nelson.
Picard Alley, N. fr. 257 Clinton to 99 William.
Pine, N. fr. 282 Swan to 125 Sycamore.
  Booth alley.
  23 S. Division.
  55 N. Division.
  87 Eagle.
  129 Clinton.
  181 William.
  277 Broadway.
  318 Cypress.
  355 Sycamore.
Pink, E. fr. 227 Lord to 144 Montgomery.
  37 Smith.
  77 Montgomery.
Pink Alley, E. from 9 Bond to 24 Lord.

STREET DIRECTORY.

Pioneer (Uniontown), E. from Packer to Buffalo creek.

Pittsburgh, S. fr. Parnell to Lehigh (second street west of Abby).
Brunck.
Mystic.
Hancock.
Scranton.
Edmunds.
Lehigh.

Playter, N. fr. Curtiss to 1087 Broadway.
23 Peckham.
87 Lovejoy.
175 Grimes.
247 Broadway.

Pleasant Ave., 4th street east of Avenue A running N. fr. Leroy ave to Rodney. Changed to Marigold, Mar. 20, 1893.

Pleasant Place, 1st street east of Jefferson running north from Florida to E. Delavan av.
Lexington ave.
Rodney.

Plymouth Ave., N.W. fr. 306 Hudson to 116 Breckenridge.
63 Pennsylvania.
131 Jersey.
157 Porter ave.
199 York.
269 Connecticut.
339 Vermont.
409 Rhode Island.
479 Massachusetts.
547 Hampshire.
School.
Albany.
California.
Arkansas.
West Ferry.
Breckenridge.

Pooley Place, E. fr. 357 Dewitt to 468 Grant.

Pomona Place (formerly Olive street, in 5th ward), 3d street south of So. Park ave. (for-

merly White's Cors. rd.) running N. E. fr. Seneca to Buffalo crk.

Poplar Ave., N. fr. 836 Walden ave. to Doat (4th street east of Bailey ave).

Portage (form'ly Bayer) N. from 490 E. Utica to Glenwood ave.

Porter, N. from 84 West Ferry to 17 Bouck av. Changed to Gelston.

Porter, E. fr. 213 Heacock to Griffin street. Changed to Roseville, March 20, 1893.
37 Van Rensselaer.
121 Hydraulic.
160 Griffin.

Porter Ave., E. fr. Lake Erie to The Circle.
23 N. Y.C.R. R. tks.
63 Erie canal.
111 Fourth.
147 Lakeview ave.
183 Front ave.
221 Seventh.
259 Niagara.
295 Prospect ave.
337 Fargo ave.
377 West ave.
425 Plymouth ave.
463 Jersey.
483 Thirteenth.
523 Fourteenth.
532 The Circle.

Portland, 4th street S. fr. 951 Abbott rd. running N. E. to Cazenovia creek.
Cumberland ave.
Cazenovia creek.

Potomac Ave. (formerly Clinton ave.), E. from Erie canal and 1471 Niagara to 1474 Delaware ave.
21 Niagara.
75 West ave.
111 Dewitt.
187 Herkimer.
231 Congress.
251 Grant.

287 Emily.
319 Tryon pl.
351 Hoyt.
385 Baynes.
485 Richmond ave.
Norwood ave.
Ashland ave.
Elmwood ave.
611 Bidwell p'kway.
Brantford pl.
721 Chapin parkw'y
Windsor ave.
851 Delaware ave.

Potter, N. fr. 48 William to 173 Broadway.
34 Gay.
74 Broadway.

Potter's Corners Plank Road, S. E. fr. 1448 Abbott road to city line.

Pratt, N. from 448 Eagle to 379 Genesee.
35 Clinton.
131 William.
269 Broadway.
367 Sycamore.
451 Genesee.

Pratt and Wadham Slip, opp. foot of Michigan.

Prenatt, east fr. Euclid pl. to Buffalo creek.
Smith.
Owahn pl.
Prenatt alley.
117 Lee.
200 Maurice.
232 Orlando.
266 Babcock.
495 Buffalo creek.

Prenatt Alley, fr. 322 Abbott road to Prenatt.

Preston, N. fr. 244 West Ferry to Auburn ave.
22 Arnold.
45 Breckenridge.
Boyd.
Auburn Ave.

Prime, N. W. fr. 24 Main to 13 Commercial.
35 Dayton.
55 Hanover.
83 Lloyd.
107 Commercial

STREET DIRECTORY.

Princeton Place (formerly Weimert), S. W. from 2105 Seneca to Cazenovia creek.

Prospect, N. fr. 236 E. North to 1751 Main. Changed to Masten.

Prospect Ave. (formerly Ninth street), N. W. from 165 W. Huron to 1017 Niagara.
45 Georgia.
113 Carolina.
183 Virginia.
251 Maryland.
321 Hudson.
391 Pennsylvania.
469 Jersey.
531 Porter ave.
601 Connecticut.
669 Vermont.
739 Rhode Island.
817 Massachusetts.
879 Hampshire.
923 School.
949 Niagara.

Prosser Ave, 1st street south of Clinton st. (east of Bailey ave.) running east fr. Snow ave. to Spaulding av.
Roberts ave.
Spaulding ave.

Puerner Ave., E. tr. 27 Avenue A (near Parade House) to Kehr.
E. Parade ave.
Josephine.
Marshall.
Kehr.

Puffer, E. fr. 1727 Main to Bailey ave.
13 Masten.
Chester.
Waverly.
Purdy.
Alexander pl.
155 Jefferson.
Hager.
363 Scajaquada cr'k
Humboldt pk'y.
Rex place.
Rickert.
539 Avenue A.

Winchester ave.
Bitter.
Harrison ave.
Chelsea pl.
Dutton ave.
Sheriden ave.
Grider.
Carl.
Schuele ave.
Wyoming ave.
Cambridge ave.
Cornwall ave.
Northumberland ave.
Norfolk ave.
Leslie.
Herbert ave.
Killhoffer.
Bailey ave.

Pulaski, N. fr. Clinton to Griswold (4th st. east of Weiss).

Purdy, 2d street E. of Michigan running N. fr. Laurel to Puffer.
E. Utica.
39 Glenwood ave.
91 Woodlawn ave.
143 E. Ferry.
Harlow pl.
Elsie pl.
Dexter.
Lyth pl.
Puffer.

Putnam, north from 468 Breckenridge to 371 Bouck ave.
Auburn ave.
Bouck ave.

Quarry, S. fr. E. Hertel ave. to Cement (first street west of Bailey ave.)

Quay, E. fr. 119 Main to 138 Washington.

Queen, E. fr. William to junction of N. Ogden to east city line.

Queens Place, 1st street west of Humboldt parkway running N. fr. Florida to Mohican ave. Changed to Regina pl., Mar. 20, 1893.

Quincy (formerly Miller), S. fr. 1427 Broadway to Amity.
Grand.
Amity.

Race, 1st street north of Hertel ave. running east from Military rd to Cass.
Simon.
Clayton.
Page.
Sunset.
Grove.
Greeley.
Norris.

Railroad (form'ly Mill), east from 421 Hamburgh to 19 Griffin.
111 Red Jacket.
167 Heacock.
Van Rensselaer.
Hydraulic.
Griffin.

Ralph Alley, N. fr. 142 Burton to 713 Virginia.

Ramsdell Ave., 1st st. south of Kensington ave. (near north city line), running west fr. Delaware avenue to Grove.
Eugene.
N. Elmwood ave.
Grove.

Randall, N. fr. 20 Superior to 349 William.

Randle, 1st street east of Scajaquada creek (ne'r eastern city line) running south from Genesee.

Range Ave., 3d street west of Bailey avenue running south fr. E. Hertel avenue to Cement.
Hewett.
Cement.

Rano, E. fr. 653 Tonawanda to Harold ave.
Mayer ave.
Albert ave.

STREET DIRECTORY.

Welland.
Norman ave.
Bleeker ave.
Harold ave.

Rapin Ave., N. fr. 488 Walden ave. to Doat.

Rawlins (formerly Leo) S. fr. Genesee to Doat (2d street west of Bailey ave.)

Raze, N. fr. 916 Eagle to 347 Howard. Changed to Clare, Mar. 20, 1893.
  3 James.
  45 Clinton.
  Fritz alley.
  68 Bristol.
  Dan Domingo al
  105 Oneida.
  Steuben alley.
  Olga place.
  S. Railroad ave.
  165 Howard.

Red Jacket, N. from 514 Elk to 589 Seneca.
  29 Fulton.
  65 Perry.
  99 Scott.
  167 Railroad.
  181 Exchange.
  199 Carroll.
  233 Seneca.

Redmond, 9th street E. of Colvin running N. fr. St. Lawrence ave. to Kenmore ave. (ne'r north city line).

Reed, N. fr. 876 Broadway to 951 Genesee.
  Sycamore.
  Genesee.

Rees, N. fr. 286 W. Forest av. to Scajaquada creek.
  Bradley.
  156 Letchworth.
  Fisher.
  Jessemine.
  Scajaquada cr'k

Regent, E. fr. 995 Bailey ave. to Greene.

Regina Place (formerly Queens pl. 1st street

west of Humboldt parkway running N. from Florida to Mohican ave.

Reimann, 4th street N. of William running east from Greene to city line.
  Longnecker.
  Ideal.
  Benzinger.
  Gold.
  Davey.
  N. Ogden.
  Schiller.
  Goethe.
  City line.

Reservation, N. fr. 536 Amherst to Grote.
  Logan.
  Grote.

Rex Place, 1st street E. of Humboldt parkway running north from Puffer.

Rey, E. fr. 183 Mortimer to 586 Jefferson.

Rhein, 2d street east of Bailey ave. running S. fr. Walden ave. to W. S. R. R. tracks.

Rhine, 1st street east of Moselle, running N. from Genesee to East Ferry.

Rhode Island, E. fr. 795 Front avenue to 394 Richmond ave.
  37 Seventh.
  71 Niagara.
  109 Prospect ave.
  151 Fargo ave.
  187 West ave.
  223 Plymouth ave.
  259 Thirteenth.
  295 Fourteenth.
  331 Fifteenth.
  351 Lowell pl.
  387 Bremen.
  427 West Utica.
  Brayton.
  Eighteenth.
  Nineteenth.
  401 Chenango.

530 Essex.
535 Richmond ave.

Rich, N. fr. 948 Genesee to 679 Best.

Richards Ave., 2d street north of Eley, running north fr. Main to north city line.

Richfield Ave., 1st street south of Tifft running east fr. So. Park ave. (form'ly White's Corners road) to Boulevard.

Richlawn Ave. (formerly Euclid ave.), 3d st. east of Fillmore ave. (formerly Avenue A), running north fr. Leroy ave. to Rodney st.

Richmond Ave., fr. The Circle to 475 West Forest ave.
  56 Jersey.
  89 } Summer.
  90 }
  96 Sixteenth.
  140 York.
  150 Seventeenth.
  222 Connecticut.
  241 Bryant.
  306 Vermont.
  321 W. Utica.
  355 Anderson pl.
  391 Lexington ave.
  394 Rhode Island.
  Highland ave.
  471 W. Ferry.
  472 Massachusetts.
  525 Breckenridge.
  587 Auburn ave.
  Bouck ave.
  649 Bidwell pl.
  W. Delavan ave.
  Potomac ave.
  Bird ave.
  W. Forest ave.

Ricker Ave., 1st street north of Seneca running east from Fillmore ave. Changed to Dillon, Mar. 20, '93.

Rickert, S. fr. Puffer to Scajaquada creek (1st

street east of Humboldt parkway).

Riley, E. fr. 1321 Main to Humboldt p'kway.
  Ellicott.
  Holland pl.
  101 Michigan.
  177 Masten.
  327 Jefferson.
  Willow pl.
  Roehrer.
  Wohlers.
  Humboldt parkway.

Ripley Place, N. W. fr. 516 Connecticut to 420 Vermont (this block was formerly the first block of Eighteenth street and changed to Ripley pl. in 1889).

Ritt Ave., 7th street N. of Hertel ave. running east fr. Military road to Clayton.

River, N. W. fr. 203 Erie to 342 W. Genesee.
  53 Slip No. 1.
  84 Lake.
  117 Slip No. 2.
  147 W. Genesee.

Roberts Ave., 2d street east of Bailey avenue running south from Clinton street to W. N. Y., & P. R. R. tks.

Robie, W. from Main to Parkside avenue (1st street north of Humboldt parkway).
  Crescent ave.
  Woodward ave.
  Parkside ave.

Rochester, 1st street W. of Abby running S. fr. Parnell to Lehigh.
  Brunck.
  Mystic.
  Hancock.
  Scranton.
  Edmunds.
  Lehigh.

Rochevot Alley, N. fr. 29 Burton to Virginia.

Rock, N. W. fr. 343 West Genesee to Slip No. 3.

Rockland, 2d street S. of Kensington avenue running east fr. Bailey ave. to Eggert.
  Suffolk.
  Orleans.
  Ulster.
  Eggert.

Rodney, E. fr. Halbert to Liberty ave. (4th street north of Leroy avenue).
  Fillmore ave.
  Holden.
  Hill.
  Richlawn ave.
  Marigold.
  Pleasant ave.
  Manhattan ave.
  Wemple ave.
  Montclair.
  Federal ave.
  Liberty ave.

Roeder, E. fr. 215 Ave. A to Moselle. Changed to Glenwood ave.

Roehrer, 1st street east of Jefferson running N. fr. Best to E. Ferry.
  Dodge.
  Northampton.
  Kingsley.
  Riley.
  Landon.
  E. Utica.
  Glenwood ave.
  Winslow ave.
  Woodlawn ave.
  E. Ferry.

Roesch Ave., E. fr. Niagara to Skillen (1st street north of Germania Park).
  Palace ave.
  Tonawanda.
  Baxter.
  Kertz.
  Eckhert.
  Ullman.
  Argus.
  Elgas.
  Teutsch.
  Ziegeler.

Newfield.
Skillen.

Roetzer, N. fr. 146 Walden ave. to Genesee.

Rogers, N. fr. Bidwell pl. to 475 W. Forest ave. (now Richmond avenue).

Rohe, 1st street north of Walden ave. running east fr. Bailey ave. to Sumner pl.

Rohr, N. fr. Walden ave. to Genesee, 3d street E. of Parade grounds.

Roland Ave., 1st street north of Tifft, running east from Abby to Hopkins.
  Germania.
  Hopkins.

Rommel, 3d street east of N. Y. C. (Belt Line) R. R. running north from Broadway.

Roos, N. fr. 268 William to 395 Broadway.

Root, E. fr. Erie canal to 382 Fifth.

Rosalia, 2d street east of Pierce Steam Heating Works, running N. fr. N. Y. C. R. R. (Belt Line) at Cross Cut Junction to Hertel ave. (also 2d street east of N. Elmwood ave. running south fr. Hertel ave.)

Rose, N. fr. 938 Virginia to 365 E. North.
  77 Carlton.
  141 High.
  290 E. North.

Roseville (formerly Porter) east fr. 213 Heacock to Griffin.
  57 Van Rensselaer.
  121 Hydraulic.
  160 Griffin.

Ross Ave., E. fr. Tonawanda to Bleecker ave

STREET DIRECTORY.

(4th street north of Ontario).
Condon ave.
Bleeker ave.

Rother Ave., N. fr. 1164 Broadway to Walden avenue.
Stanislaus.
Sycamore.
Walden ave.

Royal Ave. (formerly Newell ave.), east fr. Niagara to Mayer av. (3d street north of Ontario).
Tonawanda.
Mayer ave.

Ruhl Ave., E. fr. Military road to Clayton (4th street north of Hertel ave.)

Ruhland Ave., 3d street east of N. Y. C. R. R. (Belt Line) tks. running south fr. Walden ave. and across Sycamore to an inner lot.

Rumsey (formerly Hagen) 2d street east of Bailey ave. running south from East Delavan ave.

Russell, W. fr. 2500 Main to Parkside ave.
Fairfield.
Greenfield.
Crescent ave.
Summit ave.
Woodward ave.
Parkside ave.

Ruth Ave., 8th street east of Tonawanda, running N. W. from Ontario to Esser ave.

Rutland, 2d street S. fr. 951 Abbott road running N. E. to Cazenovia creek.
Cumberland ave.
Cazenovia creek.

Ryan, N. E. from 2013 Seneca to Frank ave. (2d street south of

Mineral Spring road).

Sage, 2d street south of White's Cors. plank road, running east fr. Seneca st. to Buffalo creek.

Saginaw, E. from Hamburgh and south of Sandusky.

Salem, 7th street south fr. 951 Abbott road running N.E. to Cazenovia creek.
Cumberland ave.
Cazenovia creek.

San Domingo Alley, 3d street north of Clinton running east fr. Emslie to Clare.
Bond.
Lord.
Smith.
Montgomery.
Clare.

Sandusky, E. fr. 237 Louisiana to 18 Smith.
2 Louisiana.
28 Kentucky.
54 Tennessee.
86 Vincennes.
108 Alabama.
134 Vandalia.
170 Hamburgh.
200 Sidway.
230 Katharine.
262 Fitzgerald.
280 Reservation line
455 Smith.

Sanford, N. fr. 180 East Forest ave. to 135 Leroy ave.

Saranac Ave., 1st street east of Colvin running north fr. Hertel ave. to Taunton pl.
Tacoma ave.
Taunton pl.

Saratoga, N. fr. Ontario (first street east of Tonawanda).

Sarvis, 2d street west of Delaware Ave. Cemetery, running N, fr.

Hertel ave. to Olive.

Sawyer Ave., 3d street north of Eley running north from Main to north city line.

Sayre (formerly Logan No. 2, in 25th ward) 2d street north of Hertel ave. running west fr. Military road to N.Y. C. R. R. tracks.

Scheu, N. fr. Clinton to Humboldt street (5th street east of Weiss). Changed to Weaver ave., October, 1891.

Scheu Ave., 9th street south of Abbott road running east fr. Abby to Hopkins.
Germania.
Hopkins.

Schiller, N. fr. 1742 William to 1995 Broadw'y.
Queen.
Ludington.
Lovejoy.
Vanderbilt.
Reimann.
Broadway.

Schmarbeck, N. fr. 1310 Broadway to W. S. R. R. track.

School, N. E. fr. 995 Niagara to 161 Albany.
21 Prospect ave.
53 Fargo ave.
87 West ave.
121 Plymouth ave.
149 Albany.

Schuele Ave., N. fr. East Ferry to East Delavan ave. (2d street E. of Grider).
Puffer.
E. Delavan ave.

Schutrum, N. from 1560 Broadway to W. S. R. R.

Schuyler, E. fr. 11 Hagerman to 2 Fillmore ave. and 888 Seneca.
21 Emslie.

STREET DIRECTORY.

Griffin.
197 Seneca.
Fillmore ave.

Scott, E. fr. 97 Main to
248 Chicago (closed
bet. Chicago and Ala-
bama) and from 369
Alabama to 358 Smith.
19 Washington.
37 Beaver.
49 Burwell pl.
67 Illinois.
93 Mississippi.
129 Columbia.
161 Michigan.
171 W. Market.
Elk st. market.
179 E. Market.
250 Chicago.
457 Alabama.
513 Hamburgh.
563 Red Jacket.
618 Heacock.
681 Van Rensselaer.
746 Hydraulic.
851 Smith.

Scoville Ave., 3d street
east of Babcock, run-
ning north fr. Blank
ave. to Erie R'y tks.
Clinton.
Manitoba.
Erie R'y tracks.

Scranton, 5th street S.
fr. 569 Abbott road
running west fr. Ab-
by to B., R. & P. R. R.
tracks.
Rochester.
Pittsburgh.
B., R. & P. R. R. tks.

Seabrook, 3d street east
of Skillen, running N.
W. fr. Fairmount ave
to O'Neil.
North Park ave.
O'Neil.

Sears, 4th street east of
Fillmore av. running
north fr. Curtiss to
1061 Broadway.
Peckham.
Lovejoy.
Grimes.

Broadway.
See Ave., E. fr. Niagara
to Norman ave.
(4th street north of
Ontario).
Tonawanda.
Norman ave.

Seifert, N. fr. Clinton to
Griswold (8th street
east of Bailey ave.)

Selkirk, N. fr. 871 Elk to
975 Seneca.
Perry.
Clifford.
Minton.
Exchange.
Seneca.

Seneca, E. fr. 223 Main
to east line of city.
9 Webster alley.
21 Washington.
Postoffice.
Custom house.
60 Ellicott.
110 Centre.
121 Wells.
142 Berrick alley.
160 Nichols pl.
175 Michigan.
198 Fitch alley.
248 Seneca pl.
279 Chicago.
375 Louisiana.
386 S. Cedar.
481 Alabama.
500 Spring.
551 Hamburgh.
579 Jefferson.
589 Red Jacket.
645 Heacock.
709 Van Rensselaer.
720 Swan.
738 Emslie.
783 Hydraulic.
823 Griffin.
888 Schuyler.
898 Fillmore ave.
899 Smith.
975 Selkirk.
987 Exchange.
1069 Peabody.
1115 Walter.
1141 Maurice.
1269 Orlando.
1186 Wasson.

1199 Babcock.
1221 Imson.
1260 Troupe.
1296 Milton.
1301 Bradford.
1325 Harrison.
1342 Lester.
1359 Dole.
1506 Bailey ave.
Keppel.
1627 Elk.
1642 Buffalo river.
1660 White's Cors. rd
Changed to S.
Park ave.
Sage.
Pomona pl.
1940 Mineral Spring.
Knorr ave.
Hayden.
2013 Ryan.
Geary.
Weyand.
Mugler.
Kamper.
2105 Princeton pl.
2166 Zittle.
2190 Cazenovia.
2215 Buffam.
2270 Indian Church
road.
Duerstein.
Edson.
2460 City line.

Seneca, West, W. fr. 224
Main to 120 Erie.
14 John.
23 Pearl.
53 Franklin.
80 Terrace.
90 Erie.

Seneca Place. (Changed
fr. Daugherty's alley
north from 248 Seneca
to 59 Myrtle.

Sessions, 2d street S. of
northerly city line
running east fr. Dela-
ware ave.

Seventeenth, N. fr. 150
Richmond ave. to 395
Vermont.
61 Connecticut.
129 Vermont.

Seventh, N. W. from 209 Court to 915 Front av.
- 39 Wilkeson.
- 108 Georgia.
- 176 Carolina.
- 246 Virginia.
- 316 Maryland.
- 385 Hudson.
- 456 Pennsylvania.
- 525 Jersey.
- 596 Porter ave.
- 664 Connecticut.
- 741 Vermont.
- 803 Rhode Island.
- 873 Massachusetts.
- 917 Front ave.

Seward (formerly Victoria, in 5th ward), 2d street south of Clinton running east fr. Barnard to city line.
- Fenton.
- Holly.
- Stanley.
- S. Ogden.
- East city line.

Seymour, E. from 610 Swan to 516 Smith.
- 44 Grosvenor.
- 113 Hagerman.
- 134 Emslie.
- 180 Bond.
- 230 Lord.
- 252 Elizabeth.
- 274 Cornelia.
- 286 Smith.

Sexton Alley, N. fr. 12 Swan to 13 So. Division. Abandoned by Common Council in March, 1893.

Sharon Ave., 4th street east of Colvin, running north fr. Bangor pl. to Kenmore ave. (north city line).

Shawnee Ave. (formerly Lexington ave., in 25th ward), 1st street north of Leroy ave. running east fr. Hill to Liberty ave.
- Richlawn ave.
- Pleasant ave.
- Manhattan ave.

- Montclair ave.
- Livingston ave.
- Liberty ave.

Shepard, 2d street west of Bailey avenue running north from 1604 Broadway to West Shore street.
- Olmstead.
- West Shore street.

Sheridan, 1st street N. of Hertel ave. running west from Main to D., L. & W. R. R. tks. Changed to Custer, March 20, 1893.

Sheridan Ave., 5th st. E. of Avenue A running north fr. East Ferry to East Delavan ave.
- Puffer.
- E. Delavan ave.

Sherman, N. from 188 Howard to 565 Best.
- 57 William.
- 165 Peckham.
- 231 Lovejoy.
- 283 Broadway.
- 425 Sycamore.
- 563 Genesee.
- 629 High.
- 671 E. North.
- 735 Best.

Sherriff Ave., 5th street north of Hertel ave. running east fr. Military road to Clayton.

Sherwood, N. from 250 Hampshire to 135 Arkansas.

Shields Ave., N. W. fr. 554 W. Utica to Massachusetts ave.

Shirley Ave., 1st street north of East Hertel ave. running east fr. Range ave. to Bailey avenue.
- Park Ridge ave.
- Lenox ave.
- Bailey ave.

Short, 3d street east of of N. Y. C. R. R.

tks. running fr. Hertel ave. to Gladstone.

Shumway, N. from 238 Howard to 791 Broadway.
- 57 William.
- 159 Peckham.
- 225 Lovejoy.
- 303 Broadway.

Sibley (formerly Barnard), 2d street east of So. Park ave. (formerly White's Cors. road) running south from Downing street to city line.

Sidney, east from Humboldt p'kway to Ave. A (2d street north of East Ferry).
- Lark.
- East Ferry.

Sidway, 1st street east of Hamburgh running north from Erie R'y to 497 Elk.
- 45 Sandusky.
- 97 Mackinaw.
- 175 Elk.

Simon, 1st street east of Military rd. running north from Race to Layer ave.

Sirett, 1st street south of 711 Abbott rd. running east of Hopkins.

Sixteenth, N. from 96 Richmond ave. to 357 Vermont, then from Massachusetts to 311 Hampshire is called Lawrence pl.
- York.
- 115 Connecticut.
- 183 Vermont.

Sixth, N. W. from 215 Court to 979 Niagara. Changed to Front ave in 1884.

Skillen, 1st street north of Hertel ave., running N. W. fr. Military rd. to 265 O'Neil.

STREET DIRECTORY.

Clarion pl.
Ontario.
Esser ave.
Fairmount ave.
Zinns ave.
Roesch ave.
N. Park ave.
O'Neil.

Slips,
COMMERCIAL, from Commercial street to Buffalo river.
COIT, from River street to Erie basin.
SLIP No. 1, fr. Erie canal to Erie basin.
SLIP No. 2, fr. Erie canal to Erie basin.
SLIP No. 3, fr. Erie canal to Erie basin.
WILKESON, fr. Erie canal to Jackson st.
PECK, HATCH, WADSWORTH and PRATT run fr. Blackwell canal to Buffalo river.
OHIO BASIN, from Ohio basin to Hamburgh canal.

Sloan, E. fr. Erie canal to 156 Church street. Changed to Bingham.

Sloan, E. fr. Black Rock harbor to 1422 Niagara.

Sloan Place, S. fr. 1397 Elk to Buffalo river. Changed to Melvin pl., March 20, 1893.

Smith, N. from Buffalo creek to 817 Broadw'y
18 Sandusky.
137 Abbott road.
187 Prenatt.
241 Elk.
278 Fulton.
313 Perry.
358 Scott.
375 Clifford.
Minton.
431 Exchange.
465 Seneca.
512 Seymour.
530 Cornelia.

567 Elizabeth.
576 S. Division.
Laban alley.
595 N. Division.
633 Eagle.
649 James.
677 Clinton.
695 Fritz alley.
709 Bristol.
715 S. Railroad ave.
725 San Domingo al.
738 Oneida.
769 Pink.
793 Howard.
853 William.
959 Peckham.
1027 Lovejoy.
1111 Broadway.

Snow Ave., 1st street east of Bailey avenue running south from Clinton street across Prosser ave. to W. N. Y. & P. R. R. tks.

Sobieski, N. from 1136 Broadway to Walden avenue.
Stanislaus.
Sycamore.
Walden ave.

Soldier's Place, at junct. of Chapin parkway, Bidwell parkway, Lincoln parkway and Bird avenue.

Sommer, N. fr. Perry to 1325 Seneca. Changed to Harrison, March 20, 1893.

Sophia, S. fr. 208 Fletcher to southerly city line.
81 City line.

South, E. fr. 442 Ohio to 2 Hamburgh.
11 Louisiana.
39 Kentucky.
44 Tennessee.
72 Vincennes.
98 Alabama.
126 Vandalia.
160 Hamburgh.

South, E. fr. Erie canal to 108 Tonawanda.

Changed to Wayne.
Southampton, E. fr. 995 Ellicott to 1154 Jefferson.
Michigan.
Masten.
Jefferson.

South Cedar, N. fr. 386 Seneca to 377 Swan.
Myrtle.
Swan.

South Division, E. fr. 309 Main to 576 Smith.
11 Sexton alley.
21 Washington.
61 Ellicott.
87 Oak.
125 Elm.
161 Michigan.
219 Chestnut.
279 Pine.
345 Cedar.
411 Hickory.
477 Spring.
563 Jefferson.
627 Grosvenor.
713 Emslie.
759 Bond.
806 Lord.
815 Smith.

South Michigan, S. from Buffalo river opp. foot of Michigan to Sea Wall.

South Newfield, 6th st. east of Tonawanda running south from Esser ave. to Clarion place.
Ontario.
Clarion pl.

South Ogden, N. fr. 308 Mineral Spring road to 1721 William.
Buffalo creek.
Seward.
Beer.
Clinton.
Griswold.
Diugens.
Bismarck.
William.

South Park Ave. (formerly White's Corner s

rd.) south fr. junction of Elk and Seneca to city line.
- 120 Cazenovia creek
- 273 Abbott road.
- Mesmer ave.
- Hubbell ave.
- 504 Triangle.
- Columbus pl.
- 606 Tifft.
- Richfield ave.
- Crystal ave.
- Bloomfield ave.
- Springfield ave.
- Whitefield ave.
- 783 Woodside ave.
- Goodliffe.
- Larabee.
- Carter.
- 960 Marilla.
- 1045 Downing.
- 1094 Hurlbert.
- 1146 City line.

South Railroad Ave., N. E. fr. 93 Emslie to 364 Fillmore ave.
- 33 Eagle.
- 43 Bond.
- 57 James.
- 95 Clinton.
- 97 Lord.
- 121 Fritz alley.
- 139 Bristol.
- 141 Smith.
- 165 San Domingo al.
- 185 Oneida.
- 199 Montgomery.
- 237 Clare.
- 289 Howard.
- 291 Fillmore ave.

South Sycamore, E. fr. 461 Sycamore st. to Adams. Changed to Beckwith.

Spaulding, 2d street S. of 711 Abbott rd. running E. fr. Hopkins.

Spaulding Ave., third street east of Bailey ave. running south from Clinton street to W. N. Y & P. R. R. tks.
- Prosser ave.
- W. N. Y. & P. R. R. tracks.

Spencer, south fr. 1095 William to lot 58.

Spencer Ave., 1st street south of East Delavan ave. running east from Herbert ave. to Bailey ave. Changed to Kirkpatrick, Mar. 20, 1893.

Spencer Ave., 2d street east of Scajaquada creek running south fr. Genesee (near east city line). Changed to Cheektowaga, Mar. 20, 1893.

Spiess, N. fr. Genesee to Bardol (3d street E. of Parade grounds.

Spring, N. fr. 500 Seneca to 151 Cherry.
- 17 Myrtle.
- 39 Swan.
- 69 S. Division.
- 99 N. Division.
- 131 Eagle.
- 153 Vary.
- 173 Clinton.
- 205 Bristol.
- 227 Superior.
- 279 William.
- 369 W. Peckham.
- 399 Hollister.
- 427 Broadway.
- 487 Champlin.
- 529 Sycamore.
- 619 Genesee.
- 651 Cherry.

Springfield Ave., 3d st. south of Tifft running east from South Park ave. (form'ly White's Cors. road) to Boulevard.

Spruce, N. W. from 304 Broadway to 31 Cherry street.
- 75 Sycamore.
- 153 Genesee.
- 183 Cherry.

Staats, north from 165 Court to 134 Niagara.

Stanislaus, 1st street N. of Broadway running east fr. Loepere to N. Y. C. (Belt Line) R. R.
- Sweet ave.
- Sobieski.
- Rother ave.
- Koscuiszko.
- Lathrop.
- N. Y. C. (Belt Line).

Stanley, 6th street east of Weiss running S. fr. Clinton to Buffalo creek. Changed to Willet, Mar. 20, 1893.

Stanley Place, 1st street east of Delaware ave. running north from Duncan to Hertel av. Changed to Fairchild pl., March 20, 1893.

Stanton, N. fr. 214 Howard to 763 Broadway.
- 57 William.
- 157 Peckham.
- 223 Lovejoy.
- 293 Broadway.

Starin Ave., 3d street west of Main running north fr. Amherst st. to Hertel ave.
- Beard ave.
- Linden ave.
- Morris ave.
- Depew ave.
- Woodbridge ave.
- Huntington ave.
- Hertel ave.

State, N. E. fr. 37 Water to 84 Canal.
- 19 Fly.
- 48 Canal.

Steele, E. fr. 2095 Main to 766 Avenue A.
- Humboldt parkw'y.
- N. Y. C. R. R. (Belt Line).
- Pauline.
- Avenue A.

Stephen Place, 2d street east of Tonawanda running north from Chadduck avenue to Eckhert.

Sterling Ave., 4th street east of Colvin running north fr. Hertel ave. to Tacoma ave.

Stetson, 2d street north fr. 962 Clinton running north from Metcalfe to Howard.

Steuben Alley, E. from Clare to Fillmore av. (1st street north of Oneida).

Stevens, S. E. from Mechanic to Erie canal.

Steward, 1st street west of Delaware Avenue Cemetery running N. fr. Hertel avenue to Olive.

Stone, E. fr. Bailey ave. to Greene (1st street south of Broadway).
Crocker.
Greene.

Stortz Ave., 4th street E. of Jefferson running north from E. Utica to Winslow ave.
Glenwood ave.
Winslow ave.

Strauss, north from 900 Broadway to 975 Genesee.
153 Sycamore.
319 Genesee.

St. Ann, 4th street east of Jefferson running north from Best to Northampton.

St. Clair, N. E. fr. 524 Ohio and junction of Louisiana to South.
42 Kentucky.
49 Lacy.
96 South.

St. James Place, west fr. Chapin parkway to Elmwood ave. (first street N. of Bouck av.

St. John's Place, W. fr. 54 Wadsworth to Orton pl.

St. Joseph Ave., S. from Walden ave. to West

Shore street (2d street west of Bailey ave.)

St. Lawrence Ave., first street south of Kenmore ave. (northerly city line) running east fr. Fitzgerald to Alden.
Campbell.
Duluth.
Gunnell.
Redmond.
Harvest.
Newport.
Alden.

S.. Louis, N. fr. Best to Northampton (third street east of Jefferson). Changed to St. Michael, March 20, '93.

St. Louis Ave., S. from Walden ave., across Sycamore (4th street east of N. Y. C. (Belt Line) R. R.) Changed to Oberlin, March 20, 1893.

St. Michael (formerly St. Louis), north from Best to Northampton (3d street east of Jefferson).
Dodge.
Northampton.

St. Paul, E. from 1081 Main to 806 Oak.
Ellicott.
Oak.

St. Stephen's Place, S. fr. 195 Abbott road to D. L. & W. R. R.

Suffolk, 1st street east of Bailey ave. running north from Sugar to Kensington av.

Sugar, E. fr. 2331 Bailey ave. to easterly city line.
Suffolk.
Courtland.
Orleans.
Hazlewood ave.
Wilkes ave.

Harriet.
Ulster.
Edison.
Hickman.
387 Eggert.
391 City line.

Summer, W. from 1130 Main to 155 York.
43 Linwood ave.
97 Delaware ave.
165 Oakland pl.
229 Elmwood ave.
273 Ashland ave.
313 Howard ave.
351 Richmond ave.
York.

Summer, East. See E. Summer. Changed to Edna pl., Mar. 20, 1893.

Summit Ave., 2d street west of Main, running N. W. from Oakwood pl., to Crescent ave.
Jewett ave.
Russell.
Amherst.
Crescent ave.

Summit Park Ave., 2d steet north of E. Hertel ave. running east from Main street to Bailey ave. Changed to Minnesota avenue, March 20, 1893.

Summit View Ave., 4th street north of East Delavan avenue running east fr. Grider street to Wyoming ave. Changed to Gratiot ave., Mar. 20, '93.

Sumner Place, 2d street east of Bailey avenue running north from Walden ave. to Doat.
Rohe.
Doat.

Sunset (formerly Alexander street, in 25th ward), third street E. of Military road running north fr. Hertel ave. to Race.

Superior, E. from 227
Spring to 315 Jefferson. (Formerly Hamilton,.
 20 Randall.
 46 Jefferson.

Sussex, E. fr. Grider to
Northumberland av.
(3d street north of E.
Delavan ave.)
 Durnam ave.
 Deerfield ave.
 Humber ave.
 Wyoming ave.
 Cambridge ave.
 Cornwall ave
 Northumberland
 avenue.

Sutton Lane, east from
3219 Main.

Swan, E. from 275 Main
to 720 Seneca.
 12 Sexton alley.
 19 Washington.
 51 Ellicott.
 88 Oak.
 101 Centre.
 124 Elm.
 127 Berrick alley.
 165 Michigan.
 224 Chestnut.
 267 Chicago.
 282 Pine.
 348 Cedar.
 377 S. Cedar.
 414 Hickory.
 481 Spring.
 563 Jefferson.
 610 Seymour.
 682 Hagerman.
 713 Seneca.

Swan, West, W. from
276 Main to 163 Terrace.
 26 Pearl.
 47 Erie.
 64 Franklin.
 79 Terrace.

Sweeney, N. from 974
Genesee to 717 Best.

Sweet Ave., N. fr. 404
Lovejoy to Walden
avenue.
 Grimes.

Kent.
Broadway.
Stanislaus.
Sycamore.
Walden ave.

Swiveller Alley, N. from
708 Virginia to 133
Carlton.

Swinburne, S. from 1451
Broadway and Amity.
 Grand.
 Amity.

Sycamore, E. from 239
Oak to 447 Walden av.
 37 Elm.
 82 Michigan.
 124 Bundy's alley.
 125 Pine.
 152 Ash.
 187 Spruce.
 212 Walnut.
 243 Hickory.
 285 Pratt.
 319 Spring.
 338 Eureka pl.
 343 Tousey.
 373 Mortimer.
 400 Kane.
 424 Camp.
 445 Jefferson.
 461 Beckwith.
 473 Madison.
 501 Monroe.
 533 Adams.
 569 Grey.
 607 Johnson.
 647 Sherman.
 683 Fox.
 715 Herman.
 748 Guilford.
 770 Reed.
 805 Strauss.
 835 Wilson.
 857 Fillmore ave.
 917 Mills.
 937 Bowen.
 960 Loepere.
 982 Sweet ave.
 1008 Sobieski.
 1028 Rother ave.
 1046 Harmonia.
 1049 Kosciuszko.
 1103 Lathrop.

 1123 N. Y. C. (Belt
 Line).
 1147 Becker.
 1148 Howlett.
 1169 Gittere.
 Ruhland ave.
 1189 Oberlin.
 1207 Kuempel ave.
 1228 Miller ave.
 1246 Titus ave.
 1266 Goodyear ave.
 1286 Koons ave.
 1373 Walden ave.

Sylvan Alley, N. fr. 390
Clinton to 231 William.

Tacoma Ave., 1st street
north of Hertel ave.
running east fr. Exeter ave. to Sterling
ave.
 Colvin.
 Saranac ave.
 Bolton ave.
 Norwalk ave.
 Sterling ave.

Tamarack (formerly
Lexington, in Fifth
Ward), 5th street S.
from 951 Abbott road
running N. E. to Cazenovia creek.
 Cumberland ave.
 Cazenovia creek.

Taunton Place, 2d street
north of Hertel ave.
running east fr. Exeter ave. to Sterling
ave.
 Colvin.
 Saranac ave.
 Bolton ave.
 Norwalk ave.
 Sterling ave.

Taylor. Changed to S.
Cedar.

Tecumseh, E. from 193
Louisiana to 67 Hamburgh.
 21 Kentucky.
 46 Tennessee.
 72 Vincennes.
 100 Alabama.
 124 Vandalia.
 162 Hamburgh.

Tennessee, N. from 44 South to 167 Mackinaw.
  65 Tecumseh.
  109 Sandusky.
  161 Mackinaw.
Tenth, N. W. fr. 244 Carolina to 247 Hudson.
  61 Virginia.
  129 Maryland.
  197 Hudson.
Terrace, N. W. from 156 Main to 180 Court.
  8 Commercial.
  35 Pearl.
  63 Franklin.
  82 Evans.
  92 Lock.
  118 W. Seneca.
  128 Erie.
  160 Henry.
  163 W. Swan.
  188 Charles.
  206 Ann.
  216 Mechanic.
  223 Delaware ave.
  240 Church.
  269 W. Eagle.
  293 W. Genesee.
  329 Court.
Teutsch, N. from Zinns ave. to Roesch ave. (second street west of Skillen).
Texas (formerly Johnson ave.), 1st street east of Bailey avenue running north from Kerns ave. to Lang avenue.
The Bank, at junction of Front av. (formerly Sixth) and Massachusetts ave.
The Circle, at junction of Richmond avenue, Porter ave., Pennsylvania, Wadsworth, Fourteenth and North streets.
The Park, W. of Main, bounded by Amherst, Parkside ave., Forest Lawn and State In-

sane Asylum gro'nds.
Theodore, S. fr. Genesee, first street east of Bailey ave.
Third (heel-path of Eric canal),north fr. Pennsylvania to Porter av.
Thirteenth, N. W. from 350 Pennsylvania to 185 Albany.
  59 Porter.
  69 Jersey.
  131 York.
  201 Connecticut.
  263 Vermont.
  331 Rhode Island.
  399 Massachusetts.
  467 Hampshire.
  497 Albany.
Thomas, 3d street north of Clinton running N. from Metlcalfe to 875 William.
  Howard.
  William.
Thompson, N.W. fr. 120 Parish to 121 Farmer.
  37 Amherst.
  105 Hamilton.
  177 Austin.
  243 Farmer.
Thompson, N. W. from Grace to Arthur (1st street west of Tonawanda). Changed to Peoria, March 20, 1893.
Tifft, E. from 784 Hamburgh turnpike to 606 So. Park ave. (formerly White's Cors.rd.)
  594 Abby.
  Germania.
  725 Hopkins.
  Folger.
  Alleghany.
  Ithaca.
  955 So. Park ave.
Tillinghast, 1st street N. of Amherst, running W. from Parkside av. to Colvin street.
Timon, N. fr. Dodge to Northampton (third

street E. of Jefferson).
Tioga, 2d street south of Hertel ave. running east fr. Delaware ave to Fairchild pl.
Titus Ave., N. from 1409 Broadway to 1246 Sycamore.
  West Shore st.
  Sycamore.
Tompkins, E. fr. Michigan to Masten (1st st. N. of Glenwood ave.)
Tonawanda, N. fr. 1649 Niagara to northwest city line.
  44 Dearborn.
  108 Wayne.
  Watts.
  222 Parish.
  233 Amherst.
  300 Hamilton.
  375 Austin.
  442 Farmer.
  505 Hertel ave.
  535 Grace.
  580 Garfield.
  607 Arthur.
  653 Rano.
  Martin ave.
  Hunt ave.
  762 Ontario.
  Briggs ave.
  Royal ave.
  See ave.
  Crowley ave.
  Ross ave.
  Laird ave.
  Chadduck ave.
  Esser ave.
  Roesch ave.
  1126 O'Neil.
  1269 City line.
Tousey, N. fr. 468 Broadway to 343 Sycamore.
  51 Champlin.
  91 Sycamore.
Town Line Road, E. fr. 2736 Delaware ave. to Eley.
Townsend, N. from 714 William to 899 Broadway.
  97 Peckham.

STREET DIRECTORY.

161 **Lovejoy.**
269 Broadway.

Townsend, W. fr. Erie canal to Lake Erie (from towpath opposite Hudson).

Tracy, W. fr. 314 Delaware av. to 277 Carolina.

Tremont Ave., 3d street east of Norfolk ave. running N. fr. Warwick ave. to Bayfield.
Duffield.
Bayfield.

Trestle Alley, N. fr. 1384 William to N.Y. C. R. R. tracks.
Lovejoy.
N.Y.C.R. R. tracks.

Triangle, N.W. from 504 So. Park ave. (formerly White's Cors.rd.) to 799 Abbott road.
Folger.
Trowbridge.
Abbott road.

Trinity (formerly Delaware pl.), W. from 376 Delaware ave. to 327 Virginia.

Trost, 1st street north of N. Y. C. R. R. (belt line) at Cross Cut Junction running E. fr. Carter to Rosalia.

Troupe, N. fr. 1260 Seneca to W. N. Y. & P. R. R.

Trowbridge, E. fr. Hopkins to Triangle (6th street south of 711 Abbott road).

Troy Alley, south from 324 Austin.

Tryon Place, N. fr. 338 Auburn ave. to 313 W. Forest ave.
81 Bouck ave.
151 W. Delavan ave
225 Potomac ave.
258 Annie pl.
291 Bird ave.

357 W. Forest ave.

Tupper, East, E. fr. 707 Main to 718 Michigan.
19 Washington.
53 Ellicott.
99 Oak.
116 Demond pl.
137 Elm.
154 Goodell alley.
167 Michigan.

Tupper, West, W. fr. 716 Main to 317 Virginia.
24 Pearl.
51 Franklin.
91 Delaware ave.
168 Carolina.
239 Virginia.

Twelfth, N. fr. 308 Virginia to 311 Maryland.
43 Keep alley.
59 Maryland.

Tyler, 1st street north of Hertel ave. running west fr. Main to D, L. & W. R. R. tks. (at Internat'nal Junction near N. city line).
Cornell.
Bruce.
D., L. & W.R.R. tks.

Ullman (in 14th ward), N. fr. 1148 Sycamore to Walden avenue. Changed to Howlett, March 20, 1893.

Ullman (in 25th ward), N.W. fr. Esser ave. to O'Neil (5th street east of Tonawanda).
Roesch ave.
O'Neil.

Ulster, 3d street east of Bailey ave. running north from Sugar to Eggert.

Union, N. fr. 250 Eagle to 89 William.
35 Clinton.
77 William.

Union Place, N. from 96 Richmond ave. to 182 York. This was formerly the first block of Sixteenth street.

Changed back to Sixteenth street, March 20, 1893.

Urban, E. fr. 105 Avenue A to 216 Moselle.
Josephine.
Kehr.
Barthel.
Moselle.

Urban Alley, N. fr. 492 High to 479 Best. Changed to Durrenberger place in 1888.

Utica, East, E. fr. 1381 Main to 162 Avenue A.
85 Michigan.
161 Masten.
228 Purdy.
264 Verplanck.
282 Welker.
311 Jefferson.
342 Dupont.
368 Hauf.
Brooklyn ave.
Stortz ave.
Roehrer.
Wohlers.
450 Duckwitz.
490 Portage.
Humboldt pk'y.
Avenue A.

Utica, West, W. fr. 1382 Main to 293 Massachusetts.
49 Linwood ave.
105 Delaware ave.
155 Atlantic.
271 Elmwood ave.
342 Ashland ave.
382 Norwood ave.
423 Richmond ave.
451 Chenango.
Eighteenth.
514 Brayton.
521 Rhode Island.
554 Shields ave.
Fifteenth.
629 Massachusetts.

Utley Alley, N. W. from 144 Wilkeson to 203 Georgia.

Vandalia, N. from 126 South to 247 Mackinaw.

49 Tecumseh.
107 Sandusky.
159 Mackinaw.

Vanderbilt, 3d street N. of William running E. fr. Greene to Schiller.
Longnecker.
Ideal.
Benzinger.
Gold.
Davey.
N. Ogden.
Schiller.

Van Rensselaer, N. fr. 627 Elk to 709 Seneca.
29 Fulton.
73 Perry.
100 Scott.
142 Roseville.
163 Railroad.
193 Exchange.
211 Carroll.
245 Seneca.

Vary, E. fr. 153 Spring to 226 Jefferson.

Vermont, east from 734 Front ave. to 306 Richmond ave.
27 Seventh.
61 Niagara.
99 Prospect ave.
141 Fargo ave.
177 West ave.
213 Plymouth ave.
249 Thirteenth.
285 Fourteenth.
329 Fifteenth.
342 Lowell pl.
357 Sixteenth.
378 Bremen.
395 Seventeenth.
413 Brayton.
429 Eighteenth.
483 Richmond ave.

Vernon, W. from 2600 Main to Fairfield.

Verplanck, N. fr. 264 E. Utica to 221 E. Ferry.
Glenwood ave.
Woodlawn ave.
East Ferry.

Victoria (in 5th ward) 2d street south of Clinton running east from Barnard to east city line. Changed to Seward, March 20, 1893.

Victoria (in 25th ward) third street N. of Leroy ave. running east from Avenue A to Hill (formerly Flint street).
Holden.
Hill.

Villa Ave., 1st street S. of northerly city line running east fr. Delaware ave.

Vincennes, E. from 72 South to 193 Mackinaw.
51 Tecumseh.
109 Sandusky.
161 Mackinaw.

Vine, E. fr. 157 Oak to 474 Michigan.
Elm.
Michigan.

Virginia, N. E. fr. Erie canal to 786 Jefferson.
23 Fourth.
47 Efner.
69 Fifth.
95 Front ave.
129 Seventh.
162 Niagara.
181 Fell alley.
195 Prospect ave.
225 Whitney pl.
251 Tenth.
271 West ave.
293 Garden.
308 Twelfth.
317 W. Tupper.
327 Trinity.
336 Keep alley.
357 Edward.
370 Cottage.
370 Mariner.
392 Elmwood ave.
407 Morgan.
414 De Rutte.
422 Park.
450 Delaware ave.
472 Meech.
492 Franklin.

521 Pearl pl.
522 N. Pearl.
552 Main.
582 Washington.
601 Rochevot alley.
614 Ellicott.
637 Weaver alley.
651 Oak.
665 Goodlin alley.
675 Demond pl.
687 Elm.
708 Swiveller alley.
711 Ralph alley.
725 Michigan.
751 Maple.
779 Mulberry.
805 Locust.
833 Lemon.
859 Orange.
887 Peach.
913 Grape.
938 Rose.
955 Cherry.
970 Beech.
997 Jefferson.

Voorhis, 2d street W. of Main running N. from Amherst st. to Hertel avenue.
Beard ave.
Morris ave.
Depew ave.
Woodbridge ave.
Huntington ave.
Hertel ave.

Wabash, N. fr. 350 Ohio to Mackinaw. Abandoned by the Common Council, Dec. 3d, 1888.

Wadsworth, N. W. from 253 Allen and Day's Park to The Circle.
2 Norris pl.
28 Hudson.
54 St. John's pl.
65 Arlington pl.
100 The Circle.

Wadsworth Place and Wadsworth Park. Changed to Arlington place in 1886.

Wagner Pl., N. from 730

Walden ave. to D., L. & W. R. R.

Wakefield Ave., second street north of Leroy ave. running east fr. 1037 Avenue A to Hill. Holden.
Hill (form'ly Flint).

Walden. Changed to Avenue A and Avenue A changed to Fillmore ave. in 1892.

Walden Ave., E. fr. 1139 Genesee to city line.
15 Bowen.
43 Loepere.
71 Sweet ave.
74 Latour.
91 Sobieski.
96 Kiefer.
113 Rother ave.
128 Rohr.
129 Koscuiszko.
Lathrop.
Harmonia.
146 Roetzer.
Wasmuth ave.
Howlett.
Barthel.
251 Gittere.
Ivy.
Ruhland ave.
Oberlin.
Kuempel ave.
318 Moselle.
Bissell ave.
Goodyear ave.
340 Bissell.
Koons ave.
447 Sycamore.
May.
488 Rapin ave.
Goembel ave.
St. Joseph's ave.
Fay.
562 Burgard ave.
599 Bailey ave.
Brinkmann.
Sumner pl.
700 Keystone.
730 Wagner pl.
Rhein.
806 Wex.
836 Poplar.
911 N. Ogden.

995 City line.

Wall, on Lake Shore fr. opposite foot Main to Hamburgh turnpike.

Wallace Ave., 1st street east of Parkside ave. running north fr. Linden avenue to Hertel ave.
Depew ave.
Woodbridge ave.
Hertel ave.

Walnut, N. fr. 376 Eagle to 317 Genesee.
37 Clinton.
127 William.
241 Broadway.
320 Sycamore.
409 Genesee.

Walter, north from 996 Elk to 1115 Seneca.
Perry.
Seneca.

Walthers, 1st street W. of Bailey av. running south fr. East Ferry. Changed to Wende, March 20, 1893.

Warner Ave. (formerly Winslow ave.), south fr. 1131 Broadway to Newton.

Warren, E. fr. 251 Chicago to Ohio slip. This street closed by Lake Erie boiler and engineering works.

Warwick Ave., 6th st. north of E. Delavan ave. running east fr. Grider to 2336 Bailey ave.
Deerfield ave.
Wyoming ave.
Cambridge ave.
Cornwall ave.
Northumberla'd av
Norfolk ave.
Andover.
Irvington ave.
Tremont ave.
Westchester ave.
Frankfort ave.

Bailey ave.

Washington, N. fr. Buffalo river to 17 High.
6 Ohio.
66 Perry.
118 Scott.
138 Quay.
147 Green.
169 Exchange.
203 Carroll.
237 Seneca.
Postoffice.
Custom house.
259 Dickens alley.
285 Swan.
297 Booth alley.
309 S. Division.
339 N. Division.
371 Eagle.
405 Clinton.
421 Broadway.
436 Lafayette.
478 E. Mohawk.
525 E. Huron.
543 Genesee.
577 E. Chippewa.
Washingt'n mkt
703 Tupper.
777 Goodell.
823 Burton.
851 Virginia.
913 Carlton.
979 High.

Wasmuth Ave., N. fr. Walden ave. to Genesee (5th street east of Parade grounds).

Wasson, N. fr. 1186 Seneca to W. N. Y. & P. R. R. track.

Water, N. W. fr. 22 Commercial to 270 Erie.
11 Maiden lane.
32 Dock.
37 State.
61 Le Couteulx.
69 Evans.
77 Norton.
95 Evans ship canal
118 Joy.
134 Erie.

Watson, N. fr. 670 Eagle to 647 Broadway.
37 Clinton.

119 Howard.
185 William.
285 Peckham.
389 Broadway.

Watts, 1st street north of Scajaquada creek running east fr. Tonawanda to Winans.

Waverly, N. from 204 Glenwood avenue to Puffer.
  47 Woodlawn ave.
  97 E. Ferry.
  Dexter.
  Puffer.

Wayne, east fr. Erie canal to 108 Tonawanda.
  11 Niagara.
  49 Dearborn.
  65 East.
  89 Tonawanda.

Weaver Alley, N. fr. 76 Goodell to 637 Virginia.
  32 Burton.
  71 Virginia.

Weaver Ave., 5th street east of Weiss running north from Clinton to Dingens.
  Griswold.
  Dingens.

Webb, N. W. from 28 Baker to 27 Mechanic.

Weber, 4th street east of Bailey avenue running north from East Delavan ave. to Sugar. Changed to Harriett, March 20, 1893.

Webster, N. W. fr. 428 W. Ferry to 465 Breckenridge. Changed to Maynard, Mar. 20. '93.

Webster Alley, S. fr. 9 Seneca to rear 201 Main.

Wecker (formerly Alexander ave.) 2d street south of E. Delavan ave. running east fr. Herbert to Bailey av.

Weimar, 1st street east of Weiss running S. fr. Griswold to Buffalo creek.
  Clinton.
  Beer.
  Buffalo creek.

Weimert, 3d street S. of Mineral Spring road running S. W. fr. Seneca street to Cazenovia creek. Changed to Princeton pl., Mar. 20, 1893.

Weiss, south fr. 187 Dingens to Buffalo creek (1st st. east of Bailey ave.)
  Humboldt st.
  Clinton.
  Beer.
  Buffalo creek.

Welker, N. fr. 282 East Utica to 247 E. Ferry.
  37 Glenwood ave.
  93 Woodlawn ave.
  141 E. Ferry.

Welland (form'ly Dana ave) 4th street east of Tonawanda running N. W. from Rano to Crowley ave.

Wells, N. from 122 Exchange to 121 Seneca.
  25 Carroll.
  45 Seneca.

Wemple Ave., 2d street east of Euclid avenue running N. from Lexington ave. to Rodney. Changed to Manhattan ave.

Wende (formerly Walthers), 1st street west of Bailey ave. running S. fr. E. Ferry.

Werrick Alley, N. from 154 Goodell to 137 Burton.

Wescott, E. from Troup to Harrison (1st street north of Seneca).

Wesley, first street W.

of Main running N. fr. Beard ave. to Hertel ave.
  Depew ave.
  Woodbridge ave.
  Huntington ave.
  Hertel ave.

West Ave., N.W. fr. 268 Carolina to Albany and N. fr. 106 Albany to Scajaquada creek.
  61 Virginia.
  129 Maryland.
  177 Malta place.
  197 Hudson.
  265 Pennsylvania.
  333 Jersey.
  389 Porter ave.
  389 York.
  467 Connecticut.
  535 Vermont.
  603 Rhode Island.
  671 Massachusetts.
  739 Hampshire.
  783 School.
  823 Albany.
  859 California.
  887 Arkansas.
  909 West Ferry.
  977 Breckenridge.
  1035 Auburn ave.
  1091 Bouck ave.
  1142 Penfield.
  1163 W. Delavan ave.
  1235 Potomac ave.
  1303 Bird ave.
  1371 W. Forest ave.
  1411 Bull.
  1471 Scajaquada crk.

West Bennett, N. from 302 Clinton to 139 William.

Westchester, first street S. of Kensington ave. running E. fr. Chautauqua to Eggert. Changed to Colchester, March 20, 1893.

Westchester Ave., 4th street east of Norfolk ave. running north fr. Warwick avenue to Bayfield.
  Duffield.
  Bayfield.

West Delavan Ave., See Delavan ave., West.

West Ferry. See Ferry, West.

West Forest Ave., See Forest ave., West.

West Genesee. See Genesee, West.

West Huron. See Huron, West.

West Market N. from 120 Elk to Main and Hamburgh canal.
  29 Fulton.
  65 Perry.
  111 Scott.
  131 Hamburg can'l.

West Parade Avenue N. fr. 634 Best to Northampton.

West Peckham (formerly Hinckley) E. fr. 369 Spring to 474 Jefferson.
  37 Mortimer.
  67 Jefferson.

West Shore, 1st street S. of Sycamore running E. from Miller ave. to Bailey ave.
  Titus ave.
  Goodyear ave.
  Koons ave.
  (Closed bet. Koons ave. and May).
  May.
  St. Joseph's ave.
  Fay.
  Bailey ave.

West Summer, N. from 90 Richmond ave. to 155 York. Changed to Summer, March 20, 1893.

West Tupper. See Tupper, West.

West Utica. See Utica West.

Wex Ave., 3d street E. of Bailey ave. running south from 806

Walden ave. to West Shore R. R.

Weyand, N. E. fr. Seneca to Frank avenue. (4th street south of Mineral Spring rd.)

Wheelock, N. from 2040 Clinton to Griswold.

Whitefield Ave., 1st st. north of Woodside ave. running east fr. So. Park ave. (formerly White's Cors. road) to Boulevard.

White's Corners Road, S. fr. junction of Elk and Seneca to City line. Changed to So. Park ave., Mar. 20, '93.

Whitlock, 2d street N. of Hertel ave. running West fr. Page.

Wnitney, 2d street N. of Amherst running W. fr. N. Elmwood ave. (formerly McPherson). Changed to Meldrum, Mar. 20, '93.

Whitney Place, N. W. fr. Junction of 177 W. Chippewa st. and 274 Georgia to 221 Hudson.
  77 Carolina.
  147 Virginia.
  217 Maryland.
  279 Hudson.

Wick, north from 1514 Broadway to W. S. R. R. tracks.

Wilbur, 5th street south of 711 Abbott rd. running E. fr. Hopkins.

Wilkeson, E. fr. Erie canal to 202 W. Mohawk.
  23 Fourth.
  64 Court.
  99 Front ave.
  114 Caldwell alley.
  133 Seventh.
  144 Utley alley.
  145 W. Mohawk.

Wilkes Ave., 3d street east of Bailey avenue running N. fr. E. Delavan ave. to Sugar.

Willard, south fr. Genesee to Doat (1st street west fr. Bailey ave.)

Willet (formerly Stanley), 6th street east of Weiss, running south from Clinton to Buffalo creek.
  Beer.
  Seward.
  Buffalo creek.

William, E. fr. 465 Michigan to City line.
  22 Mark.
  48 Potter.
  82 Milnor.
  89 Union.
  99 Picard alley.
  113 Pine.
  139 W. Bennett.
  147 Bennett.
  Clinton market.
  159 E. Bennett.
  181 Cedar.
  215 Walnut.
  231 Sylvan alley.
  234 Lutheran.
  250 Hickory.
  268 Roos.
  282 Pratt.
  298 Castor alley.
  316 Spring.
  342 Mortimer.
  349 Randall.
  362 Jefferson.
  389 Madison.
  417 Monroe.
  445 Adams.
  481 Watson.
  502 Emslie.
  538 Krettner.
  557 Sherman.
  580 Stanton.
  608 Shumway.
  634 Smith.
  661 Coit.
  687 Detroit.
  714 Townsend.
  740 Wilson.
  761 Fillmore ave.
  772 Curtiss.

841 N.Y.C.R.R. tks.
875 Thomas.
895 Metcalfe.
965 Newell.
1011 Lewis.
1039 Cassy.
1067 Depot.
1095 Spencer.
1123 Hannah.
1151 Henricka.
1161 Babcock.
1363 Erie R'y tracks.
1384 Trestle alley.
1404 Central ave.
1425 Bailey ave.
1650 Greene.
1570 Longnecker.
1588 Ideal.
1618 Benzinger.
1648 Gold.
1678 Davey.
1714 N. Ogden.
1721 S. Ogden.
Queen.
1742 Schiller.
1763 New S. Ogden.
City line.

Williamsville Road, N. fr. 1506 Seneca to N. city line. Changed in 1886 to Bailey ave.

Willow Place, north fr. 30 Kingsley to Riley.

Wilson, N. fr. 740 William to 1021 Genesee.
97 Peckham.
161 Lovejoy.
277 Broadway.
Sycamore.
Genesee.

Winans, south fr. Watts (bet. Tonawanda st. and Scajaquada cr'k).

Winchester Ave., 1st st. east of Avenue A running north from East Ferry street to East Delavan ave.
Puffer.
E. Delavan ave.

Windemere, 2d street S. of Cazenovia running west from Abbott rd.

Windsor, 2d street N. of East Delavan avenue running E. fr. Olympic ave. to Bailey av. Changed to Holborn, March 20, 1893.

Windsor Ave., 1st street west of Delaware av. running north fr. Potomac ave., junction of Chapin Parkway to The Park.
Bird ave.
W. Forest ave.
The Park.

Winona, N. from 1134 Elk to Perry.

Winslow Ave. (in 11th ward) S. from 1131 Broadway to Newton. Changed in 1891 to Warner ave.

Winslow Ave. (in 18th ward) 1st street north of Glenwood avenue running east fr. Dupont to Moselle.
Brooklyn ave.
Stortz ave.
Roehrer.
Wohlers.
Humboldt parkwy.
Fillmore ave.
Kehr.
Moselle.

Winter, N. W. fr. Massachusetts to Hampshire (1st street east of Sixteenth).

Winthrop Place (formerly Lewis place), 4th street east of Delaware ave. running N. fr. Sessions to Kenmore ave.
Villa ave.
Kenmore ave.

Woeppel, 1st street N. of East Utica, running east from Humboldt parkway to 210 Avenue A.

Wohler's, second street east fr. Jefferson running N. from Best to East Ferry.
Dodge.
Northampton.
Kingsley.
Riley.
Landon.
East Utica.
Glenwood ave.
Winslow ave.
Woodlawn ave.
East Ferry.

Woodbridge Ave., third street N. of Amherst running W. fr. Main to Parkside ave.
Beard ave.
Wesley.
Parker ave.
Voorhis.
Starin ave.
Wallace ave.
Parkside ave.

Woodlawn Ave. (formerly Barr street,, east from 1477 Main to Moselle.
Otis place.
Michigan.
Maple.
Mulberry.
Masten.
Chester.
Waverly.
Purdy.
Verplanck.
Welker.
Jefferson.
Dupont.
Roehrer.
Wohlers.
Humboldt parkway.
Avenue A.
Bitter.
Kehr.
Moselle.

Woodside Ave., east fr. 783 So. Park ave. (formerly White's Cors. rd.) to Abbott rd.

Woodward Ave. (formerly Davis ave.), 2d street west fr. Main, running N. W. from

STREET DIRECTORY.

Humboldt parkway to Crescent ave.
  Robie.
  Florence.
  Oakwood pl.
  Jewett ave.
  Russell.
  Amherst.
  Crescent ave.

Worcester Place (formerly Highland place), 3d street east of Fillmore ave. (formerly Avenue A), running north fr. East Forest ave. to Leroy ave.

Wright Ave., N. fr. East Delavan ave. (1st st. west of city line).

Wyoming, 3d street N. of Hertel av. running west fr. Military road to N.Y.C.R.R. tracks. Changed to Arizona, March 20, 1893.

Wyoming Ave., N. from East Ferry to Kensington ave. (3d street east of Grider).
  Puffer.

  E. Delavan ave.
  Litchfield ave.
  Sussex.
  Maple Ridge ave.
  Gratiot ave.
  Pembroke ave.
  Warwick ave.
  Colfax ave.
  Mendola.
  Kensington ave.

Yates, S. fr. 533 Amherst to Scajaquada creek.

York, N.E. fr. 389 West ave to 140 Richmond ave.
  35 Plymouth.
  71 Thirteenth.
  107 Fourteenth.
  141 Ketchum pl.
  142 Fifteenth.
  155 Summer.
  181 Sixteenth.
  200 Seventeenth.
  209 Richmond ave.

Young, S.fr. 1253 Broadway to N.Y.C.R.R. tracks.
  Ashley.
  Grimes.
  N.Y.C.R.R.

Zelmer, S. fr. Genesee, 2d street east of Bailey ave.

Zenner (form'ly Logan in 18th ward), 2d st. west of Bailey ave. running south from East Ferry.

Ziegeler, 7th street east of Tonawanda running N. fr. Roesch av. to O'Neil.

Zimmermann, S. from Genesee to Doat (4th street west of Bailey ave.)

Zinns Ave., E. fr. Elgas to Skillen (1st street north of Esser ave.)

Zittel, east fr. 2166 Seneca to city line.

Zurbucher, N. fr. East Ferry to Puffer (first street west of Jefferson.) Changed to Alexandria place in 1887.

Directory of Lodges in Erie County.

Eagle No. 69, Lewis Block, Swan st., 2d and 4th Friday.

Triangle No. 92, Scheu's Hall, 241 E. Genesee st., 1st and 3d Wednesday.

Custer No. 145, Buehl's Hall, cor. Michigan and William sts., 2d and 4th Wednesday.

Fidelity No. 158, Lewis Block, Swan st., 2d and 4th Monday.

International No. 164, Philipbar's Hall, cor. Niagara and Amherst sts., 2d and 4th Tuesday.

Queen City No. 220, Grant and Ferry sts., 1st and 3d Tuesday.

Arnim No. 225, Odd Fellows' Hall, Lancaster, 2d and 4th Friday.

Millard Fillmore No. 292, Metropolitan Hall, Main st., every Thursday.

Selkirk No. 295, Mystic Star Hall, cor. Broadway and Pratt sts., every Saturday.

Amherst No. 302, 191 Forest ave., every Monday.

Dowdall No. 309, 1593 Broadway, every Saturday.

Buffalo No. 315, cor. Clinton and Watson sts., every Monday.

Lake Erie No. 317, Yox's Hall, 606 William st., every Monday.

Christopher Columbus No. 325, cor. Utica and Jefferson sts., every Friday.

Hydraulic No. 307, Germania Hall, 709 Seneca st., every Thursday.

East Buffalo No. 333, cor. Babcock and Clinton sts., every Friday.

Ragau No. 335, over 256 Main st., every Friday.

North Star No. 337, Tonawanda, every Wednesday.

Bison No. 351, cor. Main and Eagle sts., every Monday.

Uniform Lodge, cor. Broadway and Madison st., every Thursday.

Girard Park Lodge, 198 Seneca st., 1st and 3d Thursday.

UNIFORMED RANKS.

Buffalo Division No. 6, Turn Hall, every Friday.

E. C. Shafer Division No. 26, Fidelity Hall, every Saturday.

Robt. Oemig Division No. 31, Fidelity Hall, every Friday.

Geo. M. Browne Division, Harmonia Hall, every Tuesday.

Eagle Lodge No. 69, K. of P.

Chancellor Commander......................GEO. H. LOPER
Vice Chancellor...............................J. E. TROUT
Prelate......................................JOS. ZACHRINGER
Master of Work................................P. D. STEIN
Keeper of Records and Seals............R. B. DAVENPORT
Master of Exchequer...........................W. S. DAVIS
Master-at-Arms............................MILAN CHISOM
Inner Guard..............................BENJ. WENEGAR
Outer Guard................................FRED SELAND

Name.	Occupation.	Address.
Adams, W. L.		Chicago, Ill
Burgard, W. M.	Gen. Agt. C.& N.W.Ry	46 Exchange st
Bullymore, T. R.	Comercial Traveler	76 W. Genesee st
Bodamar, C. H.		Marinette, Wis
Brigham, Albert	with S. O. Barnum & Son.	28 Elmwood ave
Brigham, J. F.	with S. O. Barnum & Son	47 College st
Braun, Chas	Clerk	238 Dodge st
Baker, D. N.	Shipping Clerk	29 Statts st
Buckley, J. H.	Salesman S. O. Barnum	96 W. Mohawk st
Baumeister, F.		340 High st
Chisom, Milan		801 N. Oak st
Campbell, C. B.		268 Connecticut st
Cunningham, Frank	Confectionery	469 Fourteenth st
Davenport, R. B.	with S. O. Barnum & Son	289 Hudson st
Davis, W. S.		546 Main st
Day, Geo. J.	Commercial Traveler	29 Statts st
Danforth, E. E.		Los Angelos, Cal
Cooup, C. A.		133 Harvard pl
Espy, F. D.		New York, N. Y.
Feldmiller, C. F.	Engineer	414 Bristol st
Gray, W. H.	Foreman N.Y.C. Paint Shop.	904 Bailey ave
Gorgan, Sanford		79 Days pk
Hinson, Chas. W.	Judge Municipal Court.	172 W. Eagle st
Hill, J. P.		Detroit, Mich

Name.	Occupation.	Address.
Haudricourt, Jno.		646 Elm st
Harvey, Wm.		424 Grant st
Kline, C. J.	Clerk	83 Krettner st
Kurtz, G. E.		
Kelley, W. R.	Saloon	9 Main st
Loper, Geo. H.	with S. O. Barnum & Son	199 S. Division st
Lauder, Jno.		1466 Bailey ave
McGoogan, J. S.	Pattern Maker	38 Vandalia st
McElwain, F. J.	Sewing Machine Agt.	557 Oak st
Meech, Jno. H.	Academy of Music	247 Main st
Massmann, F.		372 S. Division st
Mordaunt, Frank		New York, N. Y.
Ortt, Jas. B.		Chicago, Ill
O'Brien, Chas. S.	Prop. Popular Laundry	42 S. Division st
Pinkel, Wm. C.	Fancy Dyer	128 Seneca st
Runcie, S. H.	Trunk Mfg.	206-208 Terrace
Stein, Jno. A.	Real Estate & Law Office	22 N. Pearl st
Sackett, Jno. B.	ex-Erie Co. Treasurer	City and Co. Hall
Stein, P. D.	President Excelsior Brewery	899 Michigan st
Souser, Louis		269 Niagara st
Seland, Fred	Teamster	219 Cedar st
Spang, Adam	Saloon	259 Broadway
Stiker, F. P.	Draughtsman	453 Fourteenth st
South, N. M.	Painter	103 Central ave
Sorg, Emil G.	Clerk	18 Walnut st
Soergel, J. G.	Meat Market	1550 Main st
Trout, J. E.		877 Seneca st
Thompson, S. H.	Carpenter	286 Front ave
Thorn, W. J.		Cheektowaga, N. Y.
Taggert, I. H.	Prop. Tucker's Hotel	76 Niagara st
Ulrich, Chas	Salesman	233 E. North st
White, Jno.	Clerk	15 E. Bennett st
Waterbury, D. N.		Syracuse, N. Y.
Winegar, Ben	Teamster,	185 Cedar st
Wohlfarth, A. F.		New York City
Zachringer, Jos.		40 Shumway st
Zaches, F. L.		145 Broadway

Triangle Lodge No. 92, K. of P.

Chancellor Commander......................EMIL KIEFER
Vice Chancellor.................... ....CHRIST HARTER
Prelate.............................ROBERT HUGENSMILT
Master of Work.........................JOHN HILBURGER
Master of Finance............ }
Keeper of Records and Seals.. } ....JOHN H. DROEGMILLER
Master of Exchequer.........................JNO. B. EWIG
Master-at-Arms.........................JULIUS R. WOLFF

Name.	Occupation.	Address.
Bingel, Conrad	Contractor and Builder	618 Oak st
Barnd, Fred	B. & Geiger Steam Heating	646 Oak st
Backhause, Alfred	Laborer	197 Titus ave
Braun, Chas	Carpenter and Builder	383 Mills st
Bogenshutz, Wm. A.	Painter Foreman	397 Ludington st
Bogenshutz, J. A.	Painter	59 Monroe st
Benz, Andrew	Bartender	87 Pratt st
Droegmiller, J. H.	Driver	4 Ralph Alley
Doerflein, Conrad	Barber 892 Main	60 Locust st
Demerly, Wm. J.		194 Washington st
Ewig, John B.	Shiping Clerk	512 Clinton st
Ernst, John P.	Cooper	228 Adams st
Ebinger, Richard	Saloon	437 Emslie st
Frenz, John	Weighmaster Beals & Brown	287 Fargo ave
Frank, Julius	Shipping Clerk	267 Cedar st
Greenfield, Bernhard		261 W. Lorger St., Chicago, Ill
Glassmann, H. C.	Buffalo Fish Co	200 Masten st
Glassmann, Wm. J.	128 Scott St	110 Southampton st
Grotka, John	Butcher	186 E. Genesee st
Gritmacher, Chas	Carpenter	226 E. Utica st
Hoffman, Val	Oyster Dealer and Saloon	206 E. Genesee st
Hoffman, Peter	Millinery	197 E. Genesee st
Holler, Gust	Huckster	402 E. Genesee st
Herboldt Ph. M.	Bakery	356 Elm st
Hornung, John C.	Barber	250 Hickory st
Hachten, Fred	Meat Market	334 Elm st

Name.	Occupation.	Address.
Hefnagel, John		51 Shepard st
Haug, Fred	Shoemaker	100 Pratt st
Harter, Christ	Bartender	213 E. Genesee st
Haug, Herman		604 Clinton st
Hugenschmidt, Anthony		318 Watson st
Horn, Fred		118 Fox st
Hoffman, Chas	Grocer and Saloon	472 Clinton st
Hoffman, Christ		84 Bennett st
Hilburger, John	Saloon and Restaurant	432 Sycamore st
Joehrling, Herman	Machinist	64 Dirnberger st
Krueger, John		609 Clinton st
Knoll, John W	Physician	482 William st
Kiefer, Emil		240 Peckham st
Landraedel		819 Eagle st
Leison, Chas	Saloon and Restaurant	91 E. Genesee st
Machwirth, A	Mfg Cornice and Roofs	92 Broadway
Niebauer, Ed	With Giese & Co	2105 Seneca st
Ney, Frank	Marble Cutter	339 Herman st
Nickel, Adam	Bartender	15 Main st
Pfender, Christ		91 Genesee st
Randel, Geo. M	Barber & Truss Mfg	Genesee & Michigan
Riemer, Joe	Machinist	25 Cayuga st
Stauch, Ph	Real Estate 418 Main	104 E. Ferry st
Smith, Henry		353 Clinton st
Schumann, Wm	Baker	225 Eaton st
Schlickenrieder, Aug	Malster	302 Spring st
Schnabel, Peter	Brewer	101 Handel Alley
Schmidt, Peter		1510 Jefferson st
Voetch, Wm. Jr	Edgewater Hotel	Grand Island, N. Y.
Vanderlau, Peter		225 Kingsley st
Warnecke, C. F	Saloon	320 E. North st
Wolf, J. R		63 Cherry st
Williams, J. B	Saloon and Restaurant	341 Ellicott st
Zacher, Chas F	Mason	435 Emslie st
Zuegle, Chas	Bakery	299 High st
Zimmerman, Jacob	Butcher	40 Peach st

Custer Lodge No. 145, K. of P.

Chancellor Commander.................CONRAD STAFFEL
Vice Chancellor.......................CHAS. SCHAEFER
Prelate................................RICHARD KAST
Master of Work........................JOS. F. DORFER
Keeper of Records and Seals...............GEO. LAUCHT
Master of Finance.........................PETER BOOS
Master of Exchequer....................JULIUS HERBOLD
Master-at-Arms.............................WM. SUDROW
Inner Guard............................EDWARD LODER
Outer Guard.................................JOHN BOOS

Name.	Occupation.	Address.
Agster, Adolf	Book-keeper	34 W. Parade ave
Asmus, Henry	Musician	66 Bennett st
Atkins, Robt. F	Undertaker	68 E. Eagle st
Boom, Ed. C		526 Oak st
Buehl, Chas. A	Saloon	463 Michigan st
Baumeier, Louis	Cigarmaker	596 Genesee st
Bick, Henry J	Clerk and Musician	415 Cliton st
Best, Aug	Moulder	252 Carlton st
Boos, Peter	Foreman Kellogg & McDugal	389 Hickory st
Boos, John	Laborer	197 Stanton st
Cole, Fred	Sailor	U. S. Ship Michigan
Dorfer, Jos. F	Saloon and Res't	51 E. Genesee st
Doenitz, Fred	Jewelry Case Maker	389 Hickory st
Eagel, Wm	Tailor	21 Cayuga st
Ford, Ed. C	Foreman Engine No. 6	1416 Main st
Feldshoe, Aug	Laborer	84 Detroit st
Fink, Michael	Grocer	Lemon and High
Fisher, Christ	Laborer	439 Jefferson st
George, H. J	Grocer and Saloon	168 Howard st
Gerke, Chas. A	Laborer	212 Adams st
Geiger, John	Laborer	N. Y. C. R. R.
Grimm, Fred	Saloon	376 Chicago st
Gruber, Chas	Contractor	Walden ave
Hillmann, Ed	Photographer	Ellicott, cor. Genesee

HERMAN BAUMGAERTEL,

—— PERFECT ——

SANITARY PLUMBING

Gas and Steam Fitting.

1112 Genesee St., . . BUFFALO, N. Y.

LODGE DIRECTORY.

Name.	Occupation.	Address.
Hammer, Fred		91 Reed st
Handwerk, Carl	Laborer	Lemon st
Hangen, John	Collector, Clinton Brewery	27 Maple st
Herbold, Julius	Wagon and Carriage Builder	142 Broadway
Hertkoen, Wm	Furniture Mfg	402 Oak st
Hillmann, Adolph	Photographer	Genesee st
Hoenack, O. J	Jeweler	53 E. Genesee st
Holzworth, John J		504 Eagle st
Juergens, John	Laborer	1046 Smith st
Kiehl, Chas	Saloon	Goodell and Mulberry
Kriedman, Aug	Sec. Boss, N.Y.C.R.R.	Detroit and William
Krueger, Christ	Laborer	996 Smith st
Kroll, Wm		Erie Co. Almshouse
Koch, Bernhard	Broom Maker	219 Sherman st
Kleinschmidt, Wm	Forman Star Oil Co	23 Madison st
Keoppen, Wm	Laborer	51 Thomas st
Kumph, Wm	Bookbinder	470 Hickory st
Kurtzmann, Chas	Piano Store	854 Michigan st
Kast, Richard	Coppersmith	Exchange st
Loder, Ed	Pedler	121 Myrtle ave
Leible, John	Milk Dealer	116 Strauss st
Lang, Chas	Laborer	127 Lovejoy st
Langenbach, Albert	Clerk	101 Wohler ave
Laucht, Geo	Carpenter	283 Mortimer st
Lauffer, John	Butcher	Elm and N. Division
Losel, Jacob	Bakery	223 Pine st
Manie, Christ	Roofer	376 Chicago st
Meister, Gust	Clerk	515 Oak st
Marshke, Fred	Laborer	76 Jones st
Meyer, David	Cigarmaker	715 Genesee st
Mier, Fred	Musician	298 Mulberry st
Miller, Wm. F	Tailor	402 Elm st
Parker, Ed	Teamster	522 Elm st
Peters, H. G	Musician	80 Tracy st
Rahmsdorf, Emil		Bennett st
Rath, Andrew		624 S. Broadway, St. Louis, Mo.
Regh, Geo	Corset Mfg	59 E. Genesee st
Reeb, Martin	Saloon	686 Michigan st
Ritt, Leo M	Notary Public	207 Porter ave
Schafer, Chas	Saloon	512 Washington st
Schafer, Louis	Milk Dealer	Kenly and Humbold

LODGE DIRECTORY.

Name.	Occupation.	Address.
Sauther, J. B.	Boat Captain	198 Spring st
Schmidt, John	Fishman	24 Wohler ave
Schulteiss, Louis	Musician	297 Ellicott st
Staffel, Conrad Sr.	Cigarmaker	305 Mulberry st
Staffel, Conrad Jr.	Collector	37 Kane st
Staffel, John	Musician	37 Kane st
Strauss, Arnold	Machinist	526 High st
Stallmeister, John	Laborer	94 Peach st
Springfels, Frank	Saloon	523 Washington st
Streifert, John	Butcher	837 Emslie st
Sudrow, Wm	Wagonmaker	159 Monroe st
Sudrow, Ph	Hat Store	387 High st
Sauder, J. B.		128 Spring st
Vogt, Julius	Machinist	16 Wohler ave
Weber, Geo. M	Saloon	124 Clinton st
Wieland, Gottlieb	Restaurant	170-172 Terrace
Woesner, Geo	Coal Dealer	163 Pine st
Woltz, Chas. P	Saloon	1125 Genesee st
Wunderlich, Chas	Laborer	904 Smith st

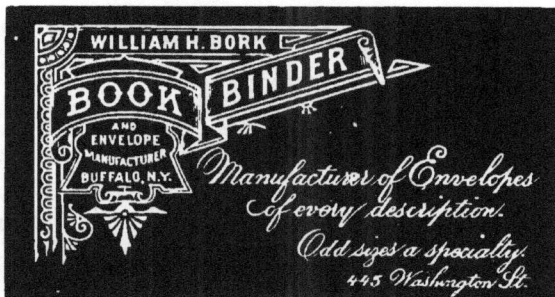

Fidelity Lodge No. 158, K. of P.

Chancellor Commander.....................WM. J. LEIFER
Vice Chancellor.................................JAS. V. LEE
Prelate...W. S. HAMPSHER
Master of Work.................................MOSE COHEN
Keeper of Records and Seals..................L. F. AVERY
Master of Finance............................CHAS. E. RICE
Master of Exchequer............................JOHN NORD
Master-at-Arms..........................JOHN M. McCOIG
Inside Guard.................... ....JAMES TUCKER
Outside Guard.............................M. YALLOWICH

Name.	Occupation.	Address.
Avery, L. F.	Turner	109 Erie st
Belgard, James	Butcher	143 Puerner ave
Bowman, A. W.		346 Davey st
Best, Ph.	Best Bros	141 Erie st
Barmon, A. W		108 Swan st
Bosberg, H	Pawn Broker	190 Main st
Barmon, A.		193 Main st
Cohen, Fred		818 Seventh St., Washington, D. C.
Cohen, Moses	Clerk	16 West Eagle st
Dreschler, J. F.		33 Oriental Terrace, Newark, N. J.
Elfenbein, Jacob	Clerk	392 Walnut st
Elfenbein, J. W.		Myersdale, Pa.
Ellsner, Morris		443 Canard St., Cleveland, Ohio.
Ellsner, A.		61 Oak st
Freedman, Ph.	Commercial Traveler	98 West ave
Fybush, J. C.		108 Orchard St., Elmira, N. Y.
Fybush, A.		338 Seneca st
Gill, Sam R.	Bartender	188 S. Division st
Grotzinsky, J. A.		Eagle and Clinton sts
Hall, Fred A.		164 Ohio st
Howell, M.	World's Dispen'ry Medical Ass'n	187 Whitney pl
Hubbard, W. C.	Clerk	300 W. Genesee st
Hines, H. H.	Patternmaker	304 Fourteenth st

Name.	Occupation.	Address.
Hampsher, W. S.	Manager	12 American Block
Hewenway		993 Washington st
Kerr, A. T.	Liquor Dealer	99 Seneca st
Luetti, R.	Barber	29 Tenth st
Levyn, Samuel S.		Livingston, Manitoba
Lee, James		164 Ohio st
Leifer, Wm. J.	Saloon	43 Chicago st
Meyers, Aaron	Manager L. B. Meyers	185 Main st
Metz, Albert H.	Bookkeeper	5 Oakwood pl
Mumpton, C. C.	Saloon	141 Canal st
McCormick, Neil		47 Main st
McQuelhin,		164 Ohio st
McCoig, Jno.		164 Ohio st
Nord, Jno	Nord Bros., Saloon	164 Ohio st
Palakoff, Chas.	Coal Dealer	334 Clinton st
Patchiss, Chas.	Steward	71 Fulton st
Perlstein, A.	Fish Dealer	17 William st
Roche, Ed. F.		596 Northampton st
Russell, R. J.	Painter	97 Jefferson st
Roberts, Walter	Lake Stewart	164 Ohio st
Reinhart, James	Tailor	321 Niagara st
St. Clair, Frank	Laborer	160 Mackinaw st
Starsky, L		Glen Hazel, Elk Co., Pa.
Swisher, James	Bartender	172 Clinton st
Smith, W. G.	Lawyer	446 Massachusetts st
Sawyer, George C.	Lawyer	319 Main st
Tucker, James		135 Canal st
Treusch, Wm. S.	Clothier	829 Seneca st
Talbot, A. J.		56 Hodge st
Vogeon, Louis	Bartender	141 Canal st
Wilson, Wm.	Builder	873 West ave
Weiskerg, A.		1037 Main st
Weiskerg, M.		13 Wadsworth st
Yellowich, M.	Peddler	Terrace near Henry
Yellowich, J.	Second Hand Store	99 Commercial st

"The Little White House."

F. KRAEBEL, Propr.   161 East Genesee Street.

International Lodge No. 164, K. of P.

Attleberger, H.............Clerk..... ....1343 West ave
Benson, R ....Baggageman.....93 Rhode Island st
Bushover, Amos.........Teamster.........75 Tonawanda st
Blylie, Levi.........Prat & Letchworth.....................
Brunt, Peter.......................................220 East st
Baker, W. E......... Shpiping Clerk............360 Hoyt st
Cook, B. A.............Bookkeeper.......396 Plymouth ave
Champlin, W. T..........Dentist.............1872 Niagara st
Cline, W. F...................................29 Danforth st
Dixon, Chas. B........Park Police.........353 Dearborn st
Duchler, Ph..526 Amherst st
Duchler, Henry ....66 Clay st
Duchler, Geo....................................118 Seventh st
Dorian, J. S........Reporter Int'l Gazette........436 East st
Draper, Jno.......................................141 Hawley st
Eckert, G. H..............................68 Elmwood ave
Fuhrman, Fred...........Molder...........197 Thompson st
Grant, A. R...............................Tonawanda, N. Y.
Guenther, H.............................1829 Niagara st
Grant, Chas.................................1937 Niagara st
Harris, Walter...
Houck, W. C.... ...Pratt & Letchworth...................
Hill, W. C........U. S. Lighthouse Keeper..2124 Niagara st
Knoll, Ed..............Car Repairer..........167 Farmer st
Klein, W. F...........................Niagara Falls, Ont·
Keiser, Wm..................................551 W. Utica st
Lawrence, Richard.......Saloon...........233 Tonawanda st
Molder, Chas.......... Horseshoer......... 12 Tonawanda st
Myers, Jno. J...........Molder..........15 Military Road
Moffat, Millard................................254 Dearborn st
Moonen, Chas............Saloon............238 Amherst st
Moon, Geo.........Boathouse and Saloon....2006 Niagara st
Moodie, J. W.......Pratt & Letchworth...790 Prospect ave
McCall, Eugene.......Boots and Shoes... ...204 Amherst st
Noble, Henry J........Yardmaster............188 Grace st
Noonen, Jno.........Customs Inspector....47 Military Road

LODGE DIRECTORY.

Name.	Occupation.	Address.
Ott, Henry	Pratt & Letchworth	21 Barry pl
Paxton, James	Molder	1927 Niagara st
Phillipbar, F. W	Saloon	1865 Niagara st
Robbins, W. T	Clerk	124 Congress st
Ringer, G. A	Foreman Machwirth Bros	268 West ave
Rosser, W. C		1880 Niagara st
Robberts, J. A	Lawyer, 404 Main St	1195 Main st
Seitz, Wm	Seitz Bros	361 Dearborn st
Stricker, Geo. H	Jeweler	1883 Niagara st
Stark, Christ		379 Dearborn st
Shean, Jno. F	Engineer	599 Grant st
Smith, Thos		120 Reese st
Thompson, J. C	Physician	243 Dearborn st
Terryberry, J. W		148 Hawley st
Wannacott, S		189 Grace st
Weisskers, M		98 East st
Wolf, Jacob		158 Anna pl
Wannacott, J. W		45 S. Division st

Queen City Lodge No. 220, K. of P.

Name.	Occupation.	Address.
Ackerman, A. J.	Architect	5 North st
Allen, C. S.	Real Estate	50 Arkansas st
Allen, A. J.		212 Hampshire st
Brown, W. H.	Contractor and Builder	327 Hampshire st
Brown, I. C.	Physician	411 Fourteenth st
Burch, O. B.	Locksmith	86 California st
Cansdale, E. G.	Saloon	514 Front ave
Cone, D. A.	Cone Co	93 Nineteenth st
Cornwall, G.	Patternmaker	1203 Niagara st
Dunlea, M.	Horse Shoer	530 Rhode Island st
Eckel, L. P. J.	Architect	191 York st
Gasson, G. D.	Tailor	505 W. Utica st
Gibson, D. C.	Baggageman	43 Arkansas st
Gibson, Glen		Fort Plains, N. Y.
Hoyt, R. H.	Hoyt & Loomis	39 Mechanic st
Hughes, G. M.	Carpenter	115 Fifteenth st
Hoffman, W. E.		
Iffer, Chas.	Bookkeeper	3 Niagara st
Jones, R.	Jones & O'Donnell	336 Dodge st
Keener, E.	Co-operative Stove Co.	402 Connecticut st
Kent, J. V.	Kent Bros	317 Tryon Place
Lemunyon, T. D.		31 Niagara st
Logan, I. C.		204 Fourteenth st
Mather, A. A.		147 E. Utica st
McConnell, A. D.	Contractors' Supplies	73 W. Eagle st
O'Connor, C. B.		Cor. Michigan and Virginia sts
Parkhurst, D. L.		503 W. Utica st
Perran, H. T.	Architect	942 Front ave
Peter, W. G.		192 Thirteenth st
Prince, —	Traveling Agent	192 Eighteenth st
Robinson, J.		Suspension Bridge, N. Y.
Ryan, G. W.	Grocer	512 Front ave
Schmolle, W.		12 American Block
Schmolle, A. B.		12 American Block
Smith, C. M.	Printer	154 Chenango st
Smith, Frederick	Architect	446 Massachusetts st
Schmuck, Jos.	Foreman	520 Front ave
Spitzer, Chas.	Saloon	335 Masschusetts st

LODGE DIRECTORY.

Name.	Occupation.	Address.
Stinson, B. F.	Stinson & Peacock	210 York st
Steele, O. C.		Batavia, N. Y.
Staggers, J.	Saloon	Riley, cor. Michigan
Thompson, R. E.	Thompson & Marshall	570 Fargo ave
Thompson, O. F.	Commercial Traveler	Grider st
Tyler, C. E.		Franklin st
Wilson, J. L.		445 Massachusetts st

JACOB WEILBACHER,

—— CHOICE ——

Beef, Mutton, Lamb, Veal, Pork, Ham, Bacon,

Corned Beef, Tongue, Etc.

Poultry and Game in season.   236 BROADWAY.

ADAM SPANG,

SAMPLE ROOM

Choice Wines, Liquors & Cigars

120 N. Division St.   Near Elm.

F. J. DORFER'S

Lunch & Sample Room

Genesee Orchestrion Hall.

51 EAST GENESEE ST., BUFFALO, N. Y

CHARLES OISHEI,

Attorney ₰ Counselor-at-Law

No. 360 Main St., Room 8.

NICKOLAUS DEHOS,

FINE GROCERIES.

Wines, Beer, Liquors

.   .   **and Cigars.**

124 Mulberry St.,   Buffalo, N. Y.

Arnim Lodge No. 225, Lancaster.

Chancellor Commander..................PHILIP GUETLICH
Vice Chancellor.........................LOUIS KELLEY
Prelate ....FRED WARNER
Master of Work.........................W. N. REYNDERS
Keeper of Records and Seal ....JOS. BAUER
Master of Finance......................N. SCHWEIGERT
Master of Exchequer....................PETER LINK
Master-at-Arms ....J. P. SOMMERS
Inner Guard............................A. M. FREY
Outer Guard ....WM. DELZER

Name.	Address.
Abendschein, Ben	Lancaster, N. Y.
Barnard, Frank	"
Bauer, Jos	"
Delzer, Wm	"
Drudge, Jos	Clarence, N. Y.
Eck, Louis	Lancaster, N. Y.
Eby, Peter	"
Ensinger, Erhard	"
Frey, A. M.	"
Guetlich, Ph	"
Grau, John	"
Handel, Fred	"
Johnson, Tracy	East "
Kobel, Michael	"
Kelley, Louis	"
Koch, John	Blossom, N. Y.
Leininger, John	Lancaster, N. Y.
Leininger, John N	"
Link, Peter	"
Link, J. F.	"
Meyers, Geo	"
Milleham, Robt	"
Miller, Geo	"
Mueller, Jos	"

LODGE DIRECTORY.

Name.	Address.
Reynders, W. N.	Lancaster, N. Y.
Reimer, John	"
Reynders, Aug.	No address
Reynders, Rudolph	Lancaster, N. Y.
Schweigert, N.	"
Scheifla, Gottlieb	"
Suttell, Anton	"
Scheifla, Henry	"
Scheifla, Fred	"
Scheifla, Chas.	"
Sandel, Geo.	"
Sturm, Levi	"
Sommers, J. P.	"
Seibert, H.	Alden, N. Y.
Schmeiser, Julius	Buffalo, N. Y.
Tursmann, Coe	Lancaster, N. Y.
Ullmann, Henry	"
Weinmann, Peter	"
Wenz, Julius	"
Warner, Fred	"
Winling, Michael	"
Waag, Fred	Buffalo, N. Y.

Mill'rd Fillmore Lodge No. 292, K. of P.

Chancellor Commander................WESLEY O. PLANTZ
Vice Chancellor..........................E. D. CHESBRO
Prelate....................................JNO. J. RICHARDSON
Master of Work.................. ....LA FAYETTE HILL
Keeper of Records and Seals.................J. C. HILTON
Master of Finance............. ....A. J. DANCE
Master of Exchequer......................L. STETTENBENS
Master-at-Arms..............................GEO. BLAKE
Inner Guard.................................FRANK KRAFT
Outer Guard ....JNO. WAGNER

Name.	Occupation.	Address.
Allen, Wm.		Erie, Pa.
Anken, Frederick	Bartender	796 Jefferson st
Alshaft, Stephen J.	Furier	113 Mulberry st
Adams, James		1759 Genesee st
Adams, Fred. J.		1759 Genesee st
Anderson, James		981 Niagara st
Armstrong, J. B.		987 Broadway
Bulman, John P.	Clerk	209 S. Division st
Browne, Geo. M.	Corporation Counsel	82 Anderson pl
Bristol, H. V.	Book Agent	26 W. Summer st
Bonn, Amos		New York City, care Clipper
Berger, Harry		821 Gratiot St., St. Louis, Mo.
Beck, F. M.	Showman	651 West ave
Burns, John	Painter	71 Efner st
Bisson. John	Tailor	209 S. Division st
Beck, J. M.	Carriage Mfg	41 E. Eagle st
Barnes. Fred		207 Mortimer st
Bliss, F. H.	Photographer	85 Lexington ave
Bryan, F. D.		309 Oxford Ave., Providence, R. I.
Blake, Geo.	Merchant	2317 Niagara st
Becker, J. H.		Elmore, Ohio.
Burns, Wm. F.	Saloon 48 Evans St.	226 Elm st
Bonnah, Victor A.		202 Main st

LODGE DIRECTORY.

Name.	Occupation.	Address.
Birgler, Jos	Bartender	479 Hickory st
Bingeman, C	Grocer and Saloon	High near Michigan
Barmore, Sam		Bellaire, Ohio
Bock, M	Junk Dealer	204 Eagle st
Block, Moritz	Cloak Manufacturer	957 Delaware ave
Brown, Henry	Brown & Friend	57 Seneca st
Cross, Wm		145 N. Division st
Cross, C. A	Actor	Clipper. New York
Creamer, Frank J	Professor	Connerville, Ind
Cook, John A	Blacksmith	50 Logan st
Cable, Wm. J	Upholsterer	254 Genesee st
Carlton, Alexander	Porter	754 Main st
Cowles, B. I	Excursion Boats Owner	67 Main st
Cloherty, Richard	In care of J. Crossdale, Chicago, Ill.	
Crawford, J. A	Brakeman	598 N. Division st
Caldwell, Samuel	Foreman	330 Pine st
Callahan, Michael	Assessor	503 N. Division st
Chesbro, Emory	Carpenter and Builder	114 Ash st
Crowell, D. C	Saloon	1622 Main st
Cashman, H. C	Actor	N. Y. City, care Clipper
Desbecker, Benj	Wholesale Clothier	388 Virginia st
Dill, George A	Saloon and Dance Hall	253 E. Genesee st
Draught, Wm. S	Street-car Conductor	515 Broadway
Davis W. S	Actor	N. Y. City, care Clipper
Dance, Albert J	Machinist	290 Koons ave
Dressel, Victor H	Clerk	17 W. Eagle st
Drew, G. P	Commercial Traveler	111 Ellicott st
Ebling, Henry M	Machinist	441 Thirteenth st
Ehricke, C. H	Cigarmaker	99 Seventh st
Evans, David	Cashier Coal & Iron Exchange	457 Fargo ave
Fix, George W	Barber	Connecticut and 17th st
Fahy, John J	Propertyman	13 Milnor st
Frank, Jos		189 Madison st
Fiscus, Julius	Hostler	155 E. North st
Fredricks, Chas. F	Marine Captain	202 Main st
Frank, George	Ticket Broker	Chicago, Ill.
Frank, J. H		Chicago, Ill.
Frank, A. T		Chicago, Ill.
Greenberg, K	With Warner Bros	414 Franklin st
Glasser, Michael	Contractor	823 Genesee st
Geiger, John	Laborer	778 Michigan st

249 Genesee St.

—THIS HALL TO-LET FOR—

Lodges, Drills, Receptions, Balls, Parties and Entertainments at Reasonable Rates.

None but First-Class Parties
Need Apply.

GEO. A. DILL, Prop.

LODGE DIRECTORY.

Name.	Occupation.	Address.
Grimes, Jos. W		Marysville, Kentucky
Goldstein, Louis		150 Broadway
Gnann, W. F		205 Rhode Island st
Grosser, Max F		53 Mortimer st
Ganger, Theodore	Machinist	141 E. North st
Gillespie, Chas		269 Efner st
Garson, Jos		164 Putnam St., Cleveland, Ohio
Hirsh, S		Niagara Falls, N. Y.
Hargreaves, Jacob	Scene Painter	206 Pine st
Hill, La Fayette	Liquor Peddler	361 Franklin st
Harris, Thos	Silver Plater	442 Dewitt st
Hodge, J. J		Loudsay, Ont
Hohensee, H. F	Machinist	338 Mortimer st
Hilton, C	Agent	100 E. North st
Hardt, H. H. W	Shoemaker	248 Adams st
Hodgson, James	Blacksmith	1283 West ave
Hibbard, H. H		Pen Yan, N. Y.
Heiser, Fred		690 Michigan st
Hof, Herman		531 John St., Cincinnati, Ohio
Hulmes, W		East Saginaw Mich
Hoffman, John		222 Cedar st
Heller, Frank		5 Sycamore st
Howell, John F	Pop Mfg	560 Lexington ave
Howe, Wm. K	Express Messenger	173 Woodlawn ave
Johnson, C. H	Saloon and Restaurant	19 W. Eagle st
Jacob, J. C	Machine Hand	82 Shumway st
Jehle, Fred. J	Poultry Dealer	45 Peach st
Jones, Wm. J	Clerk	62 Morgan st
Kiepe, Wm. J. J		133 Madison st
Krieke, J. G		236 Whitney pl
King, Harry		The Academy, Niagara Falls
Klinger, Frank	Cooper	194 Madison st
Kiener, John Jr	Musician	306 Pratt st
Klein, Jacob	Barber	43 Best st
Korn, Geo		350 Spring st
Koch, Jacob	Saloon	371 Michigan st
Koehler, F. F		
Kobler, Ph. J	Carpet Fitter	344 Pratt st
Kraft, Herman	Musician	328 Pratt st
Kraft, Frank	Machinist	400 William st
Lederer, F. J	Printer	672 Jefferson st

LODGE DIRECTORY.

Name.	Occupation.	Address.
Loersch, Jos.	Wall Paper Dealer	404 Broadway
Locken, Chas	Stage Carpenter	182 Ellicott st
Luck, F. W. Chas	New York City, Care Clipper	
Lang, Christ J		58 E. Genesee st
Leach, Geo.		149 E. Ferry st
Latour, Geo.	Salesman	321 Elm st
Levy, Moses	Live Stock Dealer	137 Eagle st
Lettau, Jos. M.	Saloon	77 Canal st
Moore, Ed. J	New York City, care Clipper	
Manhardt, F. P.	Printer	33 E. Huron st
Munger, F. E.		Law Exchange
Mathews, Chas. B.		309 West ave
Menges, H. J.	Cabinet Maker	453 Madison st
Mueller, Henry	Mason	21 Monroe st
Moore, Den		Atlanta City, N. J
Merkling, John	Musician	64 Mulberry st
Mumm, J.	Contractor and Sewer Builder	168 Best st
Morden, B. L.	Cigarmaker	206 Genesee st
Marklin, James		981 Niagara st
Marsh, James	Bookkeeper	Am. Ex. Bank
Moulton, G. E. R.	309 Oxford St., Providence, R. I.	
Miller, Ph.	New York City, Care Clipper	
McEnery, John		875 Michigan st
McElvein, Walter J.	Painter	22 Maryland st
McDermott, Thos. E.	Shoe Mfg	244 Main st
McPherson, Wm.		44 Church st
McCormick, James	New York City, care Clipper	
McNulty, J. A.	New York City, care Clipper	
McKenna, Wm. A.	Bartender	91 Commercial st
Nagel, Geo. W.	Bartender	Gold Dollar Saloon
Nawn, Thos. J.	New York City, care Clipper	
Nagel, Geo.	Machinist	554 E. North st
Orr, Chas.	ex-U. S. Pension Agent	55 Eagle st
Otto, Chas. W.		249 Monroe st
Owen, Chas.	Saloon	50 W. Seneca st
O'Neal, Ed. P.	Saloon	91 Commercial st
Oppenheimer, A.	Oppenheimer & Co.	25 N. Pearl st
Prenavau, Napoleon	Saloon	191 Main st
Peet, Geo. W.	Foreman	73 Clinton ave
Pfanner, J. P	Agent	99 E. Eagle st
Provost, W. S.		26 Webster st

LODGE DIRECTORY.

Name.	Occupation.	Address.
Plantz, Wesly O.	Agent	127 Southampton st
Price, Melvin		Corfu, N. Y
Pegram, Orlando		Yonkers, N. Y
Quandt, Wm. H.		264 Connecticut st
Rosenau, Sol	Merchant	72 N. Pearl st
Rosenau, E.	Live Stock Dealer	386 Virginia st
Rohn, W. E.		705 Jefferson St., Toledo, Ohio
Rynar, Chas.		143 Main st
Roth, Julius R.	Paint Store	1236 Lovejoy st
Roller, Frank M.		38 Hawley st
Richardson, J. J.	Foreman	1150 West ave
Reeves, A. H.		Jerome and Dumont sts., Brooklyn, N. Y
Robinson, R. G.		724 N. Eighth st., Philadelphia Pa.
Rauch, J. J.	Sewing Machines	443 Sycamore st
Riedie, T. E.		64 Virginia st
Schuele, Jacob	Tobacco and Cigars	253 Sycamore st
Shatzel, Ed. H.	Decorator	50 E. Genesee st
Spadi, C. W.	Agent	412 Genesee st
Snyder, C. W.	Carpenter	268 Bowen st
Stettenbenz, Louis	Collector	561 Oak st
Singleton, C.		81 S. Division st
Stata, P. S.	Patrolman	141 Thompson st
Schuh, Albert L.	Bookkeeper, care Buffalo Scale Co.	
Stata, P. S.	Saloon	1864 Niagara st
Schroeder, Chas	Barber	391 Niagara st
Schlagter, Al. W.	Cigarmaker	96 Exchange st
Smith, Morris	Machinist	42 Perry st
Schuknecht, Chas.	Bartender	253 Genesee st
Sturm, Rudolph	Cabinet Maker	59 Locust st
Strauss, Emanuel		1069 Delaware ave
Sandheim, H.		Bradford, Pa.
Seibert, Simon	Assemblyman	298 Jefferson st
Schoenhut, Chas.	Paperhanger	283 Broadway
Sleap, E. A.	Moving Vans	194 Glenwood ave
Swartz, Jos.		34 Carlton st
Thompkins, Chas. V.	Machinist	341 Ellicott st
Turpell, F. L.	Carpenter	228 Seventh st
Van Dusen, W. J.		Silver Creek, N. Y.
Vogt, Henry	Moulder	87 Guilford st
Witcomb, Chas. H.	Patrolman	No. 1 Police Station
Whitesides, James		152 Erie st

Name.	Occupation.	Address.
Wall, Morris	Pants Mfg	98 Lexington ave
Weil, Sam	Clothing	158 Ohio st
Warner, Leopold		132 Morgan st
Warner, Ludwig	A. Warner & Co	157 Huron st
Warner, J. R.	Warner & Co	993 Main st
Warner, Ed.		991 Main st
Welter, John M	Painter	239 Sycamore st
Welte, David F	Painter	705 Genesee st
Wagner, Chas. H	Painter	114 Ash st
Wallace, Ed		115 Tupper st
Walker, H. H		New York City, care Clipper
Wagner, John	Polisher	237 Sycamore st
White, Wm. F	Saloon and Restaurant	237 Sycamore st
Wells, Jas. A		Fort Thomas, Ky.
Winter, John		82 Pratt st
Willson, G. W		10 Staniford St., Boston, Mass.
Wolsey, C. T	Physician	12 S. Division st
Wood, Jas. D	Engineer	117 W. Eagle st
Williamson, H. T	Clerk	Tremont House
Wesp, Ph	Starchmaker	166 Howard st
Wolf, Louis J		65 Ellicott st
Williams, Robt. M		377 First Ave., Winnepeg, Manitoba
Watson, A	Real Estate	375 Elm st
Zier, John H	Butcher	1 Washington market

ECKEL and ACKERMAN.

ARCHITECTS.

OFFICES,
46 NIAGARA ST.   BUFFALO, N.Y.

Chas. Foltzer,

Sample .

. Room !

470 Broadway,

Buffalo, N. Y.

Selkirk Lodge No. 295, K. of P.

Chancellor Commander................WM. J. SUTHERLAND
Vice Chancellor.............................JAS. CARSON
Prelate....................................G. A. REINHARDT
Master of Work...............................R. W. HALL
Keeper of Records and Seals.............C. CONSCHAFTER
Master of Exchequer.....................J. A. KLAMROTH
Master of Finance ....JAS. BEAMAN
Inner Guard..............................CHAS. BARRON
Outer Guard...............................FRANK BARBER

Name.	Occupation.	Address.
Antonitiz, John	Agent	314 Ellicott st
Anthony, W. F.	Teamster	1094 Fillmore ave
Burgard, Wm	Saloon	20 to 24 Broadway
Barron, Chas	Fireman	164 Ohio st
Barness, J. B.	Firmean	59 Woeple st
Bray, Thomas	Groom	293 Monroe st
Brazee, E. O.	Decorater	163 West ave
Bauer, Anthony	Machine Hand	681 Eagle st
Beaman, James		473 Broadway
Bamburg, J. F.	Barber and Musician	367 Walnut st
Beer, Fred	Broom Sewer	124 Fillmore ave
Burkhardt, Jacob	Barber	363 Jefferson st
Beckhof, Fred		98 Luthern Alley
Becht, B.		150 Peach st
Burghardt, H. G.	Policeman	243 Emslie st
Burton, Daniel	Steward	257 Seneca st
Burns, Chas	Switchman	1205 Broadway
Blackley, Robert	Saloon	419 Michigan st
Braley, Wm	Street-car Conductor	127 Dumont pl
Cox, Geo	Blacksmith	177 W. Tupper st
Carl, A. R.	Store	376 Dewitt st
Charles, J. M.	Boatman	38 Charles st
Cavanaugh, D.	Agent	666 Elm st
Christmon, John	Contractor	58 Strauss st
Cary, Jos. P.	Rivetor	76 Front st

LODGE DIRECTORY.

Name.	Occupation.	Address.
Charles, J. E.	Boatman	Foot of Charles st
Conschafter, Chas.	Cabinetmaker	392 Madison st
Carl, Oswald		Box 683, Pullman, Ill.
Carson, Jas.	Painter	302 Michigan st
Dehn, Wm. E.	Switchman	201 Krettner st
Daws, Chas. K.	Baggageman	87 Farmer st
Dykeman, John		Brantford, Ont.
Durr, Wm.	Machinist	271 Jefferson st
Douglas, Harry	Painter	293 Monroe st
Doyle, Peter	Saloon	1775 Broadway
Erthel, J. P.	Candy Maker	950 Jefferson st
Fletcher, Cameron	Cabinetmaker	1112 Lovejoy st
Fuchs, Michael	Decorator	577 Broadway
Filbrick, C. F.	Advertiser	198 Carroll st
Frank, E. J.	Brakeman	152 Madison st
Finigan, Wm. P.	Sailor	174 Terrace
Fredricks, Henry W.	Saloon	70 Cherry st
Fribolin, Louis	Machinist	607 Jefferson st
Glover. John R.	Tug Captain	Matham's Tug Office
Graham, C. S.	Wagner Palace-car Co	140 Walnut st
Guenther, Chas.	Butcher	191 Oneida st
Guenther, Wm.	Tinsmith	392 Madison st
Hanley, P. G.	Bridge Builder	Lancaster, N. Y.
Hallock, Levi	Bridge Builder	73 Gold st
Hasselbach, Martin	Cheese Mfgr	594 Jefferson st
Hole. Fred	Bartender	707 S. Division st
Hannon, Michael	Heater	164 Ohio st
Herschler, Christian	Machinist	648 Carroll st
Hall, R. W.	Horseshoer	139 Madison st
Henshaw, R. W.		Springville, N. Y.
Herman, Godfried	Car Repairer	289 Fillmore ave
Hass, W. B.		17 Bushnell ave
Hyer, Douglas	Switchman	37 Stone st
Jainer, Wm. H.	Cigarmaker	16 Peach st
Jainer, Wm.	Machinist	212 Pine st
Jones, H. R.	Machinist	259 Madison st
Kenyon, Russell	Saloonkeeper	16 Broadway
Kranz, Chas. C.	Painter	110 Grape st
Koehler, F. W.	Doctor	578 Broadway
Klamroth, J. A.	Proof Reader	230 Chester st
Lempke, Chas.	Iron Worker	616 Fulton st

LODGE DIRECTORY.

Name.	Occupation.	Address.
Lauer, J. H.	Clerk	42 Richard st
Lehr, Henry C.	Plumbing	885 Broadway
Leonard, J. M.	Saloonkeeper	106 Georgia st
Lester, John	Tracklayer	573 Broadway
Lidman, H. E.	Steamship Agent	1086 Broadway
Lee, James	Livery Stable	131 Erie st
Momberger, Geo.	Merchant Tailor	356 William st
Momberger. Christ.	Merchant Tailor	356 William st
Momberger, J. A.	Framemaker	410 Monroe st
Mason. Jas.	Street-car Conductor	191 Jefferson st
Mumpton, B. U.	Saloon	818 S. Division st
Mumpton, J. N.	Grocer, Saloon, Meat Market	106 Georgia st
Mock, Nicholas J.	Assessor	City and County Hall
Metzler, Adam	Machinist	569 Clinton st
Meyers, John Jr.	Clerk	199 Eaton st
Moore, Thos. L.	Brakeman	14 Queen st
Madden, John	N. Y. C. Car Shops	
Marsinke, E. F.	Wagner Palace-car Co	143 Grape st
Morten, Hugh		885 Delavan ave
Meyown, Sam B.		147 Tennessee st
Muenich, Geo.	Painter	246 William st
Mayer, Andrew	Collector	
Murphy, Patrick	Bridge Builder	Lancaster. N. Y.
McLaughlin, Sam	Street-car Conductor	10 Kehr st
McGinn, Jos.	Painter	152 Seneca st
McQuay, Samuel	Hostler	519 Jefferson st
Nord, Alexander	Bartender	164 Ohio st
O'Keefe, J	Yard Conductor	1100 Bailey ave
Oney, Delien	Teamster	235 East st
Panimo, Sal.	Millhand	405 Main st
Piper, Hugo	Moulder	798 Sycamore st
Prier, Geo.		457 Broadway
Patton, Samuel J	Marine Fireman	266 W. Ferry st
Ruiel, Chas.	Cabinetmaker	43 Goembel ave
Rapp, Fred C.	Cutter	380 Madison st
Raber, Emanuel	Saloon	148 Riley st
Rupert, Jos.	Keeper Erie Co. Penitentiary	391 Myrtle ave
Randel, John	Saloon	181 Ellicott st
Rheinbach, Jos.		218 Sherman st
Ruth, F. H.	Saloon and Restaurant	132 Sycamore st
Rose, Herman	Barber	438 Jefferson st

LODGE DIRECTORY.

Name.	Occupation.	Address.
Ruhl, Henry	Cigar Mfgr	702 Genesee st
Schlegel, Job	Cabinetmaker	238 Shumway
Sutton, Albert	Car Inspector	81 Shepard st
Stimal Wm	Blacksmith	53 Mortimer st
Smith, Arthur	Steward	178 Swan st
Stockel, A	Saloon	49-51 Bartol st
Siler, Hubbard D. C.	Wood Machinist	318 Benzinger st
Spang, Conrad	Mill Hand	561 Elm st
Stemler, Albert T.	Janitor High School	
Stoers, J. E.	Carpenter	92 Wood ave
Shelton, T. B.	Real Estate and Insurance	116 Franklin st
Steigerwald, John		
Smith, C. E.	Engineer	164 Alabama st
Selfridge, S. B.		West Humbold Parkway
Sheppy, Chas. L.		1550 Michigan st
Spang, Chas	Saloon	621 Jefferson tt
Stubey, Louis	Bartender	438 Monroe st
Shields, Wm. R.	Blacksmith	25 Pooley pl
Silverson, Morris	Tobacconist	435 William st
Stamford, Michael	Bartender	63 Tousey st
Sutherland, W. J.	Bookbinder	110 Clinton st
Schwartzmeier, Mich	Saloon	Jefferson & Sycamore sts
Tremont, George	Switchman	33 Chilly st
Thrope, Albert	Laborer	494 Jefferson st
Talty, Stephan	Laborer	78 Porter st
Turner, Samuel R.	Electrician	486 Elk st
Webb, Thomas	Engineer	303 Breckenridge st
Wesp, Christian	Pop Mfgr	37 Howard st
Westphal, Oscar E.	Tinsmith	260 Southampton st
Wander, Henry	Yard Conductor	80 Morland st
Wilson, Peter G.	Blacksmith	37 Burgard pl
Young, Wm	Machinist	141 Genesee st

Amherst Lodge No. 302, K. of P.

Chancellor Commander.......................F. E. FERRIS
Vice Chancellor............................E. R. CHILDS
Prelate....................................C. SCHRADER
Master of Finance..........)
Keeper of Records and Seals.. } ....JOHN PALLARD
Master of Exchequer...........................E. ROOP
Master-at-Arms...............................P. BITTNER
Master of Work...........................E. G. HALBLAUB
Inside Guard................................P. PEACOCK
Outside Guard..............................WM. MURRY

Name.	Occupation.	Address.
Bohn, Geo.............		Foot of Mills st
Bittner, P...	Foreman E. L. Co., Black Rock.	1233 West ave
Brady, Frank...........	Moulder...........	977 Grant st
Barber, H. E..........		Carmine pl
Burger, E. L...........	Wetherby, Ontario Co., N. Y.	
Bruss, C. F..........	M. D............	203 Amherst st
Barnette, J. M.........	Carpenter...........	109 French st
Boxall, A. C...........	Engineer..........	26 Twelfth st
Brown, E. M............		Kail st
Brooks James..........	Soapmaker...........	20 Pooley pl
Chamberlin, H.....	Agt. Cresent Transit Co...	18 Roesch ave
Carpenter, A. L......	Carriage Trimmer..	Parish & Niagara
Conden, A.............	Barber...........	180 Austin st
Conger, D. B..	Foreman Richmond & Taylor..	1353 West ave
Cekey, J. R............		1502 Niagara st
Childs, E. R..... ...	Foreman Buffalo Top Co....	19 Gelston st
Charles, J. F..........		128 Walden ave
Darker, Peter...........	Mason...	cor. Grote and Peter sts
Dill, John.............	Carpenter.........	70 Delavan ave
Doyle, J. M........	works N. Y. C. R. R.....	241 Amherst st
Donavan, Thos...........		
Fitzgerald, Jos........	Carpenter...........	71 Pooley st
Fite, Thos...........	Carpenter.........	1601 Niagara st

LODGE DIRECTORY.

Name.	Occupation.	Address.
Frisbee, B. J.	Traveling Agt	Bailey ave
Gahan, W. J.	Lumber Inspector	24 Glor st
Gavin, Thos.	Engineer	158 Delavan ave
Gleason, D. A.	Engineer	1420 Elk st
Henning, Theodore	Saloon	268 Amherst st
Hummel, Henry	Barkeeper	230 Tonawanda st
Holder, Wm	Laborer	26 Pooley pl
Jenner, Theodore	Milk Dealer	154 Hertel ave
Jagoe, W. H.	Yardmaster	152 Potomac ave
Jackson, C. H.	Musician	213 East st
Kirby, W. H.	Yardmaster	243 Gorton st
Kusterer, Louis F.	Meat Market	233 Amherst st
Kappel, Frank	Brakeman	42 Young ave
Leibe, Geo	Night Watchman	97 Kail st
Lindsey, A.		1423 Niagara st
Lobdell, W. A.	L., Gibbs & Gunnel	237 Thirteenth st
Linburg, J. F.	Saloon	176 Austin st
McIntosh, J. L.	Plumber	240 Triangle st
McKenzie, Wm	Machinist	1101 Niagara st
McGregor, M.		
Messler, Wm	Printer 218 Main	452 Tonawanda st
Mahoney, Thos	Weighman	80 Michigan st
Mercer, Wm	Machinist	81 East st
Mennen, Chas		238 Amherst st
Mann, Wm	James Mann & Sons	1028 Grant st
Mousel, J.		1565 Niagara st
Moran, J.	Buffalo Gen. Electric Light Co.	1283 West ave
Murry, Wm	Fireman	45 Dart st
Oberacker, Wm	Barber	97 Kail st
Polland, Jno	Milk Dealer	417 Dewitt st
Peacock, Peter		417 Dewitt st
Roop, E. M.	Paper and Jewelry Box Mfg	44 Kail st
Ressinger, Geo. F.		235 Amherst st
Scherer, Wm		28 Kail st
Scherer, Geo		cor. Eagle and Pine sts
Straker, Jno	Wagon Maker	247 Amherst st
Schrader, Chas	Foreman Car Inspector	247 Amherst st
Simon, Chas	Grocer and Saloon	cor. Kail & Austin sts
Smith, Ed	Saloon	1591 Niagara st
Salesky, G.	Buffalo School Furniture Co.	41 Hawley st
Straker, James	Car Repairer	Michigan st

LODGE DIRECTORY.

Name.	Occupation.	Address.
Theillen, Jac	Saloon 1530 Niagara	113 W. Forest ave
Willox, Geo	Barber 122 Amherst St	77 Kail st
Yakom, E. O.		19 Ferguson st

Dowdall Lodge No. 309, K. of P.

Name.	Occupation.	Address.
Atford, Hiram J		136 Scoville Ave., Cleveland, Ohio
Annis, Wm. J		170 S. Division st
Brinnen, J. W	Saloon and Restaurant	1236 Bailey ave
Beason, J. W		709 Clinton st
Bacher, Jno.	Saloon and Restaurant	523 Broadway
Bacher, Fred		523 Broadway
Behling, H	Jeweler	1108 Lovejoy st
Brubeacher, W. H		King and Gold sts
Baker, J. Y		89 Goethe st
Bauer, Jos	Armstrong & Bauer	604 Virginia st
Boland, J. C		1430 Broadway
Barnhardt, J		44 Young ave
Bachman, C		23 Landon st
Britt, Jas		392 Florida St., Milwauke, Wis.
Curtes, R. B. P.	Tinsmith	1 King st
Clark, Alonzo		141 Central ave
Cable, Ed	Switchman	44 Young ave
Cimmerer, L. J.	Saloon and Restaurant	1593 Broadway
Crane, T. C	R. R. Conductor	18 Gatchel st
Conway, Con	Switchman	70 Gatchel st
Campbell, C. H		552 Perry st
Coy, W. W		
vid	Air Brake Inspector	1100 Bailey ave
Danser, E. G	M. D	392 Walden ave
Dale, Jos	Carpenter	82 Central ave
DeForest, F. C	Operator	258 Seneca st
Decker, J. H	Glasser	189 Doll ave
Darmody, James		1100 Bailey ave
DeForest, J. W	City Engineers' Office	228 Seventh st
Drake, W. W		Gold and King sts
Florence, J. S	Carpenter	108 Doll st
Grow, J. C	Car Inspector	513 Jefferson st
Gurtner, H. D	Laborer	33 Stanton st
Glass, David	Car Repairer	18 Krettner st
Girvin, Chas		7 King st
Goffrey, Michael		205 S. Division st
Grant, Peter	Carpenter	359 Fulton st
Green, F. C		

LODGE DIRECTORY.

Name.	Occupation.	Address.
Gisel, August	Sewer Contractor	15 Southampton st
Hornbeck, Oliver	works N. Y. C. Car Shop	8 Central ave
Hutchinson, Jos	Switchman	554 N. Ogden st
Harvy, Jas		426 Florida St., Milwaukee, Wis.
Harrington, Jno. W	Yard Conductor	287 S. Railroad st
Hoffman, Aug		380 N. Central ave
Howe, Wm. M	Coach Builder	1238 Jefferson st
Hooley, Patrick	Street Car Conductor	474 Jefferson st
Heusinger, R	Shoemaker	916 Virginia st
Heller, Henry	Saloon	959 Broadway
Hartman, J		418 Jefferson st
Judd, Wm. J	Foreman N. Y. C. Car Shop	968 Lovejoy st
Jordan, O. J	Physician	Walden ave
Juergens, J. W		490 Dodge st
Knoll, Chas. S		143 Central ave
Koester, Fred	Carpenter	407 Central ave
Klocke, Chas	Grocer and Saloon	1165 Lovejoy st
Koch, V	Laborer	461 Broadway
Logan, T. F	Yardmaster	626 Exchange st
Lynch, Jno	Switchman	1374 Bailey ave
Lacy, Frank	R. R. Conductor	62 Wick st
Lambert, J. H	Switchman	933 Clinton st
Luke, W	Teamster	1633 Bailey ave
Lyth, Jno. A		394 Central ave
McGuire, Daniel		Sloan P. O., Cheektowaga, N. Y.
McDonald, Jno	N.Y.C. Car Shop	King & Garfield sts
Merkerel Frank	Painter	Broadway
Mertz, W. A	Carver	122 Leo ave
Murphy, Frank	Painter	177 Dodge st
Nagle, J. F		347 Spring st
Nagle, E. A		347 Spring st
O'Grady, Daniel	Grocer and Saloon	1644 Broadway
Owens, Jno. J	Saloon	1198 Bailey ave
Oswald, Chas	Laborer	356 Benzinger st
Peevers, B. A	Dry Goods and Millinery	1146 Lovejoy st
Pedlowe, E. S	Co. F., 13th Infantry, Forth Leavenwoth, Kas.
Pfohl, P		Cheektowaga, N. Y.
Quinn, Chas		
Ross, W. D		201 S. Division st
Rathburn, Chas	Switchman	1399 Broadway
Rachmyer, Jerry		7 King st

LODGE DIRECTORY.

Name.	Occupation.	Address.
Rachmyer, W. W.		7 King st
Rockey, Geo.	Street Car Conductor.	212 Sycamore st
Shafer, J. C.		1430 Broadway
Schmidt, Geo	Cigarmaker	840 Jefferson st
Sheehan, J. H.	Saloon	12 Broadway
Stanley, Wm. T.		848 Fillmore ave
Taylor, E. E.	Painter	76 Ludington st
Thorne, E. H.	Physician	692 Genesee st
Thorne, J. J.	Paper Hanger	660 Eagle st
Wheeler, J. C.	Physician	1137 Bailey ave
White, Harry		409 Swan st
Wilcox, R.		Suspension Bridge, N. Y.
Willis, W. R.	Night Caller	1308 Bailey ave
Yates, J. S.		Bensinger and Reiman sts
Zinc, Herman		34 Empire st
Zimmermann,		87 Orange st

Buffalo Lodge No. 351, K. of P.

Name.	Occupation.	Address.
Bittner, Earnest	Fireman	33 Troup st
Beeson, Fred W		790 Clinton st
Batt, David	Blacksmith	203 Hamburg st
Buse, John	Carpenter	97 Watson st
Braeder, Chas	Moulder	11 Oneida st
Brennen, Martin	Barber	248 Adams st
Bittner, Geo	Teamster	1197 Perry st
Bartholomew, Wm	Supt. Buffalo Barrel Co	261 Babcock st
Brown, Nicholas		23 Watson st
Bovee, Chas	Lineman	236 Cedar st
Bauer, Henry	Cigar Mfy	49 Milnor st
Biddeman, Jos	Confectioner and Tobacco	231 Oneida st
Buchenroth, John	Teamster	1016 Clinton st
Camin, Louis		261 Hickory st
Casey, Patrick	Laborer	23 Watson st
Crockson, Levi	Bolt Maker	271 Lewis st
Churchill, H. W	Supply Clerk L.S.&M.S	335 Howard st
Conschafter, Louis	Undertaker	483 William st
Durr, Abraham	Engineer	276 Jefferson st
Dingeldey, Peter	Photographer	732 Jefferson st
Dettling, Paul		Clinton and Watson sts
Day, Geo. E		749 Broadway
Forbes, Geo	Foreman LS&MS Paint Shop	137 Shumway st
Fisher, Frank C	Saloon and Grocer	604 Clinton st
Fisher, John	Fireman City and Co. Hall	616 Fulton st
Fenstermacher, W	Driver Fire Dept	607 Clinton st
Gramlich, Fredrich	Upholsterer	594 Clinton st
Gladstone, P	Clerk	14 William st
Grebner, Henry	Patrolman	78 Krettner st
Georges, Jos	Undertaker	682 Broadway
Graesser, Herman	Carpenter	138 James st
Graeber, Chas	Advertising Agent	208 Monroe st
Hughes, James		1053 Elk st
Hager, Anthony	Heater	159 Cedar st
Hauptman, Geo	Moulder	224 Peckham st
Hanna, Elmer E		19 Gorham st
Hoerner, Andrew	Moulder	308 Watson st
Hoepfluger, Theo	Saloon	116 Peckham st

LODGE DIRECTORY.

Name.	Occupation.	Address.
Hauptman, Michael	Laborer	224 Peckham st
Habitzreiter, Frank	Moulder	342 Guilford st
Hunt, Wm		138 Northampton st
Hulbert, Frank	Broom Maker	190 Hickory st
Haffa, Geo. J		609 Clinton st
Jackson, John	Turner	290 Oak st
Johel, Oswald Sr	Saloon and Restaurant	Ellicott and Huron
Johel, Oswald Jr	Machinist	79 Watson st
Kuttendreier, Max	Machinist	205 Fox st
Keller, William	Moulder	354 Spring st
Keppert, Ph	Blacksmith	616 Fulton st
Kuhn, Henry	Carpenter	92 Monroe st
Lavagea, Michael	Ship carpenter	248 Orlando st
Lannsdell, Fred	Agt. Milson Fertilizer	89 Jones st
Leonard, Wm	Marine Engineer	99 Adams st
Lieppert, Michael	Laborer	817 Eagle st
Lang, John		93 Maurice st
Laux, Chas	Bolt Maker	259 Adams st
Lanspach, Aug		385 Pratt st
Leininger, Geo		79 Lemon st
Lamond, Alex	Cooper	232 Madison st
Lewis, Geo. W. Jr	Physician	311 Delaware ave
Loyall, R. L		115 Lord st
Luippold, Christ C	Planing Mill	261 Jefferson st
Lucas, Ed		866 Eagle st
Long, Robt. C		309 Elm st
Mutter, Wm	Clerk	668 Clinton st
Matot, Jos	Carpenter Foreman	567 E. Utica st
Marshall, Albert	Switchman	82 Bogardus st
Mohring, John	Insurance	37 Howard st
Mallnow, Chas	Gents' Furnisher	673 Clinton st
Miller, Jos	Cigar Mfgr	308 Riley st
Moldenhauer, Leo	Cigarmaker	123 Spruce st
McIntyre, Robt	Yardmaster N. Y. C. R. R	90 Howard st
McIntire, W. H	Carpenter	38 Gilbert ave
Neimeier, Anthony	Tailor	501 Clinton st
Newman, Herman		18 Montgomery st
Neunder, Wm	Plumber	68 Locust st
Peterson, John	works Kellogg & McDougal	117 Babcock st
Peters, Theo	Boilermaker	626 Eagle st
Pine, Frank	Laborer	594 Clinton st

Central Star

Laundry

502-520 Broadway.

Gentlemen's Fine Work a Specialty

OFFICES

33 East Eagle Street.

2 East Swan Street.

TELEPHONE 1036-1.

Name.	Occupation.	Address.
Paine, O. R.	Machinist	266 Walnut
Pagels, John	Engineer	21 Monroe st
Peters, F. C.	Teamster	626 Eagle st
Ripple, Fred	Paperhanger	690 Clinton st
Redle, Herman	Brewer	272 Jefferson st
Rowell, F. B.	Clerk	571 Howard st
Rathman, Henry	Plumber	278 Carlton st
Skane, Jas.		23 Watson st
Smith, Wm.	Book Binder	641 Fulton st
Switzer, Alex	Moulder	46 Bristol st
Schwan, Wm.	Cooper	
Schworm, Louis		35 Howard st
Speich, Ignatz	Saloon	29 Howard st
Sperry, Ferdinand	Moulder	13 E. Peckham st
Sperry, Edward	Plumber	623 Clinton st
Schaebkan, Theo.		883 Clinton st
Schott, Chas.		
Scurry, Jos.		503 Sherman st
Sendker, Alfred	Shoe Mfgr	309 Michigan st
Turo, Aug.		1047 Elk st
Tromans, Geo.	Machinist	210 Sycamore st
Theobald, Fred Jr	Clerk	150 Emslie st
Tenjost, Wm.	Clerk	564 William st
Villiaume, Jules	Superintentent	91 Watson st
Wild, Robt	Machine Hand	99 Watson st
Wurtz, Ph.	Clerk	564 William st
Wyman, Rolin		675 Clinton st
Williams, Samuel D.	Upholsterer	16 Marshal st
Williams, Robt.	Engineer	89 Watson st

Lake Erie Lodge No. 317, K. of P.

Name.	Occupation.	Address.
Anderson, Geo.	Street-car Conductor	—— Seneca st
Ahlgrim, Frederick	Laborer	586 Adams st
Arnheim, Frank		32 Stanton st
Ballou, Fred J.	Woodworker	205 Sherman st
Bachman, Henry		1058 Smith st
Bussmer, Theobald	Cooper	117 Sherman st
Bensch, Emil	Car Inspector	73 Howard st
Beuther, Gustav		94 Adams st
Becker, Henry	Saloon	631 Howard st
Doersam, Henry	Tailor	304 Madison st
Dimming, Fred	Machinist	594 Mills st
Duke, Gustav	Machine Hand	33 Spruce st
Dittmer, Frederick	Tinsmith	405 Jefferson st
Diemer, John	Painter	246 Fox st
Dick, Geo.		226 Fox st
Evert, Frederick	Brickmaker	348 Bristol st
Ebling, Carl	Boilermaker	88 Stanton st
Fleischauer, Fred	Tailor	978 Jefferson st
Fleischauer, Fred	Moulder	380 Sherman st
Goerss, Henry	Machine Hand	35 Davis st
Goerss, Carl		—— Stanton st
Grupp, Geo.	Machinist	157 Monroe st
Gross, Ph	Moulder	248 Madison st
Goldfoot, Elmer	Linseed Oil Works	356 William st
Glaser, Martin	Machinist	197 Walnut st
Hausen, Wm	Fireman B. F. D.	418 Bristol st
Heider, John	Saloon	163 Washington st
Hoffmann, Fred	Teamster	30 Keppel st
Hartmetz, Fred		554 Washington st
Holz, Carl		194 Riley st
Haslow, Carl	Laborer	180 Stanton st
Haensch, Paul		1730 Clinton st
Holdermiller, Wm	Butcher	116 Thomas st
Haidle, Fred C.	Sidewalk Contractor	124 Peckham st
Hauser, Jos		42 Casey st
Haese, Wm	Saloon	481 Howard st
Horst, Henry	Blacksmith	103 Coit st
Hanzel, Louis		427 Bristol st

LODGE DIRECTORY.

Name.	Occupation.	Address.
Himmer, John	Laborer	212 Fox st
Hackmer, John	Machinist	55 Thomas st
Joerus, Henry C	Butcher	202 Howard st
Jonas, Henry	Laborer	119 Shumway st
Joerg, John	Laborer	511 William st
Koehn, Fred	Teamster	41 Peach st
Krinich, Fred		— Fillmore ave
Keil, Frank	Saloon	1044 Genesee st
Kick, Henry	Butcher	14 Spencer st
Kuffahl, Fred	Bricklayer	52 Grey st
Koehn, Wm	Saloon	253 Sherman st
Koppermann, Ernst	Machinist	Hopkins & Ullmer ave
Koch, Gustav	Machinist	81 Shumway st
Lesswing, Fred	Moulder	113 Metcalfe st
Lesswing, Jacob	Machinist	288 Emslie st
Lagemann, Carl	Tailor	335 Monroe st
Lorenz, Adolph	Carpet Weaver	21 William st
Loesch, Ed. C	Cigar Mfgr	205 Krettner st
Langes, William	Butcher	79 Stanton st
Met, Bernhard		146 Walden ave
Miller, Jos		42 Schmarbeck st
Menz, John		24 Raze st
Miller, Martin		1074 Smith st
Meinzer, Conrad		57 Lovejoy st
Moyer, Francis		953 Seneca st
Meissner, Henry	Car Repairer	37 Sherman st
Meinzer, Ph	Blacksmith	85 Stanton st
Mittermeyer, Fred	Saloon	473 Jefferson st
Nagel, Gottlieb	Moulder	510 Carlton st
Nagel, Carl		405 Hickory st
Nagel, Wm	Supt. for Kellogg & McDougal	247 E. Utica st
Nagel, Gottlieb	Laborer	424 Pratt st
Oldenburg, Wm	Engineer	28 Thomas st
Pellion, Wm		883 Clinton st
Polland, Henry	Laborer	245 Madison st
Reinhardt, Emil S	Moulder	30 Sherman st
Rick, Wm	Moulder	283 Howard st
Rick, Chas	Laborer	125 Shumway st
Roesch, Chas	Laborer	129 Peckham st
Schlinz, Wm. F	Machinist	61 St. Josephs ave
Sehrer, Peter	Butcher	124 Hold st

Name.	Occupation.	Address.
Schlee, Earnst H...	Boxmaker.	77 Shumway st
Sommer, Edward	Butcher	177 Lewis st
Schafer, Frederick	Butcher	244 Madison st
Schepening, Conrad		129 Stanton st
Schrader, Ferdinand	Brass Finisher	36 Fox st
Schutrum, Carl	Grocery and Saloon	Sherman and Fox st
Sahr, Emil	Carpenter	89 Lovejoy st
Schurr, John		313 Adams st
Stark, Eugene C	Physician	220 E. Eagle st
Schrader, Henry	Blacksmith	435 N. Ogden st
Schneider, Christian	Butcher	481 Howard st
Schartel, Michael		555 Adams st
Simon, Frank		643 Sherman st
Theisz, Henry	Patrol Driver	641 William st
Weber, Frederick	Cooper	36 Sherman st
Wahlenmayer, Frederick	Jeweler	558 William st
Wohlfeil, Amandus	Carpenter	89 Lovejoy st
Yox, John	Saloon.	606 William st
Yox, Hartman	Supt. Linseed Oil Works	——Jefferson st
Yenke, Frederick	Car Repairer	10 Stanton st
Zelt, Leo	Machinist	256 Sherman st
Zink, Balthaser	Saloon	85 Howard st

Christopher Columbus Lodge No. 325.

Chancellor Commander.....................ALBERT C. LUX
Vice Chancellor..................................JNO. KNEIS
Prelate...LOUIS GEYER
Master of Work...........................DR. C. B. LE VAN
Keeper of Records and Seals.........JNO. L. HORNBERGER
Master-at-Arms...........................LOUIS HOLZMAN
Master of Finance ....G. ADOLPH KAYSER
Master of Exchequer.....................HENRY F. DORST

Name.	Occupation.	Address.
Adler, Chas. W	Saloon	264 E. Genesee st
Bonsteel, A. U	Salesman	Great Valley, N. Y.
Bloom, James	Painter	146 Ellicott st
Butterfield, H. G	Salesman	408 Masten st
Bayer, Chas	Civil Engineer	544 E. Utica st
Cleland, Harry	Salesman	158 Woodlawn ave
Dorst, Henry F	Letter Carrier	341 Glenwood ave
Davis, Chas. H	Dentist	Redlands, Cal.
Donahue, T. F.	Mechanic	45 Pearl st
Fitch, Chas. W	Salesman	116 Southampton st
Fisher, F. M.	Carpenter	Town Line, N. Y.
Felch, Albert S	Pharmacist	1315 Jefferson st
Geyer, Louis	Shoe Dealer	1313 Jefferson st
Gastel, Joseph	Clerk	363 E. Utica st
Grecinger, George	Policeman	352 E. Utica st
Heerwagen, Fred	Wholesale Produce	286 Glenwood ave
Hill, Richard	Painter	43 Winslow ave
Holzman, Louis	Merchant Tailor	193 Eaton st
Hoyer, H. G.	Mechanic	550 Elm st
Hornberger, J. L.	Letter Carrier	392 Glenwood ave
Josephs, Wm. R.	Pharmacist	505 Sycamore st
Klueck, Gerhard	Bakery	1189 Jefferson st
Kneis, John	Photographer	21 Purdy st
Kobler, Andrew	Shoe Dealer	1528 Main st
Koehler, Henry F	Blacksmith	787 Oak st
Kayser, G. Adolph	Furniture Dealer	1239 Jefferson st

Name.	Occupation.	Address.
Le Van, Clarence B.	Physician	1223 Jefferson st
Lambrix, Henry	Plasterer	251 Glenwood ave
Lorms, L. J.	Baker	1289 Jefferson st
Lux, Albert	Letter Carrier	1404 Michigan st
Moher, F. C. H.	Architect	E. Utica op. Verplank
McBean, H. C.	Vessels Supplies	33 Main st
Myers, D. E.	Undertaker	1199 Jefferson st
Miller, Jacob	Salesman	49 Green St., Albany, N. Y.
McKay, Frank N.	Letter Carrier	1415 Michigan st
Niederpruem, N.	Contractor	348 E. Utica st
Neumann, John G.	Upholsterer	352 Emslie st
Neubeck, Louis H.	Florist	494 Masten st
Niel, Chas.	Contractor	299 E. Utica st
Oehmig, Robt.	Erie Co. Treasurer	485 E. Utica st
Ort, Wm.	Contractor	167 Steele st
Polland, Geo. A.	Milk Dealer	130 Leroy st
Pring, John G.	Policeman	10 Winslow ave
Roehmer, A. G.	Attorney	394 Main st
Shafer, E. C.	Manufacturer	405 E. Utica st
Schultz E. G.	Manufacturer	554 Glenwood ave
Schumm, Frank	Grocer	400 E. Utica st
Smith, Claude C.	Jeweler	961 W. Ferry st
Smith, E. P.	Painter	941 Main st
Schreiber, Wm.	Foreman	336 Glenwood ave
Urschel, John	Laborer	130 Leroy ave
Weis, Peter	Saloon	1323 Jefferson st
Weis, Daniel	Saloon	93 E. Utica st
Witzig, Frank J.	Painter	Ebenezer, N. Y.
Weber, F. C.	Painter	92 Perry st
Wesp, Peter	Manufacturer	184 Howard st
Wendling, Chas. J.	Manufacturer	877 Seneca st
Widner, J. E.	Physician	Englewood, Ill.

Niagara Falls Line

— TO —

NIAGARA FALLS AND
ELDORADO BEACH.

. . STEAMER HARRISON . .

Leaves Main Street at 9 A. M. and 2:30 P. M.
Ferry Street Dock, 15 minutes later.

SLOAN & COWLES, Lessees,

104 Main Street.

☞ Six Excursion Steamers to charter.

Telephone 968.   "S. and C."

Hydraulic Lodge No. 327, K. of P.

Chancellor Commander...................WM. GRIFFIN
Vice Chancellor....................... ....R. L. HOWEY
Prelate...............................A. E. CHAPMAN
Master of Work...........)
Keeper of Records and Seals.. ∫ ....MATT. J. MERZIG
Master of Finance............... ......JOHN MOSTBERGER
Master of Exchequer.....................PETER REHORN
Master-at-Arms..............................H. J. BUSH
Inner Guard........................ ....WM. MAMPLE
Outer Guard...........................PETER BECHTEL

Name.	Occupation.	Address.
Applegate. H. W	Laborer	Buffum st
Babcock, A. L	Teamster	505 Seneca st
Becker, M. J	Becker & Sons	192 William st
Bechtel, Peter	Cabinetmaker	631 Elk st
Blaser, Michael	Cigarmaker	754 Eagle st
Baumgaertner, J	Truck Builder	675 Seneca st
Bush. Herbert J	Carpenter	767 Seneca st
Buehler, Michael	Saloon	836 William st
Baumgaertner, Jos	Engineer	675 Seneca st
Becker, Geo. J	J. P. Becker & Son	192-194 William st
Buttler, Geo	Engineer	13 Wenona st
Bingham, Alfred	Scroll Sawyer	178 Myrtle ave
Chapman, Albert E	Tobacco, etc	556 S. Division st
Clancey, Wm. J	Steam Fitter	556 S. Division st
Converse, G. H	Flagman	669 Myrtle ave
Claus, Ed		Erie, Pa.
Curtis, W. J		858 Seneca st
Christensen, Peter		475 Swan st
Cable, Geo. H	Fireman	778 S. Division st
Clancey, J	works 317 Washington st	556 S. Division st
Downs. Jos	Watchmaker	831 Seneca st
Dietschler. Henry	Plumber	51 Hydraulic st
Deuchler, Henry	Deuchler & Keller	761 Seneca st
Dryer, F. J	Teamster	184 Southampton st

LODGE DIRECTORY.

Name.	Occupation.	Address.
Dau... Bernhard	Blacksmith	497 Babcock st
Epting, John	Merchant Tailor	714 Swan st
Elliott, W. J	Railroad Fireman	558 Swan st
Eaton, W. T		South Buffalo
Elliott, R. J	Engineer	490 Elk st
Fitzgerald, E. J		39 Vary st
Fleming, J	Caller Erie R. R	550 Fulton st
Fields, H. H	Life Insurance Agt	19 Emslie st
Greiner, E. J	Saloon	435 Seneca st
Griffin, John	Laborer	714 Exchange st
Gun, James	Blacksmith Foreman	26 Walter st
Howey, Robert L		616 Clinton st
Hirsch, Jno	Machinist	651 S. Division st
Howley, M. F	Gents' Furnisher	807 Seneca st
Henson, Robt		65 Monroe st
Hessler, Thos. N	Locomotive Engineer	684 S. Division st
Jerold, Frank		10 Pearl st
Keller, Andrew	Keller & Deuchler	761 Seneca st
Leary, J. M	Paperhanger	381 Myrtle ave
McCleary, M. L		448 Seneca st
McCormick, M. J		92 Troup st
McBride, E. H	Printer	1298 Seneca st
McMahon, P. J	Saloon	13 Seneca st
Mostberger, W. T	Machinist	83 Emslie st
Mostberger, John	Foreman Car Repairer	83 Emslie st
Mabey, Alfred G	with P. C. Millett	78 Delaware pl
Mueller, Ernest		96 Washington st
Molter, Aug	Butcher	127 Louisiana st
Moran, Michael	Laborer	155 Peabody st
Merzig, Matt	County Clerks' Office	87 Emslie st
Meyer, Adolph		122 Peckham st
Mample, Wm. R	Moulder	308 Fulton st
O'Neil, J. M	Physician	854 Seneca st
Pitz, P. F	Degot & Co	108 James st
Reicke, D. C		Downing pl
Raymond, Alfred A	Coachman	222 Northampton st
Rehorn, Peter	Saloon	709 Seneca st
Rehorn, A	Carpenter	703 Seneca st
Rehorn, H. J	Collector	703 Seneca st
Seymore, Thos	works Union Dry Dock	71 Elk st
Schneider, Geo	Teamster	123 Spruce st

LODGE DIRECTORY.

Name.	Occupation.	Address.
Sangers, Jas		435 Seneca st
Sergeant, H. C	Agent	39 Bennett st
Trost, Louis	Comp. Educationist	9 Bond st
Then, Simon	Coal and Wood	391 Smith st
Treehouse, Alfred		491 S. Division st
Wind, Henry	Saloon	278 Jefferson st
Weber, Jno	Machine Hand	491 Babcock st
Woodcock, W. G		520 Washington st
Wilson, Andrew J		695 N. Division st
Welzel, Geo	Switchman	720 Exchange st

East Buffalo Lodge No. 333, K. of P.

Chancellor Commander.................M. W. MATTHEWS
Vice Chancellor........................GEO. V. FISCHER
Prelate.................................... .JNO. MCBRIDE
Master of Work.......................HERMAN VERGIL
Keeper of Records and Seals ....C. E. SMITH
Master of Finance............................CHRIST FAY
Master of Exchequer........................JNO. DOSTER
Master-at-Arms.............................CHAS. H. KOCH
Inner Guard..............................PHILIP BECKER
Outer Guard................................WM. SEIFERT

Name.	Occupation	Address.
Bryans, Robt.	Teamster	599 Howard st
Boldt, Louis	Saloon	1212 Clinton st
Boldt, Wm.	Brakeman	24 Bushnell ave
Broker, Geo.	Brakeman	86 Mulberry st
Beck, Philip	Carpenter	1204 Clinton st
Doster, John	Carpenter	18 Jones st
DeGuchery. E.	Switchman	S. Buffalo
Fisher, Geo. V	Moulder	773 Bailey ave
Fay, Christ	Carpenter	237 Oneida st
Godfrey, Jas. J	Tinsmith	40 Imson st
Ginther, Wm.	Switchman	77 Troup st
Hubbard, Julius.	Brickmaker	1323 Clinton st
Jacob, Geo.	Wood Turner	50 Hickory st
Kraft, H.		434 Sycamore st
Koch. Chas. H.	Butcher	704 Carroll st
Matthews, M. W.	Engineer	1329 Clinton st
Miller, Jno.	Saloon	33 Holt st
Moreman, F.		Rochester, N. Y.
Manchester, H. L.	R. R. Fireman	1226 Clinton st
Meyer, Henry	Carpenter	365 Bristol st
McBride, Jno.	Tinsmith	1298 Seneca st
O'Donnell, Daniel	Baggageman	24 Scoville ave
Pfoehl, F. W.	Grocer.	1334 Clinton st

LODGE DIRECTORY.

Name.	Occupation.	Address.
Polker, Chas	Teamster	18 Gilbert ave
Poth, Jno	Collector	20 Baitz ave
Rassback, F. E.	Saloon	5 Deshler st
Rainow, Jas. N.	Engineer	156 Peabody st
Schulz, Chas	Car Inspector	441 Bristol st
Scifert, Wm	Mason	499 Bailey ave
Schriber, Peter	Switchman	105 Smith st
Smith, C. E.	Engineer	1347 Clinton st
Seifert, Fred	Butcher	1047 Elk st
Stroke. Chas. J.	Foreman	19 Manitoba st
Tobias, W. F.	Brakeman	Emporium, Pa.
Tiffany, W. C.	Art Dealer	241 Seneca st
Vergil, Herm	Teamster	27 Scoville ave
Veeder, John R.	Clerk	Brown's Hotel, Seneca st
Wilson, W. A.	Switchman	
Weber, Frank	Moulder	Cheekowaga, N. Y.

Ragau Lodge No. 335, K. of P.

Chancellor Commander......................H. D. FISHER
Vice Chancellor...........................N. NEUBAUER
Prelate...................................I. BARNHART
Master of Work............................JNO. ENNIS
Keeper of Records and Seals...........JOHN C. V. KRAFT
Master of Finance.........................E. FORBES
Master of Exchequer.....................S. J. SCHERER
Master-at-Arms...........................F. R HAMMOND
Inner Guard...........................JOS. M. SCHERER
Outer Guard...............................W. E. HUNT

Name.	Occupation.	Address.
Allen, Chas. J.	Glass Cutter	187 Franklin st
Allen, Thos. G.	Physician	437 Elk st
Atkins, R. J.	Undertaker	Tremont House
Aiken, R. E.	Commercial Traveler	508 Prospect ave
Baker, Roland E.	Grocer	254 Allen st
Baker, A. B.	Clerk	39 Vary st
Brooks, J. A.	Photographer	515 Main st
Brooks, Thos. G.	Lake Stewart	170 Terrace
Bentz, Henry G.	Physician	894 Michigan st
Buckley, James	Confectioner	96 Mohawk st
Barnhardt, Isaac	Stationery Engineer	42 Bates ave
Church, F. E.	Barber	53 Genesee st
Clark, Asa	Printer	1770 Niagara st
Clarkson, Wm. J.	Carpenter	1770 Niagara st
Dake, F. E.	Upholsterer	247 Franklin st
Ennis, John		88 Seymour st
Eydt, J.	Bricklayer	240 Southampton st
Eckward, Carl	Music Dealer	61 Broadway
Egan, Frederick W.	Master Plumber	163 E. Ferry st
Friendly, Adolph	Commercial Traveler	469 Vermont st
Fisher, H. D.	Managing Clerk	35 School st
Forbes, Elmer	Painter	250 Eagle st
Frank. Geo. Jr.	Machinist	93 Chenango st

Crystal ➤

➤ Beach.

The Ideal Family Resort.

Boating, Fishing, Bathing, Etc., Etc.

A Delightful Place for Excursions, Picnics, Church, Sunday School and Society Gatherings, Etc.

For Excursion Rates. Dates, Etc., apply to

LODGE DIRECTORY.

Name.	Occupation.	Address.
Guttentag, Philip	Clothier	147 Main st
Goldringer. Sam	Saloon	244 William st
Goldstein, K. M.	Printer	439 Genesee st
Guenther, H. J.	Oyster Dealer	361 Michigan st
Hammond, F. R.	Salesman	436 Washington st
Hunt, W. E.	Car Builder	29 Poplar ave
Haselmeier, R. C.	Tonsorial Parlors.	Court st., near Main
Jones, L. E.	Ornamenter	217 Monroe st
Jenicke, Charles	Insurance Agt	212 Fox st
Kraft, Jno. C. V.	(**Kraft & Stern, Printers**)	365 Washington st
Killip, John W	Salesman	242 Franklin st
Kline, Henry		1481 Fifth ave., Troy, N. Y.
Lang, Chas	Weighmaster	662 William st
Lodge, Chas	Painter	228 Thirteenth st
Metzler, Wm	Machinist	569 Clinton st
Mason, Geo. W	Clerk	108 Genesee st
Murphy, M. F	Salooner	Huron and Ellicott sts
Meyer, J. Michael	Carpet Fitter	212 Bristol st
Neubauer, N	Cigar Mfgr	76 Cayuga st
Olden, John E	Painter	198 E. Eagle st
Redlich, W. C	Painter	222 Sycamore st
Reid, John	Tinsmith	151 Chester st
Staub, John J	Painter	30 Webster st
Strayer, W. J	Barber	145 E. Eagle st
Smith, D. J	Ship Carpenter	70 Terrace
Smith, Lewis	Physician	300 Elk st
Smith, Chas. J	Grocery Clerk	285 Pearl st
Sherman, Elihu R	Lawyer	19 Coit Block
Scherer, S. J	Photographer	515 Main st
Scherer, Jos. M	Photographer	515 Main st
Scherer, Frank	Photographer	515 Main st
Traut, A. C	Bookbinder	145 E. Eagle st
Wissmiller, Wm. E	Carpet Fitter	498 Hickory st
Wissmiller, G. P	Carpet Fitter	498 Hickory st
Wood, Lyndon D	Attorney-at-Law	533 Auburn ave
Willett, Lewis E	Real Estate Dealer	366 Prospect ave
Wright, J. W	Salesman	Tremont House

North Star Lodge No. 337, Tonawanda

Chancellor Commander.......................LEROY TODD
Vice Chancellor...........................J. C FITZGERALD
Prelate..................................GEO. W. CHASE
Master of Work............................WM. MCKENZIE
Keeper of Records and Seal...........WM. H. PATTERSON
Master of Finance.........................JOHN DODDS
Master of Exchequer.....................O. A. DOCKHAM
Master-at-Arms......................EUGENE DRUMMOND

Name.	Address.
Apps, Wm................................	Tonawanda, N. Y.
Aldrich, H. B...........................	" "
Biddlesom, —............................	" "
Candler, Ed.............................	" "
Donalds, Francis........................	" "
Goldschmidt, Sol........................	" "
Gorse, Wallace C........................	" "
Grant, A. R.............................	" "
Hayes, Jos. W..........................	" "
Harrison, Lewis........................	" "
Howard, Henry..........................	" "
Hecht, David...........................	" "
Hughes, G. W...........................	" "
Lundy, Pemberton M. D..................	" "
McTyeier. R. P.........................	" "
Phillips, Daniel P.....................	" "
Suttner, W. A..........................	" "

Bison Lodge No. 351, K. of P.

Chancellor Commander...................BURT J. SINK
Vice Chancellor...........................JOS. M. RYAN
Prelate...................................JACOB KRABEL
Master of Work.......................ALBERT J. KUEBLER
Keeper of Records and Seals............WM. F. LEONARD
Master of Finance.......................FRED KRAEBEL
Master of Exchequer...................ERNEST H. BEYER

Name.	Occupation.	Address.
Beyer, Ernest H.	Plumber	346 Ellicott st
Bugg, Colin, J.	Paperhanger	267 Broadway
Daly, Francis J	Saloonkeeper	51 E. Eagle st
Fullerton, Jas. C.	Lawyer	490 Niagara st
Frank, John.	Contractor	
Guillow, Geo. W.	Musician	328 Elm st
Hauser, Frank J.	Policeman	455 Oak st
Hussey, Chas. G.	Canvasser	Cherry and Locust sts
Jakel, Edward.	Contractor	1225 Jefferson st
Kuebler, Albert J.	Policeman	78 Maple st
Kraebel, Fred.	Saloonkeeper	161 Genesee st
Kraebel, Jacob.	Collect'r	998 E. Genesee st
Kane, Edward.	Plasterer	70 Swan st
Kraemer, Herman.	Asphalt Contractor	308 Jefferson st
Leonard, Wm. F.	Central Star Laundry	206 Woodlawn ave
May, Peter J.	Hotel Keeper	367 Washington st
Maloy, Harry E.	Paperhanger	16 York st
Metzger, Anton.	Saloon and Boarding House,	182 Broadway
O'Brien, John	Sailor	54 Erie st
Patton, Jas.	Policeman	122 William st
Ryan, Jos. M.	Laundryman	141 E. Ferry st
Retcl, Michael.	Physician.	247 Broadway
Stark, Wm. A.	Awning Mfgr	139 E. Genesee st
Sink, Burt J.	Foreman Barber Asphalt Co.	17 Morley Pl
Stadermann, Julius.	Jeweler	137 E. Genesee st
Schmidt, Fred.	Clerk Municipal Court	Municipal Bldg

LODGE DIRECTORY.

Name.	Occupation.	Address.
Sink, Frank	Foreman	149 Kensington ave
Stang, John	Bartender	161 E. Genesee st
Saalfield, Henry	Saloon and Restaurant	17 W. Eagle st
Tiernay, John		149 Kensington ave
Volker, Wm. J	Lawyer, Room 13, Hutchinson Bldg
Wittman, Jos	Real Estate	890 W. Ferry st
Zipprich, Wm	Saloonkeeper	131 Carroll st

Uniform Lodge, K. of P.

[No List Received.]

Winchester Lodge, K. of P.

[No List Received.]

Buffalo Division No. 6, U. R. K. of P.

Colonel................JULIUS J. HERBOLD, 142 Broadway
Colonel................CONRAD STAFFEL, 305 Mulberry st
Major.... ....JNO. B. WILLIAMS, 341 Ellicott st
Captain.....................C. L. STAFFEL, 52 Kane st
Lieutenant...............JULIUS FRANK, 895 Walden ave
Herald.......................WM. SUDROW, 361 Emslie st
Right Guide................JNO. C. MOHRING, 37 Howard
Left Guide................. F. J. DORFER, 51 Genesee st

Beaman, J. F..............................473 Broadway
Dorfer, F. J..............................51 Genesee st
Frank, Julius............................895 Walden ave
Glassmann, Herman........................200 Masten st
Glassman, Wm..........................110 Southampton st
Gladstone, —.......................... 170 Hickory st
Hilburger, Jno.................. Sycamore and Camp sts
Hoffman, C....................:..........84 Bennett st
Hogenschmitt, R..........................318 Watson st
Harter, —............................... 213 Genesee st
Krueger, J. F.........................1856 Clinton st
Kiefer, E................................240 Peckham st
Moore. T. F...........................1787 Broadway
O'Kefe. Jno................................. 116 Eagle st
Regh, Geo.............................59 Genesee st
Reeb. Martin............................686 Michigan st
Springfels. Frank.....................525 Washington st
Schaefer. Chas.........................512 Washington st
Stanford, M..............................63 Tousey st
Sheppy, C...........................:..217 Swan st
Tenjost, Wm.......................... 564 William st
Yellowich, Jul........................116 W. Eagle st
Zacher, C. F.............................435 Emslie st

E. C. Shafer Division No. 26, K. of P.

Captain... ....ALBERT J. DANCE
Lieutenant................................WM. J. CABLE
Herald...,.........................CHAS. SCHOENHUT, JR
Guard.............................WESLEY O. PLANTZ
Sentinel.............................CHAS. V. THOMPKINS
Recorder.................................GEO. A. BEERS
Treasurer........... ....JOS. LOERSCH

Aikin, R. C.
Bisson, John
Burns, John
Bonnah, V.
Bulman, J. P.
Blaser, M.
Dill, Geo. A.
Fitch. Chas.
Fiscus. J.
Fitzgerald. C.
Fredricks, Chas.
Geiger. Jno. G.
Goldringer, S.
Grant. A. R.
Hill, La Fayette
Hall, F. L.
Hammond, F.
Harrison, L.
Hayes, J. W.
Kenyon, R.
Krieke, Jno. G.
Kraft, F.

Lederer, F. J.
Latour. G. A.
Mueller, Henry
Morden, B.
Murphy, M.
Mason, G. W.
McDermott, T. E.
Pollandt. G. A.
Riecke, D. C.
Schlagter, Albert
Sturm, Rudolph
Scherer, J. M.
Sutton, Wm.
Shuh, A. L.
Stettenbenz, L.
Shafer, E. C.
Scherer, S. J.
Wagner, Jno.
Wolsey, C. T.
Welter, Jno. M.
Wissmiller, W. E.
White, Wm. F.

R. Oehmig Division No. 31, U. R. K. of P.

[NO LIST RECEIVED.]

G. M. Browne Division, U. R., K. of P.

Captain .... MICHAEL RETEL, M. D.
First Lieutenant.................... ALBERT J. KUEBLER
Herald...................................... BURT J. SINK
Right Guide .... WM. A. STARK
Left Guide.... .... FRED J. M. KRAEBEL
Treasurer............................. LOUIS GOLDSTEIN

Adler, Chas. W.
Auken, Fred
Barron, Chas.
Burton, D.
Browne, Geo. M.
Bloom, James
Beyer, Ernest H.
Bugg, Colin J.
Ertell, John P.
Fullerton, Jas. C.
Fredrick, Henry W.
Goldstein, Louis
Jakel, Edward
Kuebler, A. J.
Kraebel, Fred J. M.
Kane, Ed.
Kraebel, Jacob

Kraft, John C. V.
Kraemer, Herman
Leonard, Wm. F.
Metzger, Anton
May, Peter J.
Retel, Michael
Raber, Manuel
Rose, Chas. H.
Ryan, Jos. M.
Sink, Burt J.
Stark, Wm. A.
Saalfield, Henry
Sink, Frank
Theobald, Fred Jr.
Volker, Wm. J.
Weber, Geo. M.
Zipprich, William

Mt. Clement Lodge No. 364, K. of P.

[JUST INSTITUTED. NO LIST RECEIVED.]

KRAFT & STERN, Printers
365 Washington Street.

⇒ DRINK ⇐

M. BECK BREWING CO.S'

———————— PURE ————————

Lager

———— TO BE HAD AT ————

ALL FIRST=CLASS BARS

IN THE CITY.

Past Chancellors Association.

President...........................CHAS. W. HINSON
Vice-President............................L. E. JONES
Secretary.....................B. A. COOK, 80 Baynes St
Treasurer ....P. D. STEIN

Boos, John
Boos, Peter
Best, Aug.
Beaman, John F.
Burch, O. B.
Bulman, J. P.
Cook, B. A.
Conschafter, Chas.
Dorian, J. S.
Dance, A. J.
Davis, W. S.
Ennis, John
Eaton, Wm. T.
Fitch, Chas. W.
Fybusch, Aaron
Gerard, J. W.
Hubbard, W. C.
Hanna, —
Hinson, C. W.
Hachten, Fred
Haller, Gust E.
Jones, L. E.
Judd, W. J.
Kuebler, A. J.

Klas, Peter
Kraebel, Fred
Miller, John
Myers, John Jr.
McElwain, F. J.
Nagel, Chas. A.
Parke, W. J.
Reinhardt, Emil S.
Rice, Chas. E.
Stein, P. D.
Staffel, Conrad
Siller, H. C.
Stanly, W. T.
Schlee, Ernest H.
Stark, Wm. A.
Thompson, Ralph E.
Virgil, Herman
Williams, J. B.
Wagner, Chas. W.
Wissmiller, W. E.
Woodcock, W. G.
Yox, Hartman
Yates, Jos. S.
Zachringer, Jos.

District Deputies.

Forty-first District—F. J. McElwain, Eagle Lodge No. 69.
Forty-second District—C. Staffel, Custer Lodge No. 145.
Fifty-ninth District—L. E. Jones, Ragau Lodge No. 335.
Sixtieth District—C. Conschafter, Selkirk Lodge No. 295.

Excelsior

Brewery.

Cor. Clinton and Pratt Sts.,

Buffalo, N. Y.

—— BOTTLED BY ——

Langenbach & Gerbereaux,

466 Eagle Street,

Telephone. Seneca 308.

BUFFALO, N. Y.

Hackmen's Legal Rate of Fare.

For conveying one passenger any distance not exceeding one mile, 50 cents; and for each additional passenger, 25 cents.

For over one mile and not exceeding two miles, 50 cents.

For over two miles, $1.00.

Children between eight and 12 years of age, half the above price only; under eight no charge to be made.

For vehicle by the hour, for one or more, $1.50 for every hour, with privilege of stopping as often as required. If by the hour, must be so specified at the time of engagement; otherwise deemed to be by the mile, to be measured by the most direct traveled route.

For the use of such vehicle by the day for one or more passengers, $8.00.

Public Buildings, Blocks, Halls and Hotels.

Academy of Music—245 and 247 Main.
Agency Building—42 and 44 Niagara.
Ailinger's Hall—West Forest avenue near Hawley.
Alamo Hall—Abbott Road cor. Triangle.
Alhambra Theatre—88 and 90 Commercial.
American Block—Main between Court and Eagle.
American Exchange Bank—No. 16 West Seneca.
Ancient Landmarks Hall (Masonic)—Main corner Court.
Argus Hall—Niagara cor. Hamilton.
Arlington Hotel—No. 134 Exchange.
Assembly Hall—No. 577 Main.
Association Hall—West Mohawk corner Pearl.
August Fuchs' Office Building—Main corner Mohawk.
Austin Fire Proof Building—110 Franklin cor. West Eagle.
Baecher's Hall—No. 797 Main.
Bank of Buffalo—No. 236 Main.
Bank of Commerce—No. 188 Main.
Bapst Building—Seneca corner Washington.
Barker Block No. 152 Seneca.
Brainard House—William near Cassy.
Braner's Hall—No. 145 High.
Board of Trade Building—Seneca corner Pearl.
Broadway Hall—Nos. 349 to 353 Broadway.
Broezel Hotel—Seneca corner Wells.
Brown's Building—Main corner Seneca.
Brown's Hotel—Seneca corner Michigan.
Buffalo Gymnasium—Washington cor. East Mohawk.
Buffalo Club House—Cor. Delaware avenue and West Chippewa.
Buffalo Commercial Bank—West Seneca cor. Pearl.
Buffalo Driving Park and Industrial Fair Grounds—East Ferry corner Jefferson.
Buffalo Female Academy—Delaware Avenue and Johnson's Park.
Buffalo General Hospital—High near Oak.
Buffalo High School—Court corner Franklin.
Buffalo Homeopathic Hospital—Cottage cor. Maryland
Buffalo Hospital (Sisters of Charity)—No. 1883 Main.
Buffalo Library Building—Washington cor. Broadway.
Buffalo Loan, Trust and Safe Deposit Co.—449 Main.

PUBLIC BUILDINGS, ETC.

Buffalo Medical College—High near Main.

Buffalo Orphan Asylum—403 Virginia.

Buffalo, Rochester & Pittsburg Railroad Depot—Exchange corner Michigan.

Buffalo Savings Bank—Washington cor. Broadway.

Buffalo State Hospital—Entrance, Forest ave. near Elmwood ave.

Buffalo Women's Hospital—191 Georgia.

Builder's Exchange—Court cor. Pearl.

Burkhardt Building—15 W. Eagle.

Carlton Hotel—Exchange cor. Washington.

Central Labor Union Hall—Huron cor. Ellicott.

Central Park and Hall—631 Jefferson.

Catholic Institute—Main cor. E. Chippewa.

Catholic Protectory—Limestone Hill.

Central Hotel—170 Exchange.

Central Park—631 Jefferson.

Chapin Block—West Swan between Main and Pearl.

Chapter House—Johnson Park near Carolina.

Church Charity Foundation Home—Rhode Island near Niagara

Citizens Bank—William cor. Sherman.

City Bank—319 Main.

City and County Hall—Franklin Square, bet. Franklin, Delaware Avenue, Church and W. Eagle.

Coal and Iron Exchange—255, 257 and 259 Washington.

Coit Block—W. Swan cor. Pearl.

Columbia Building—103 to 107 Seneca.

Columbia National Bank—103 Seneca.

Concert Hall (rear of Music Hall)—Main cor. Edward.

Continental Hotel—Exchange cor. Michigan.

Courier Buildings, 197 and 199 Main and 188 to 216 Washington.

Court St. Theatre—Court near Pearl.

Crandall House—965 William.

Custom House—Washington cor. Seneca.

Deaf Mute Institute—125 Edward.

Delaware, Lackawanna & Western R. R. Passenger and Freight Depots—ft. of Main.

Drovers' Hotel—N. Y. C. stock yards near North Central avenue.

Eagle House—367 Washington.

East Buffalo Hotel—965 William.

Emergency Hospital—S. Division cor. Michigan.

Empire Savings Bank—308 Main.

Erie County Almshouse—Main near city line.

Erie County Jail—Delaware ave. corner Church.

Erie County Morgue 241 Terrace.

Erie County Penitentiary Fifth, bet. Hudson and Pennsylvania

Erie County Savings Bank - Main, Niagara, Church and Pearl.

Erie R. R. Passenger Depot Exchange corner Michigan.

Exchange Building—196 to 202 Main.

Farmers and Mechanics Bank 198 Main.

Fillmore House - Michigan corner Carroll.

Fire Department Headquarters - Court corner Staats.

Fireman's Hall 198 Seneca.

Fidelity Hall - 249 Genesee.

Fitch Creche Building -159 Swan.

Fitch Institute - Swan corner Michigan.

Fornes Building - Court corner Pearl.

Fort Porter —Front avenue between Vermont and Massachusetts.

Franklin Block - Franklin between Erie and W. Seneca.

Franklin Hall – over 50 W. Eagle.

French's Block—Washington corner E. Huron.

Genesee Hotel, The –Main cor. W. Genesee.

German-American Bank - Main cor. Court.

German Bank of Buffalo - Main corner Lafayette.

German Insurance Company Building Main cor. Lafayette.

German R. C. Orphan Asylum—Best near Fox.

German Young Men's Association Building—Main cor. Edward.

Germania Block—820 Main.

Germania Hall—707 and 709 Seneca.

Goodell Hall—Rear Buffalo Female Academy.

Grand Trunk Railway Depots—Erie st., and Michigan cor. Exchar

Granite Block—Main bet. Seneca and Swan.

Greene's Block—Washington cor. N. Division.

Grimm's Hall—Seneca cor Michigan.

Grosvenor Library—Washington cor. Broadway.

Grove Block—850 Main.

Gruener's Hotel—20 E. Huron.

Hager Block—Lloyd cor. Canal.

Harmonia Hall—264 Genesee.

Harugari Hall—Over 258 and 262 Genesee.

Harvey Block—Main cor. Swan.

Hayen Building—Main cor. Seneca.

Hellreigel's Hall—Elm cor. Genesee.

Hermitage, The—52 Court.

Hesper Hall and Parlors—Swan cor. Washington.

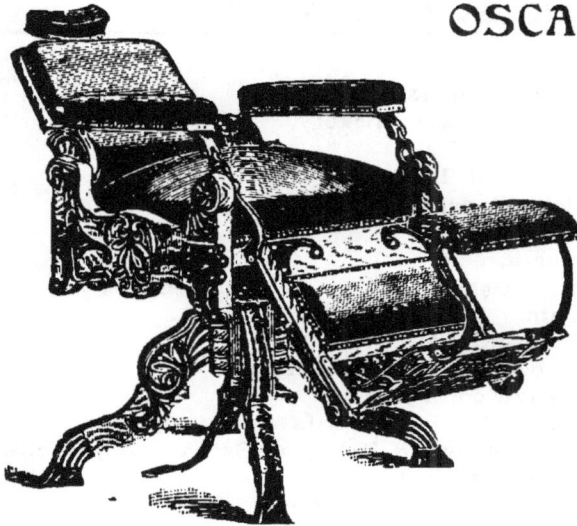

Hoffman House—873 William.
Home for the Friendless—1500 Main.
Honnecker's Hall—Sycamore cor. Hickory.
Hutchinson Block—867 to 873 Main.
Hydraulic Bank—Seneca cor. Hydraulic.
Ingleside Home—Michigan near Balcom.
Iroquois Hotel—Main cor. Eagle.
Kaiser's Hall—198 Seneca.
Kehr's Hall, (changed to Genesee Hall in 1887)—249 Genesee.
Kreis Hall—232 William.
Kreiss Hall—692 and 694 Michigan.
Kremlin Block—Main bet. Niagara and W. Eagle.
Kremlin Hall—West Eagle cor. Pearl.
Lafayette Square—Main, Washington, Lafayette and Clinton.
Lake Shore & Michigan Southern R. R. Depot—Exchange opp. Wells.
Law Exchange—Niagara cor. Eagle.
Lehigh Valley Building—Main cor. Seneca.
Lehigh Valley R. R. Depot—Michigan cor. Exchange.
Lewis Block—S. W. cor. Washington and Swan.
Lewis Hall—Niagara cor. Breckenridge.
Liberty Block—West Chippewa cor. Pearl.
Liedertafel Hall—Main cor. E. Chippewa.
Lincoln Hall—497 William.
Live Stock Exchange—William cor. Depot.
Lyceum Theatre—447 and 449 Washington.
Magdalene Asylum—485 Best.
Mansion House—Main cor. Exchange.
Manufacturers & Traders' Bank—Main cor. W. Seneca.
Marine Bank—220 Main.
Market Hall—Ellicott opp. Market.
Markets: Elk Street—Elk, Perry and Market. Washington—Washington, Chippewa and Ellicott. Clinton—Clinton, William and Bennett. Broadway—Broadway near Fillmore avenue.
Masonic Temple—41 to 45 Niagara.
Maternity Hospital—(Buffalo Women's Hospital), 191 Georgia.
Matthews' Building—Washington cor. Exchange.
Merchants Bank—208 Main.
Merchants' Exchange, Board of Trade Building—West Seneca cor. Pearl.
Merchant's Hotel—144 Exchange.
Metropolitan Bank—Main cor. E. Mohawk.
Metropolitan Hall—551 and 553 Main.

PUBLIC BUILDINGS, ETC.

Moeller House—95 and 97 Main.
Mohawk Office Building—Main cor. E. Mohawk.
Monnon's Hall—Amherst cor. Churchill.
Morgan Building—534 and 536 Main.
Municipal Court Building—34 to 38 Delaware avenue.
Music Hall—Main cor. Edward.
Mutter's Hall—Clinton cor. Watson.
Mystic Star Hall—Broadway cor. Pratt.
National Hall—Ellicott near Genesee.
Nellany Block—Main cor. Mohawk.
New Era Hall—Main cor. W. Swan.
Newsboys and Bootblacks' Home—29 Franklin.
New York Hotel—158 Exchange.
New York Central R. R. Depots—Exchange opp. Wells and Erie st.
New York, Chicago & St. Louis Depot (Nickel Plate)—Michigan cor. Exchange.
N. Y. State Arsenal—Broadway bet. Potter and Milnor.
New York, West Shore & Buffalo R. R. Depot—Exchange opp. Wells.
New York, Lake Erie & Western R. R. Depot—Michigan cor. Exchange.
Niagara Bank of Buffalo—71 W. Forest avenue.
Niagara Hotel, The—Porter avenue cor. Seventh.
Normal School—Jersey bet. 13th and 14th.
North Buffalo Catholic Institute—Dearborn cor. Amherst.
Odd Fellows' Halls—Over 29 Seneca and Michigan cor. Cypress and Niagara cor. Hamilton.
Olympic Theatre—155 Canal.
Orden Der Freiheit Halle—Ellicott cor. E. Huron.
Ortner's Hall—1995 Niagara.
Park Superintendent's Office—Park at terminus of Jewett avenue.
Pankow's Hall—291 William.
People's Bank—257 Washington.
Philippbar's Hall—Niagara cor. Amherst.
Police Headquarters—Franklin cor. W. Seneca.
Postoffice—Washington cor. Seneca.
Providence Lunatic Asylum—Main near Humboldt parkway.
Queen City Bank—341 to 345 Main.
Queen City Hall—Wadsworth cor. Wadsworth place.
Red Men's Hall—Main cor. W. Eagle.
Revere Block—Erie street near Erie Canal.
Richelieu Hotel—39 Swan.
Russ' Hall—Broadway cor. Madison.

PUBLIC BUILDINGS, ETC.

Saturn Club House—Delaware avenue cor. Edward.
Scajaquada Hall—Niagara near W. Forest avenue.
Scheu's Hall—241 Genesee.
Schroeder's Hall—610 Genesee.
Schwabl Hall—353 Broadway.
Seventy-fourth Regt. Armory—Virginia cor. Fremont place.
Sherriff's Hall—68 and 70 Forest avenue.
Sherman House—1715 Niagara.
Southern Hotel—Seneca cor. Michigan.
Spaulding's Exchange—Main cor. Terrace.
Star Theatre—Pearl cor. W. Mohawk.
Steingoetter's Hall—463 Michigan.
Sticht's Hall—Ellicott cor. E. Huron.
St. Mary's Asylum for Widows, Foundlings and Infants—126 Edward.
St. Stephen's Hall—Triangle bounded by Franklin, W. Swan and Terrace.
Stafford House—Washington cor. Carroll.
Stendt's Hall—198 Seneca.
Studio Building—35 Niagara.
The Genesee Hotel—Main cor. Genesee.
The Buffalo Loan, Trust and Safe Deposit Company—449 Main.
The Niagara Hotel—Porter avenue cor. Seventh.
Third National Bank—273 Main.
Tifft Block—Washington cor. Mohawk.
Tifft House—Main bet. Lafayette and Mohawk.
Townsend Block—Main cor. W. Swan.
Tremont House—Seneca cor. Washington.
Tucker's Hotel—Exchange cor. Michigan.
Turn Hall—329 and 331 Ellicott.
Union Bank—Main cor. W. Mohawk.
United States Court House—Washington cor. Seneca.
United States Custom House—Seneca cor. Washington.
United States Hotel—Terrace cor. Pearl.
United States Signal Station—Board of Trade Building.
United States Life Saving Station—Buffalo River, foot Erie.
Vesta Hall—Over 527 Main.
Wagner's Hall Eagle cor. Jefferson.
Weed's Block—Main cor. Swan.
Wells' Block—Michigan cor. Eagle.
Western, New York & Pennsylvania R. R. Depot—Exchange opp. Wells.
Western Savings Bank Main cor. Court.

PUBLIC BUILDINGS, ETC.

Western Union Telegraph Building   Main cor. Seneca.
White Fire Proof Building - 282 to 298 Main and 18 to 24 Erie.
World's Dispensary Medical Association — 663 Main.
Young Men's Association Building — Washington, Broadway and Clinton.
Young Men's Catholic Association Building   Franklin cor. Swan.
Young Men's Christian Association Building — Mohawk cor. Pearl.
Vox's Hall   Howard cor. Watson.
Zittle Hall — Seneca near Cazenovia.

www.ingramcontent.com/pod-product-compliance
Lightning Source LLC
Chambersburg PA
CBHW020536270326
41927CB00006B/610